THE SELECTIVE TRAVELLER IN
PORTUGAL

The Selective Traveller in
PORTUGAL

by
Ann Bridge and
Susan Lowndes

New and Revised Edition

McGRAW-HILL BOOK COMPANY

New York   Toronto   London   Sydney

First published 1949
Revised American Edition 1961
New and Revised American Edition 1967

Library of Congress Catalog Card Number: 67-28344
New and Revised edition
07733

PRINTED IN GREAT BRITAIN
BY EBENEZER BAYLIS AND SON, LTD.
THE TRINITY PRESS, WORCESTER, AND LONDON

ACKNOWLEDGEMENTS

W E wish to express our warm thanks to the many people who have shown us particular buildings or works of art, answered our questions, given us information and assisted us in various ways. We would like particularly to mention Dr. Reinaldo dos Santos, who put his unrivalled knowledge of art at our disposal on more than one occasion; the late Snr. Antonio Ferro and Dr. Tavares de Almeida, of the Secretariado Nacional de Informação, who helped us in the arrangements for many journeys; and Snr. Antonio Porto d'Assa Castelo Branco, of the photographic section of that institution, who with unfailing patience allowed us to look through their unique collection, and supplied many of the photographs for this book; Dr. João Couto, of the Museum of Ancient Art in Lisbon; Eng. José Mateus de Almeida de Mendia, formerly Director-General of the State Forestry Service, and his local forestry Officers; the officials of the Agronomical Research Institute at Sacavem and of the Laboratorio de Tecnologia at Alcobaça; the Head of the Instituto Botanico at Lisbon, Dr. Flavio Resende, and his assistants—especially Dr. Luis Gonçalves Sobrinho, who identified many hundreds of flowers for us. Colonel Mario Cardoso, of Guimarães, who twice showed us over Citânia de Briteiros, deserves especial thanks; we are also grateful to the many Curators of provincial museums who showed us their treasures, and in particular to Dr. Vasco Rebelo Valente, Director of the Soares dos Reis Museum at Oporto, who lent many photographs; also to Dr. João de Figueiredo, Conservador of the Palace of Vila Viçosa, who devoted a whole day to showing us the Palace, as well as supplying delightful hospitality.

Dr. Carlos A. G. Estorninho, Dr. Antonio Duarte and Snr. Jorge P. Rosa of the staff of the British Institute, Lisbon, gave great help in the library. Snr. João Baptista Martins, Chefe da Secretaria of the Santa Casa da Misericordia in Bragança was most kind in showing that city and its beauties to two strangers.

Mrs. Hubert Jennings and Mrs. Garland Jayne have always shared their unequalled knowledge of Portuguese art, architecture and history with the two authors, and the late Norwegian Minister.

ACKNOWLEDGEMENTS

M. Alf Hasfel, Miss Dorothy Tait, Mrs. H. Chapman, Mrs. Muir, Mrs. MacIvor, Mme. Becke Baptista, Dr. Robert K. Brady, Maurice Symington, Esq., and Leonard Downes, Esq., all gave us information and answered our queries.

Especial thanks are also due to Gerard Graham, Esq., of Oporto, who afforded exceptional opportunities for studying the making of Port, both up the Douro and at Vila Nova de Gaia; to Walter Grabham, Esq., of Madeira, who supplied unique geological and botanical information about the island; to Graham Blandy, Esq., of Madeira, for his specialised knowledge of local history, and to Horace Zino, Esq., of Funchal, for information regarding the making of Madeira.

Mrs. Scoville and the late W. B. Rumann, Esq., both kindly lent photographs.

Finally, we wish to express our gratitude to the many people whose names we do not know, but whose kindness and courtesy made toil a pleasure—the village priests and the nuns in convents who spared the time to show us their churches and buildings, and the peasants, both men and women, who so often, so cheerfully, and so graciously explained their methods of husbandry, spinning or weaving to strangers.

Readers of the later editions of this book have sometimes inquired why there are no detailed maps. The reason is that their inclusion would have greatly increased the price of the book and the Michelin Map of Portugal, the best in the opinion of the authors, can be bought everywhere. In Portugal it costs 10 esc. There is a sketch map of Portugal at the beginning of this volume, and one of Madeira at the end.

CONTENTS

LIST OF ILLUSTRATIONS

LIST OF ILLUSTRATIONS

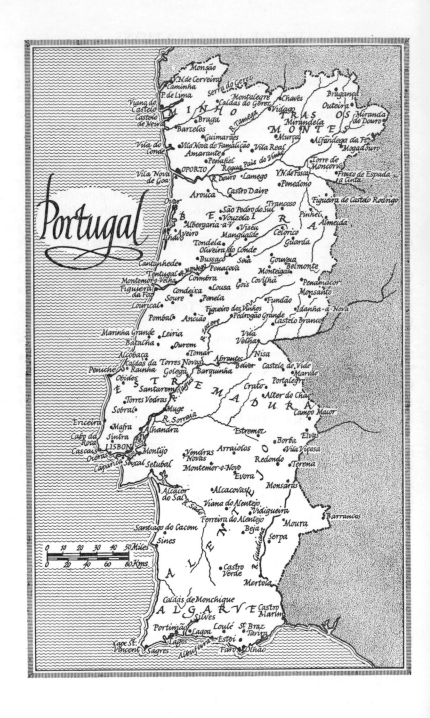

CHAPTER I

HISTORICAL LANDMARKS

FOR the traveller in a new country certain things are urgently important. He will not wish to miss any of the indisputably *unique* sights or beauties—as who returns from Verona without having seen the Pisanello frescoes, visible nowhere else on earth, to be greeted with cries of reproach from the luckier or more learned; nor will he care to have passed over things not unique, but of major importance. (This is in fact less likely to happen, since even hotel porters have a way of directing visitors to Rome to St. Peters or the Coliseum.) But in the hurried days of modern travel—so unlike the spacious maunderings, in one's private coach, of the 18th century—it is not easy for anyone but the specialist to extract from the never-sufficiently-to-be-admired completeness of Baedeker or the *Guides Bleus* what he will most want to see, what will chiefly interest him; the wealth of detail in these compendious (and quite indispensable) works is in itself baffling. If not a need, there is at least a place, today for the selective guide-book, an anthology rather than an omnibus volume. And the aim and purpose of the present book is precisely to provide such an "anthology" of the varied, unusual and beautiful things to be seen in Portugal.

But no country can be understood, even its outstanding monuments cannot be at all appreciated, without some idea, however vague, however simplified, of the shifting movements of history which led to or made possible their construction; nor without some conception of the combination of soil, climate, agriculture and attitude to life of the present inhabitants—who are probably much the same, in most respects, as their forbears—upon whose activities the whole life of a nation depends. Therefore in this opening chapter some of the landmarks in Portuguese history will be briefly and simply noted—rather in the manner of those pocket-knives on sale in China in the 1920's, which had the names and dates of the Chinese Dynasties usefully engraved along their ivory sides; and in the succeeding one some account will be attempted of the fascinating, though rapidly changing, Portuguese agriculture of today, and of the

I

life of the inhabitants. "Manners and Customs"—so ran the heading of an early chapter in all Victorian books on foreign parts; and it was seldom the least interesting one. What is so absorbing is the inevitable and intimate connection between both the historic past and these manners and customs, and the monuments at which the tourist gapes, the products which he eats and drinks and buys—a connection it is hoped here to bring out.

Reference has already been made to the "unusual" things to be seen in Portugal, and about two of these, at least, a word is necessary at the outset:—the *azulejos*, or glazed tiles, which play such a peculiar but predominant part in indoor and outdoor decoration, and that native and unique form of florid—and floral—late Gothic architecture known as Manueline. Whole streets of houses with fronts of highly-glazed, brightly-coloured tiles; the walls of whole churches, inside and outside alike, as well as passages and staircases in public buildings, decorated in the same startling fashion instead of the homely and familiar brick, stone or plaster, are liable to strike the stranger with something like repulsion; the whole business seems to him at first exotic almost to the point of outrage. In the same way those arches and doorways where the white stone itself seems almost to twine and twist upwards, as boughs, as leaves and flowers, foliating and floriferating in indescribable exuberance, strike many people, after the calm austerity of our Northern string-courses and modest mouldings, as grotesque, or shocking, or merely comic. It is only after weeks, perhaps even months, in Portugal that they begin to "get their eye in", as they say, to azelejos and Manueline—and then it is too late; the 'plane or the boat is about to carry them away, now at last nostalgically wishing that they had seen more, and paid more, much more attention to what they did see, while they had the chance. This happens so often that it seems only fair to implore the traveller, from the word go, to *accept* these two unique features of Portuguese architecture; to realise that they are unique, and for that reason alone worth careful looking-at; to take on trust, if necessary, for the first little while that they are by many accounted beautiful, and that in time he may well come to think them so himself; but that, whether he ever thinks so or not, they have their own history, differences, and values, as well as their own special and by no means trivial place in the world's aesthetic heritage, and should not, therefore, ignorantly or carelessly be written off as merely funny or ugly. Some of the later Manueline is in fact frightfully ugly, and may honestly be recognised as such—one of the authors of this book, confronted for the first time with the monstrous exterior of the West window of the Church of Christ at Tomar, with its crazy symbolic wreathings of anchors and octopuses, felt physically sick, and had to go and sit somewhere out of sight of the stone insanity and be revived with brandy! But all is not ugly, though all is strange—and the patience and sympathy of the traveller is invoked, not in the interests of Manueline, which does not care, but in his own.

I

Our first landmark comprises pre-history, including the Celts. There are traces of Palaeolithic and Mesolithic "hunting cultures" in Portugal; agriculture was probably introduced by a copper-using race which came in both overland and by sea from the Mediterranean and south Spain, probably about 2500 – 2000 B.C. The descendants of these people went on to colonise Brittany, Ireland and west Scotland, and by 1800 – 1700 B.C. they were trading with Britain—so ancient is the tradition of commerce between the two countries! Their main monuments are 'collective tombs", family vaults used over generations, either rock-cut, as at Palmela, Cascais, and Alapraia near Estoril, or built of stone above ground, like the Alcalá tombs in the Algarve; these latter structures are the ancestors of British tombs like New Grange or Maes Howe. Little is known of the Portuguese Bronze Age, but by, say, 1500 up to 500 B.C., one may state with fair certainty that the native inhabitants of Spain and Portugal were the "Iberians" of the classical writers.

The great Celtic invasions of Western Europe swept into the Peninsula, bringing an iron-using economy, in the late 5th and 4th centuries B.C.; and the Celts, as usual, have left a firm imprint—in names, in buildings, and in ornament. Some of the local names for birds, still used by the country people, are practically the same as those used by the Gaelic-speaking Highlander to-day; and in the tesselated pavements referred to as "Luso-Roman" one finds the interlaced ornament so characteristic of the great crosses of Ireland and the West Highlands. Most remarkable of all are the "castros" or hill-cities of northern Portugal, the *Citanias*, as they are called.

The most famous of these, because so far the most fully excavated, Citânia de Briteiros, on a hill near Guimarães, with its series of three greater outer walls round the lower slopes is a truly astonishing place, covering several acres, with paved roadways, stone channels for the water supply, water-tanks with elaborate stone spouts, and every variety of house—round, rectangular and one, two, or three-roomed, some with forecourts; there are one or two large circular structures with stone benches set all round against the walls which suggest a parliament or meeting-house, and inevitably recall the 11th-century Romanesque City Hall at Bragança, with its stone bench for the town councillors running all round it; and even more, since that is roofed, the similar early Council-chambers at Belmonte and Aguiar da Beira, which were built without roofs. Some of the houses, the circular ones especially, are of what is called "helicoidal" construction—that is to say the large rectangular stones composing them are set, not flat, but on their corners, making a sort of diamond pattern; the topmost row stand up today like teeth. It is a fascinating subject for speculation whether the sight of these peculiar buildings may have influenced the 11th- and 12th-century builders of the castles of northern Portugal, causing them to decorate their own walls with the sharply-toothed crenellations which are such a characteristic feature of many, notably of the one at near-by Guimarães itself.

The builders of Citânia and the neighbouring hill-town of Sabroso had obviously attained to a considerable degree of culture; in the Sarmento Museum at Guimarães may be seen their pottery, ornaments, and, most remarkable of all, a stone doorway to a house, carved with the familiar interlaced ornament, astonishingly elegant; during the 2nd and 1st centuries B.C. south-west Britain and north Spain and Portugal were part of a common province sharing elements of the same Celtic culture. In the museum, too, is the famous "Pedra Formosa", the Beautiful Stone, which for so long puzzled archaeologists, but is now known to have formed part of a tomb or shrine, since a similar example has been found *in situ*, when the new road to Citânia was being constructed. What is sad is that the great work of excavation at Briteiros, to which Dr. Martins Sarmento devoted most of his life, was undertaken at a time when stratographic excavation was little understood, so that the finds at different levels have been greatly confused; those now in charge of the excavations are however alive to this defect, and it is to be expected that much more accurate and useful work will be done in future on these most important sites.

What is less pardonable, indeed quite disastrous from the scientific point of view, is that in recent years the Portuguese Commission on Ancient Monuments, with a passion for restoration not, alas, equalled by their archaeological experience, have taken upon themselves to *reconstruct* portions of the walls and, still worse, the gateways, according to their own ideas! The visitor to Citânia from other lands stands almost speechless, between the astonishing wealth and importance of this extraordinary site on the one hand, and on the other the intrepid ignorance which has ventured so to sacrifice scientific values to a mistaken sense of what constitutes improvement.

It seems certain that the Phoenicians not only traded up the coasts of Portugal, but established settlements there. The fisher-people of Nazaré and Aveiro are by tradition of Phoenician origin, and their appearance bears out the legend; the name of the promontory of Peniche, not far from Nazaré, possibly confirms it. Another confirmation is in the curiously shaped pottery jugs, still sometimes to be bought at country fairs, which are made, unmistakably, in the shape of the Goddess Ashtaroth. And before leaving pre-history, mention must be made of the fertility cults of Tras-os-Montes, which have left their traces in the three magnificent granite statues of boars, related to the similar ones of central Spain—two at Bragança and the famous Porco de Murça at the latter town—as well as the astonishing features which still accompany the Festa of São Gonçalo at Amarante.

II

After the Celts, the Romans; and with them history begins. The occupation lasted from the 1st to the 5th century A.D.; under Augustus, Portugal was divided into three provinces, whose seats of government were at Braga (*Bracara Augusta*) in the north, Santarem (*Scalabitanum*) in the centre, and Beja (*Pacensis*) in the south. A network of roads covered the country, with some fine bridges, many of which still remain; there were wealthy cities, of which the largest so far excavated is the magnificent site at Conimbriga, not far from the later Coimbra, to which it gave its name. Few large buildings have survived except the foundations of the aqueduct at Elvas, and the "Temple of Diana" at Evora. But the wealth of Roman remains is astonishing, and full-scale excavation has really only just begun. To give an idea of this unexplored wealth, at and near the little-known site of Medobriga near Portalegre, three amateur archaeologists found in a single afternoon's hurried exploration three bridges, one complete with a watch-tower, and a Roman road connecting them, with a neolithic or Iron-Age road about ten inches below it; two whole streets of Roman houses out in the fields, with paved roads and stone gutters; and a large villa with a fresh inscription (one was already known) in the farm-yard, and the original paved approach. Close by a farmer was planting a new olive-yard, and round every hole in the sticky clay lay endless fragments of pottery; those which survived his labourer's spades, including some exquisite glass bottles, could be bought by the first comer for roughly ten shillings the half dozen! Portugal is in fact an archaeologist's Paradise.

But the other great memorial to the Roman occupation of Portugal is Portuguese itself, which, in spite of the fragments of other tongues embedded in it, like pebbles in a matrix, is indisputably a Latin language. The claim of the Portuguese that their speech today represents the nearest approach to Latin as spoken by the Romans cannot, however, be sustained, if only because the language has been debased by their habit of contracting some words and expanding others. The Latin *cor*, heart, is in Portuguese *coração*; on the other hand the Latin *color*, colour, is *cor*. As well might Americans claim that *sox* is the historic way of spelling socks!

III

Portugal, like all other parts of the Roman Empire, was swamped towards the close of the 5th and the beginning of the 6th century by the invasions of the various Teutonic tribes—in this case mainly the Visigoths. Like the Celts, they left an imprint on the language—both personal names and country names for birds are clearly of Teutonic origin. (The word for goose is not the Latin *anser* or the French *oie*, but *ganso*, like the German *Gans*.) In the north in particular the proportion of blue eyes and blond hair is high

LISBON: CHAPEL IN CHURCH OF S. ROQUE

STRIPPING THE MAIZE COBS

NORTH OF PORTUGAL: "CANASTRAS" TO STORE MAIZE OUT OF REACH OF RATS

among the country-people, another legacy of the Visigothic influx. They also produced some curious rough sculptures and stone barrel-shaped tombs, specimens of which may be seen in the Ethnological Museum at Belem, at Lisbon. In time they were Christianised, and to their period belong one or two of the early northern churches, though not as many as is popularly supposed—the most undoubted and important is the exquisite S. Frutuoso outside Braga. The Cedo-feita at Oporto, in spite of its inscription, was almost entirely rebuilt much later. These solid structures, with their extreme simplicity and round arches, though sometimes carelessly called "Romanesque" correspond closely to our English Saxon churches.

IV

The fourth great landmark in Portuguese history to be inscribed on our knife-handle is the Moorish occupation, which lasted roughly from the 8th century to the middle of the 12th, when in 1147 Santarem and later in the same year Lisbon, the latter with the help of English and Flemish Crusaders, were recovered from the infidel. The eight-hundredth anniversary of the recapture of Lisbon was celebrated in the summer of 1947 with great splendour of pageantry, but the most unforgettable moment was when, on the first night of the celebrations, an immense illuminated cross sprang into light on the battlements of the Castelo de S. Jorge, above the town, and all the bells of the city clanged out together. In the south the Moors remained a whole century longer, till the recapture of Faro in 1249. The external traces of their presence are perhaps less important than their influence on culture and on the social structure, but they are still visible. The heavy metal grilles to the lower windows of private houses is a thoroughly Mussulman arrangement, and persists even in 18th- and 19th-century structures; so is the habit of building houses round an enclosed courtyard, with blank windowless walls giving on the street. In the south, especially in the Algarve, the southern-most province of all, the chimney-pots consist of high narrow oblongs of mortar, pierced to allow the smoke to escape, and pierced in indubitably Arabesque designs; here the roofs tend to be flat, everything is lime-washed to a blinding whiteness to resist the heat, and towns such as Tavira and Olhão are so purely

Moorish in appearance that the visitor can easily imagine himself in some Moroccan city—indeed it is hard to believe that one is not. But the greatest contribution made by the Moors to Portuguese art and architecture was the introduction of glazed tiles for use in both interior and exterior decoration; *azulejo* is an Arabic word meaning "smooth", and has no connection with the prevalent blue of the later tiles. The earliest ones of all, made by the Moors or under their immediate influence had raised *cloisons* or divisions marking off the areas of the different colours, and often contained black; these are now very rare, but some may still be seen in the Palace at Sintra, and near the pool in the garden at the Quinta da Bacalhoa. But the idea introduced by the Moors has persisted ever since, and in the intervening centuries has produced some exquisite, and unique, forms of decoration. Tiled walls have many merits: they never fade, they need not be renewed, and are practically indestructible save by earthquake or fire; they can be washed, they are cool, and they are often most beautiful. The same can hardly be said of any other mural treatment except marble.

The extent to which the laws and social structure of Portugal still retain and reflect the Mahomedan influence will probably not be noticed by the casual visitor, but it is very marked. Portuguese women, even among the powerful families of the upper classes, as a rule have few of the political interests, exert little of the political influence which have been common for three or four centuries among their counterparts in England or Hungary or France; only in recent years have a notable proportion of girls gone to the universities. The legal position of women is inferior; few may vote, and on her marriage the administration of a woman's property passes to her husband; she cannot get a passport without his written application. The *Code Napoléon*, which was adopted by Portugal about 1840, after the Liberal wars, is probably responsible to some extent for this state of affairs—the Code, notoriously, rated women's rights rather low. And much of this, it is true, was the case in England up to the third quarter of the 19th century; but though *de jure* an Englishwoman may have had few rights, *de facto* she was often a power in the family and beyond, consulted and deferred to by sons or husband. This is seldom so in Portugal—nor do the women on the whole appear to seek such a position. More and more young women are now working, but the well-to-do wife who paints, plays, or studies birds or archaeology or botany on her own account is very much the exception. They are good though over-indulgent mothers and competent housekeepers, but they really lead enclosed lives, seeing chiefly their relations and a few female friends; for a married woman of good social position, or a young girl, to have her own men friends, and eat with them in restaurants, or go about with them, is still very rare.

Many of the intellectual and professional classes are trying hard to alter this state of affairs; they inquire with passionate interest into what sort of lives women lead in England or America. Curiously enough writing is considered quite a respectable occupation for ladies, and a surprising number of women have books of verses or essays, or novels, to their credit. But owing to the lack of experience and of the habit of reading, these efforts, with one or two notable exceptions, show little of the robust vigour of feminine writing in America and the rest of Europe. And for all this it is probably still reasonable to blame the Moors, since Spain and Portugal, which suffered the Moorish occupation, as the rest of Europe did not, are alike in these respects.

V

The fifth great landmark in Portuguese history was its becoming an independent kingdom in the first part of the 12th century. In 1095 King Léon of Castile handed over the government of the coastal duchy of Portugal, then still a dependency of the Kingdom of Castile, to his son-in-law, Count Henry of Burgundy. Princess Theresa, Henry's wife, seems to have become attached to her new place of residence—so much so that on her husband's death in 1114 she tried to annul her own country's rights of suzerainty. One wishes one knew more about the motives which prompted her to this subversive act; she sounds a most original character. She was not wholly successful, but her son, Dom Afonso Henriques, a resounding name in Portuguese mouths, was; he threw off the Castilian yoke, and became King Afonso I of Portugal. Having secured the independence of his tiny kingdom, which at the time of his accession only extended from the Minho to the Mondego, he set about throwing out the Moors; after clearing the northern part of the country, he proceeded to the conquest of Santarem and

Lisbon, and before his death had rid the whole of Estremadura and a large part of the Alentejo of the heathen.

To this period belong most of the great castles of northern Portugal; obviously to defend its newly-won freedom the little kingdom needed what the Border Scots called "strengths" in key positions, and many were built, including the ones at Guimarães before referred to, with its toothed battlements. From their dates, some may have been built under Castilian auspices to hold down a truculent province, and later turned against their builders; but, one way or another, this was the great castle-building epoch, and these Portuguese castles are one of the most magnificent features of a country full of architectural splendours—few towns of any size are without one. But Castile did not relinquish its rich coastal province without a struggle, and the fight for independence continued under the next four or five generations of the newly-founded dynasty:— Dom Sancho I, "O Povoador," the coloniser; Dom Diniz, who so encouraged agriculture that he was called "O Lavrador", the husbandman, husband of the Holy Queen St. Elizabeth of Portugal (who oddly enough was the great-niece of St. Elizabeth of Hungary, also a Queen, she whose forbidden loaves for the poor turned to roses in her apron when her husband challenged her); his grandson, Dom Pedro I, one of the world's great lovers, who so adored his mistress, Inez de Castro, that when he ascended the throne nearly a year after her murder by a rival faction, he had her corrupting body dressed in royal robes and crown and seated by his side, and forced his court and nobles to pay homage to her as Queen. After, he put her in a splendid Gothic tomb in the great abbey church of Alcobaça, and arranged that his own corpse should lie in another, foot to foot with hers, so that at the Resurrection the first sight his eyes should rest on would be what his mortal eyes had most delighted in, Inez's lovely face. A strange man, Pedro the Cruel—he sought to drown his anguish for his lost Inez in dancing; to the strains of the long royal silver trumpets he would even dance through the streets of Lisbon.

The struggle for independence was not yet over. More than a century after the final expulsion of the Moors from the south in 1249, another woman, Eleanor, wife of the last member of the dynasty founded by Afonso Henriques, Ferdinand I, reversed the rôle played by Theresa of Castile three and a half centuries earlier;

on *her* husband's death in 1383 she assumed the Regency, and promised the throne of Portugal to the unborn son of her only child, who had married the then King of Castile, thus re-opening the whole dynastic question. This was too much for the Portuguese after three hundred years of independence, and a revolution raised to the throne the Master of the Order of Aviz, a bastard son of King Pedro (lover of Inez de Castro), under the title of John I. He spent two arduous years fighting the Spaniards, hampered by the intrigues of the Queen-Mother, but in 1385 the invaders were finally defeated at the great battle of Aljubarrota, the Portuguese Crécy, when bowmen on foot routed the cavalry of Spain. It was in commemoration of this victory that the glorious abbey of Batalha was built, and it is charming that England and Portugal, those ancient allies, should each have its Battle Abbey.

VI

Historical periods tend to overlap, and King John I, whose vigorous action put an end to the first Portuguese dynasty and set the seal on his country's long struggle for independence, not only founded a new line, but stands at the beginning of a new era, that of European expansion overseas. He strengthened the Portuguese alliance with England, and clinched it by marrying an Englishwoman, Philippa of Lancaster, daughter of John of Gaunt. This great lady brought a strict English purity of morals, and great culture, to the Portuguese Court; it is one of Time's more curious revenges that the natural son of that resounding lover King Pedro should have married, and remained devoted to, a woman so deeply religious, and with such a high sense of personal dedication. She was greatly, and rightly, beloved, and bore the King six sons, all remarkable; but her greatest gift to her new country was her third son Dom Henrique, Prince Henry the Navigator, who was destined to play one of the greatest rôles in human history. From Sagres near Cape St. Vincent he planned, prepared and fitted out expedition after expedition to explore the coasts of Africa, always seeking a route to the East by which to bring home the spices and other oriental merchandise whose passage through the Mediterranean was almost barred by the depredations of the Moorish pirates. He made maps, he collated evidence—from as far afield as Abyssinia; he employed renowned sea-captains; when a new island or territory was discovered, true to his English blood he occupied and colonised it. Madeira in 1420, the Azores in 1431, became in this way the first beginnings of the great Portuguese Overseas Empire. But his greatest work was one of intellect, determination, and faith—to break down the fear of the unknown and to expand the limits of the possible by creating not only maps and charts, but a new technique of exploration and a corps of men trained in it—and these continued to bear fruit long after his death in 1460. The culmination of his life of selfless effort and study was reached when Vasco da Gama made the first voyage round the Cape of Good Hope to India, in 1497–99. Christopher Columbus got his training in this school; he served in a Portuguese expedition to the coast of Guinea, while he was in Portugal and Madeira from 1470 to 1484.

Wonderful man, Dom Henrique! Go and look at his portrait by Nuno Gonçalves in the great triptych in the Museum of Ancient Art in Lisbon—the sad, wise, learned face, the firm but disappointed mouth, the far-seeing eyes. Only since the Algarve has become a tourist centre have many foreigners made the journey to Sagres, the great promontory overlooking the limitless ocean, where the lonely man spent his years of unremitting toil, far from the Court and from the family he loved, but close to Faro, where he had his specialised shipyards, and where his tiny intrepid fleets came and went, bringing news, so eagerly awaited, of a new cape rounded, a new river-mouth entered, a landing on a new island—only to be told, over and over again, "Go back and learn some more; go further."

India was not the end. The voyages produced colonies; the colonies brought wealth; the process went on and on, till in 1500 Pedro Alvares Cabral, from the little town of Belmonte in Beira Baixa, carrying with him a statue of Nossa Senhora da Boa Esperança, discovered Brazil, a discovery which was to put the coping-stone on the vast edifice of the Portuguese Overseas Empire. (They still keep the statute at Belmonte in the ancient church in which Cabral was baptised, and carry it in procession once a year, in a silver-painted boat, through the narrow streets of the little hill-town.)

VII

This last discovery took place in the reign of Prince Henry's great-great nephew, King Manoel I (1495–1521), after an interval during which the wearers of the Portuguese crown had been steadily following in The Navigator's footsteps, fostering discovery, conquest, and colonisation, often at a great expenditure of life and treasure, till Portugal's overseas possessions comprised a large part, possibly more than a third, of the known world outside Europe. And with the reign of Dom Manoel we reach the seventh and perhaps the most important of our landmarks, since it represents the apex of Portugal's strength and glory. Manoel reaped where his predecessors had sown; from the new colonies wealth poured in— gold, spices, ivory, precious stones—till the small state on the extreme Western coastal strip of Europe was so rich that it really did not know what to do with its vast wealth, and the nation itself, including its sculptors and architects, was obsessed, was almost intoxicated with the mysterious wonders and splendours reported from other worlds than its own, and the romance and adventure of great ocean voyages.

The result was that astonishing architectural flowering which is now called Manueline. Buildings are one of the most natural and obvious ways in which a nation's wealth and triumph will find tangible expression, and so it was in Portugal then. Experts still argue over the various architectural impulses which, in combination with the original Gothic, produced the unique result. Certainly the Moorish influence was there, brought in direct from Morocco by architects like Francisco de Arruda, builder of the Vasco da Gama Tower at Belem, who were sent to inspect and restore the fortifications in the African colony; and from the fresh, the almost hallucinated naturalistic impulse to use knotted cables as a design for the groining of vaulted roofs, and chains, anchors, sails and coral as forms of cathedral decoration, it was but a step to including the regional flora, to letting the trunks of oak and olive act as pillars sustaining the arches framing door and window, and twining their leafy branches as tracery. And while the nautical obsession sometimes overflowed into the grotesque, as at Tomar, in other places —especially the cloisters and the Unfinished Chapels at Batalha, and the great church and cloister of S. Jeronimos at Belem— the fresh impulses and the decorative exuberance of this golden age produced some of the most beautiful examples of building in the world.

VIII

Spain had never ceased to deplore and resent the loss of Portugal, with so much of the Atlantic coast-line of the Peninsula, and several fine natural harbours; and on the death in 1580 of the Cardinal-King Henry, Manoel's celibate son, Philip II pounced with a trained army on the little kingdom, and this time succeeded in annexing it. The Spanish domination lasted for sixty years, till 1640, and was disastrous for the Colonial Empire, since the Spaniards used the troops and fleet of their new acquisition in uninteresting wars with England, Holland and France, leaving the rich Oriental colonies at the mercy of the English and Dutch. Here comes in a funny little example of how trade affects the course of history. The Dutch at that time had few or no possessions in the East Indies, but their national economy was geared to a lucrative carrying and distributing trade of the produce of the Portuguese colonies there, which they shipped from Lisbon, already a great entrepôt centre for commerce between Europe and the Orient. Philip of Spain forbade the Dutch ships to enter the Tagus—whereupon the enterprising Hollanders sailed direct to the East Indies to collect the merchandise they needed, and ended by annexing most of the undefended Portuguese colonies. From these successes they turned westwards, and captured Angola, and the greater part of Brazil. The English, regrettably, took a part in this spoliation of their ancient ally, and by the time the Spanish domination came to an end, in 1640, the East Indies, which had been Portugal's private preserve, so to speak, had seen the rise of two rival and larger colonial empires. By such a narrow margin of time, and the accident of a childless king, the fruits of Prince Henry the Navigator's great labours were brought to naught, as far as his native land was concerned.

At home, such a state of affairs could not last; the Portuguese were by now far too stubbornly grounded in independence. In 1640 the people of Lisbon rose under their Archbishop and forty of their nobles and proclaimed, as King John IV, the Duke of Bragança, the founder of what proved to be their last dynasty. This family, hailing originally from the north—there are Bragança castles at Guimarães and Barcelos, as well as at Bragança itself—had built themselves a fine house, with a hunting-park, at Vila Viçosa in the Alentejo, quite handy to Lisbon. The new King had a hard task to consolidate his country's freedom, and called in as allies its late despoilers, the Dutch, who had a good fleet and tough and well-trained troops; in exchange for their help he formally renounced the colonies of which his new allies had robbed his nation. But both he and they reckoned without the strong national consciousness and sentiments of loyalty to the motherland which had grown up in the new dominions in the New World; true, the Oriental colonies passed forever from Portuguese control, but Brazil hailed the Restoration with joy, revolted with complete success against her Dutch masters, and in 1648 the Brazilians themselves fitted out a fleet and recaptured the richest of the West African colonies, Angola and S. Tomé.

So once again Portugal was free, with a rich colonial empire— indeed for the next hundred years wealth poured in from Brazil in an unexampled stream, and brought, as it too often does, corruption both of rule and manners. Everything was too easy—no one took much trouble, because there was no need; everyone took bribes, because there was so much gold. Yet to this period the world owes some of the most exquisite buildings even of Portugal, that land of beautiful buildings. Portuguese 18th-century architecture is quite shattering, both in its abundance and its lovely elegance. Mafra; the Summer Palace of Queluz near Lisbon; the great Lisbon aqueduct; the chapel of St. John the Baptist in São Roque; the University Library at Coimbra, perhaps the loveliest library in the world—and countless splendid great rococo or baroque churches and convents all over the country sprang up, watered as it were by Brazilian gold and Brazilian diamonds, during the resplendent reign of King John V, from 1706 to 1750. None of our landmarks has left richer traces than this one. Portuguese baroque architecture, in the north especially, is a revelation—for its purity, its vigour, and its astonishing abundance. In Braga, in Lamego, in Viana do Castelo and Barcelos whole streets, whole squares, are flanked and lined with the most exquisite fronts of houses, palaces, or convents, the dark granite of the pediments and surrounds of doors and windows standing out against a background of plain whitewash; while the church façades, in the same austere materials, show an exotic exuberance of outline that somehow never loses its dignity or its grace. Let no one attempt to make up his mind whether he likes baroque or not till he has seen its unique expression in Portugal.

And within the churches, one is amazed by the glorious warmth and richness of gilt and carved retables behind and around the altars, by panelled and painted ceilings, by delicious and delicate polychrome sculptures—a form of art in which Portugal is peculiarly rich—by splendid choir-stalls, whose decoration is derived from any and every source, from Chinese lacquer to Hepplewhite; by magnificent *ambones* (twin pulpits) and splendid silver lamps or glass chandeliers. But all somehow inspired by a *gaiety* of faith and devotion which is peculiarly Portuguese.

IX

Pride comes before a fall. Nemesis struck at Portugal, and struck hard. The great earthquake of 1755 shook rulers and people alike out of their halcyon dream of wealth and ease. Something like half the capital was destroyed either by the shocks themselves or the fires which followed them; thirty thousand people are said to have been killed, and the damage ran into hundreds of millions. The disruption of commercial life was almost complete for the time being, with business houses in ruins, and goods and documents alike destoyed. But the man was ready for the hour. The great Marquês de Pombal not only took prompt relief measures, but profited by the shaken condition of the realm to gather the reins of government more firmly into his own hands. The administration was reformed; agriculture was fostered, roads built and communications improved, industry encouraged; Pombal, instead of relying purely on overseas revenues, sought to make the homeland self-supporting. Many of his measures were wise—some were not so wise; his treatment of the English merchants in Lisbon and the wine-shippers of Oporto— who under the Methuen Treaty of fifty years before had contributed greatly to Portuguese prosperity—was both ungrateful and short-sighted; but then extreme nationalist sentiment is seldom a very sound guide, especially in matters of trade.

It is a curious reflection that we owe some of the finest municipal architecture in Europe directly to earthquakes; if an earthquake is bad enough it at once leaves a clean slate, and demands re-building on a major scale. Ragusa in Dalmatia at one end of Europe, and Lisbon at the other, afford examples of this. There are always losses as well as gains. Most of mediaeval Lisbon perished, but in its place rose the superb group of buildings of the Praça do Comércio, fronting on the tossing estuary (known to generations of English merchants and seamen as "Black Horse Square") and a good part of the adjacent streets—a splendid reminder both of the earthquake and of Portugal's great Dictator.

X

From the point of view of world history the Peninsular War, from 1807 onwards, was one of the most important events in Portugal's history, since it involved the Portuguese, however unwillingly, in England's great struggle with Napoleon; but oddly enough it left little mark on the country save an abiding impression among the Portuguese of English drunkenness, a taste for French furniture and French bibelots, introduced by the Junots during their sojourn in Lisbon, and the now almost invisible lines of Torres Vedras, which dominate the imagination far more than they do the landscape. Nevertheless it has to be included, for its European importance.

XI

The Portuguese Royal Family had retired to Brazil during the Peninsular War, and the 1830s saw the dreary and complicated Miguelite Wars, between King Pedro IV, on his return from Brazil, and his brother Dom Miguel, who had seized the throne of Portugal in his absence. Brazil meantime had proclaimed its independence in 1822, and never returned to Portuguese dominion. The ideas of the French Revolution were more powerful than Napoleon's soldiers; anti-clericalism spread to Portugal, and the first dissolution of the monasteries took place there in 1834. This, alas, resulted not in fresh artistic or architectural achievements, but in the slow decay of existing ones—though the religious were thrown out, too often no use was made of their splendid buildings; some, it is true, were turned into barracks or schools or municipal offices (as at S. Pedro do Sul), but how frequently the visitor gazes in distress at the crumbling splendours of places like Bouro or Lorvão—empty mangers, without even a dog!

XII

To English people, one of the most amusing episodes in Portuguese history is its Victorian Age. For though few people realise it, Portugal had one, complete with Prince Consort!—and at about the same time as our own. On the death of Pedro IV in 1834 his daughter Dona Maria II became Queen. She married a Saxe-Coburg cousin of our Prince Albert, with the result that Queen Victoria wrote constantly and copiously to her Portuguese Royal Cousins by marriage. Many of these effusions may be read by the curious in the first three volumes of her letters. What is more, the same sort of architectural and decorative extravagances marked the period in the two countries. London has its Albert Hall, Lisbon the Palace of Ajuda; at Mafra there is a room whose furniture is entirely composed of the horns and skins of deer, in the best Balmoral tradition, and the 19th-century portions of the Palace of Pena near Sintra recall Balmoral at every turn.

XIII

Portugal became a Republic in 1910. In 1908 Dom Carlos and his eldest son were assassinated in the streets of Lisbon, and Dom Manoel II, the younger son, finding the republican party very strong, and anxious at all costs to save his country from civil war, withdrew to England, where he lived in exile till his death in 1932. He left all his Portuguese property to the State, and his body was brought back to Lisbon in a British warship, and placed in the Royal Pantheon at São Vicente there—a pleasant and uncommon example of generosity on both sides.

Portugal joined the Allies in the 1914–18 War, but her government suffered constant changes till the military *coup d'etat* in 1926, which resulted, two years later, in Dr. Salazar being brought into the government. Since then the financial position of the country has been restored, and great improvements effected in many directions.

CHAPTER II

LAND AND PEOPLE

PORTUGAL is both curiously shaped and curiously situated. It consists of a long narrow strip, varying from 75 to 135 miles in width, stretching for roughly 340 miles down the Atlantic coast of the Iberian Peninsula, of which in fact it occupies three-quarters of the total length; two of Spain's major rivers, the Douro and the Tagus, empty themselves into the sea within its borders, and two of her lesser ones, the Minho and the Guadiana, form its frontiers on the north and south respectively. In the north, the mountain system of Spain extends into Portugal in the great confused granitic masses of the Serras of Minho and Tras-os-Montes; indeed one may visualise Portugal as the gradual slope of the earth to the ocean from the high central plateaux of the Peninsula.

This is the diagram, the skeleton; the country itself is one of astonishing variety and infinite multiplicity of detail. Among the northern mountains, under the forests of pine and between the great groves of chestnuts, grow bracken, heather and fox-gloves; mists cling to the slopes, streams run down the glens—except for the vines wreathing the slender oaks and poplars, and the ox-carts creaking along the narrow roads, one might fancy oneself in Scotland. Down in the south, no such illusion is possible; the sun beats down in African heat and splendour on the great rolling sweeps of brown soil, set thickly with the shapely dark green of the cork-oaks, league after league; the cattle and pigs cluster round troughs at the wells for the water swung up by a bucket at the end of a weighted pole, or wound up by a blindfolded mule or donkey, walking endlessly in his small circle; the great fig-trees squatting on the ground like broody hens, a pattern in their greenness, the fragile almond-trees, the agaves and cacti along the road-sides—all these remind the traveller, not of Europe at all, but of Asia Minor or Morocco. Northward from the Algarve and the Alentejo lie the flat alluvial plains of the Tagus valley, the Ribatejo, where the light shapely bulls, bred for the ring, roam in huge herds over the dusty pastures, tended by men on horseback with long staves and tasselled caps hanging down their backs, and white egrets haunt the rice-fields; still farther north is the broken country of Central Portugal, of Estremadura and Beira Alta, where hill and valley, pine-woods and agriculture, maize and field-cabbage are all jumbled up together, and strings of windmills, as many as thirteen at once, stand grouped round the bare brown tops of the hills, for all the world like chaplets of shell jewellery, gleaming with mother-of-pearl, round the brown brows of a South Sea Islander. Down through this stretch —the only coherent feature in the picturesque orographical confusion—runs the Serra da Estrêla, the Mountains of the Star, slightly slanted from north-east to south-west, for over seventy miles; the highest range in Portugal, its crest rises to six thousand feet, and snow lies there from November to April—all the same, it grows crops of autumn-sown barley up to five thousand feet. Its blue outline dominates all that region, from near and far. Hidden away behind it, close to the Spanish frontier and seldom visited by foreigners, lies Beira Baixa, an open fertile country bearing splendid fruit, cherries and apples and pears, in its sunny orchards, and carrying flocks of a special breed of sheep, born almost orange-coloured and fading at maturity to a sort of *café-au-lait*—to see a flock of these delightful creatures coming down at sunset to drink at the blue-grey waters of the Zêzere is to see the strangest and prettiest sight imaginable.

And from north to south, everywhere, grow the delicate olive and the vine. Wine makes glad the heart of man, rich and poor alike, in Portugal; it is the universal drink. Port, that supreme product, grown on the buff terraces of schist up the Douro, in a stretch of country known as the *País do Vinho*, the Country of the Wine, will be dealt with in its place, which is Oporto; but there are other excellent wines too—the red wines of Colares near Sintra; the reds, and rarer whites from along the river Dão in Central Portugal; the light astringent *petillant* wine of the Minho, known as Vinho Verde or Green Wine, which prickles on the palate. This is said to be deadly to strangers, but in hot weather it is the most refreshing drink in the world. The wines are as varied as the scenery;—each district has its own, with its special qualities—but oh how good they all are, and oh how cheap! Every smallest farm has its little plot of vines, and in autumn one sees the big treading-butts, set on a four-wheeled cart drawn by stolid oxen, moving along the roads from

house to house, like threshing-machines in England; or pulled up
before some vine-wreathed porch, while a man or boy, trousers
rolled thigh-high, treads his family grapes with wine-stained legs.
In August, before the vintage, the empty wine-casks dominate the
whole countryside; the square in every village or small town is full
of them, lying under the trees—last year's, retrimmed, streaked
with brown and beige, this year's cream-coloured; outside every
other house two youths stand "rocking the cask", i.e. tilting it to
and fro to slosh the water and old iron with which it is half-filled
into every part, to cleanse the inside.

One of the most startlingly lovely things about Portugal is its
flora. It is really extraordinary that almost nothing has been written
about Portuguese wild-flowers, when one thinks of the endless
illustrated books on the flowers of Alpine Switzerland, for the
Portuguese flowers are in their way quite as spectacular, even if no
snow-capped peaks tower over them. Those rolling brown uplands
of the Algarve and the southern Alentejo are covered in April with
an amazing carpet of purple and gold, purple and white, white and
gold and scarlet—from which rise jets of sky-blue, like tiny fountains
from a carpeted Moorish courtyard: the white is moondaisies or
matricaria, the purple the open-throated *Echium plantagineum*, the
gold the two field chrysanthemums, *C. segetum* and the paler *C.
coronaria* with its band of lemon and white (parent of our garden
annual chrysanthemum "Eastern Star"); the scarlet is poppies, and
the blue fountains are the wild anchusa. Where the shadows of the
dark cork-oaks fall on this unpatterned glory, the colours deepen;
and where the arable gives place to an outcrop of barren rocky hill,
the big gum-cistus, two feet high, covers the harsh soil with an airy
cloud of immense white blossoms, like butterflies arrested in flight;
or a whole slope trembles in the breeze with the starry spikes of the
great pink asphodel, borne aloft on silver stalks, paler than apple-
blossom. There are such strange flowers too: a white lavender,
Lavandula viridis, grows on the Serras of Caldeirão and Monchique,
and a brick-pink blue-bell, *Dipcadi*; the sinister *Aristolochia*, and the
Serapias, with their long purple tongues. But when one begins on
the orchis and ophrys, there is no end to them!—their variety and
their delicate detailed beauty of green or silvery stalk, of pink or
mauve or yellow petals, of furry tongues in every shade from buff
to maroon. Up in Central Portugal, the tiny blue iris, growing from

bulbs, carpets the waste ground along the coast—alas, they die in the hand in five minutes; big yellow Spanish irises flaunt inland on the dry heaths among the lesser cistuses, white and pale yellow, or the lemon-coloured bush helianthemums; near Setubal big soft-blue irises grow beside the streams. The roadside banks are draped with the blue brilliance of three or four different lithospermums, and the dark *mata*, the furzy heathy growth under the pines, is starred with the tiny lily-like white flowers of *Anthericum*.

Further north still are the rarest botanical treasures of Portugal, the wild narcissus. Nearly all the prettiest dwarf sorts now familiar in our English gardens are Portuguese in origin. The little Hoop-Petticoat daffodil, *N. bulbocodium*, grows everywhere, but one must go to the northern provinces for *N. cyclamineus*, whose creamy petals turn back like a cyclamen's, or for the white drooping "Angels' Tears", the fragrant golden jonquils, the stouter yellow *N. Johnsoni* and the rarest of all, the lime-loving *Narcissus calcicola*, its tiny flowers no broader than one's finger-nail and piercingly sweet, which so far has only been found in two places in Portugal: in the second of these it was only discovered as recently as 1946, and by an Englishwoman. That, for the botanist as well as for the archaeologist, is one of the fascinating things about this country—all is not yet known, there is still any amount of work to be done. It is unfortunate that the only adequate book on the native wild-flowers, Pereira Coutinho's *Flora de Portugal*, is so far only available in Portuguese, and is not illustrated; even those who can use it in the original will find it very poor on its descriptions of colour, because the author worked so much from pressed and dried material. Most foreigners will find another book on the whole more helpful—the Abbé Coste's great *Flore de France*, which *is* illustrated, and covers from two-thirds to three-quarters of the Flora of Spain and Portugal. And the officials of both the Jardim Botanico in Lisbon and the Institutos Agronomicos at Sacavem and Oeiras are learned, enthusiastic, and most kindly willing to identify pressed (or *really* fresh) flowers taken to them by serious botanists.

Portugal is still, most fortunately, mainly an agricultural country: something like three-quarters of its population of nearly nine and a quarter million people are engaged in agriculture of one sort or another. Cork is one of the major products; few people realise that little Portugal, with roughly the same areas as Scotland, supplies

ALENTEJO: A LARGE PIECE OF CORK BARK BEING TAKEN OFF THE TREE

ALENTEJO: A CORK FOREST

WOMEN WORKING IN THE FIELDS

WOMEN SCUTCHING THE FLAX

the whole world with about half its cork. The trees are stripped once every nine years, and the bare trunks with their tangerine-coloured wood are one of the most characteristic features of the landscape. The cork-oak is a dual-purposes tree. They need sun almost as much as fruit-trees do, so they are planted far apart; crops are grown between them, and when these are gathered in autumn, huge droves of pigs are sent afield to eat the acorns, which are so rich that they fatten the hogs enough for the winter slaughtering. Portuguese hams are good, and every country-house has too its barrels of fat streaky bacon, wet-pickled in salt and garlic and bay-leaves (delicious once one gets accustomed to it), its sausage-like strings of home-made lard—so much cleaner and more practical than our great balloons—its various sorts of sausages; the most appetising of these is a roll of raw smoked, spiced loin of pork, slightly salted, called *paio*; it makes the best inside to a sandwich that I know.

Much of the cork is exported in its crude state, but the Portuguese have shown great enterprise in processing it, and two or three of their big cork factories are among the most up-to-date in the world; their compressed cork tiling and cork mats, made from the ground-up fragments left over when the actual bottle-corks have been punched out by machinery go to ships, hotels and hospitals in three continents. A visit to one of these concerns, like the Robinson factory at Portalegre, with its elaborate machinery and ingenious planning, is an eye-opener to most foreigners.

Olive oil is another product which is extremely important to the Portuguese, partly as their chief—and preferred—form of edible fat, partly in connection with the very valuable sardine industry; they do not export much, because after canning the sardine harvest they have not always enough for their own consumption, let alone a surplus—but in any case Portuguese oil is far too rank for foreign palates. This is no fault of the fruit, it is owing to the way it is made. When the olives ripen—usually in early December—and the silvery trees are dotted with the small black fruit, out into the fields go every man, woman and child, and shake and beat it down on to hand-woven *liteiros*, or rag rugs, from which it is gathered up and carried off in baskets to the nearest pressing-mill. The process is interesting. Two huge stone or granite wheels, four feet or more in diameter, revolve vertically on a big round granite slab with a metal border fifteen inches high, and the olives are tipped or shovelled into this—when they are ground to a pulp, the pulp in its turn is shovelled into what I can only describe as round rope berets, about two feet across, which are piled one above another in a hydraulic press and slowly compressed till the oil drips out, and is run off into a succession of metal butts full of water; in these the impurities remain in the water, and the oil is run off the surface into the next butt. The pulp is then removed from the berets and re-ground once, or even twice, in another mill, which produces a second-grade but perfectly wholesome oil. Finally the "grounds", if one may call them so, are either fed to the pigs or put on the fields as manure.

The catch about the Portuguese method is that ripe olives very quickly go rancid, and even on the estates of rich and cultivated people they are left to fester in heaps for anything from forty-eight hours to ten days before being pressed, and are then "drawn", as it is called, in hot water, which brings out the rancid flavour and odour. On the very few estates where oil such as foreigners can eat with any comfort is produced, the rule is "two hours from tree to mill", and the oil is "cold-drawn"—i.e. run off into butts of cold water. Then it is delicious. However, as the Portuguese *like* the rank taste, and in any case have no exportable surplus, this peculiar procedure affects no one but the tourist, who is liable to be almost blown out of his chair, as by a jet of poison-gas, when the salad is brought to his table.

Portugal is practically self-supporting in cereals, in spite of her very dense population—more than two hundred and sixty to every square mile, which is a higher ratio than that of France. Wheat is grown in the centre and south, barley on the northern uplands, especially in Tras-os-Montes, rice—increasingly—in the river valleys, maize everywhere. Maize is an extraordinary friend to man; in Portugal, at any rate, it has at least five uses. Sown, often, in rows between some standing crop, the thinnings are fed to cattle; so are the pollen-bearing tassels, once the grain is set in the ears. When the cobs are gathered, the outer husks serve as bedding for stock, so do the stalks and leaves, if they are too dry to be used as fodder; the clean dry inner husks are torn into fine strips and form a stuffing for pillows and mattresses. The actual grain, of course, is a staple food; the emptied cobs are used as fuel.

The Portuguese as a race have many charming characteristics, but none is more delightful or more admirable than their attitude to work, and especially to work in connection with the kindly fruits of the earth. They make a festival, a gay and social occasion, of all the principal operations by which crops are secured to man's use. Beating the trees and gathering the olives becomes a family picnic— babies sprawl in the shade while laughing youths and elders, gaily clad, collect the precious source of the useful and beloved oil; nothing is prettier, in a really ballet-esque way, than an olive-yard at harvest-time, in the soft December sunshine. Treading the wine up the Douro, for centuries one of Portugal's chief sources of wealth, will be described in detail in its place; but it is proper to say here that the whole operation is treated with a sort of reverential joy— the *ranchos*, as the teams of grape-cutters and treaders are called, walk into the *País do Vinho* as hoppers move into Kent, from as much as sixty miles away; but they come with music, guitars and tambourines, and, men and women together, sing and dance their way along the dusty roads towards an agreeable and lucrative (if arduous) employment, which moreover makes their beloved country important and rich; and the actual treading of the grapes, in the chilly *lagares*, is encouraged by music and song.

Even more social is the business of stripping the tough husks off the maize-cobs—"shucking", they call it in the States; the Portuguese word is *esfolhar*, to de-leaf. Every *quinta* or farm, some time in October, has its *esfolhada* party, to which the whole neighbourhood comes in its best clothes. The maize-cobs have been broken off the tall stems and brought into the barn in great shallow *cestos*, or baskets; the men and women sit round slitting and tearing off the tough husks, and throwing the cleaned cobs into a great golden heap, whence they are carried out to the *canastra*, a long narrow rat-proof erection set three feet above the ground on a broad granite slab, with slatted sides to allow of ventilation, and a thatched roof. There is talk, laughter and singing; also a good deal of flirtation, for a man who finds one of the rare red cobs—an *espigo rei* or King Cob, it is called—may kiss all the girls present, and a girl who gets one may kiss any man she chooses. (It is currently alleged that most young men go to *esfolhada* parties with a King Cob or two in their pockets.) But in spite of giggling, laughter and pursuits into the outer darkness, the whole heap of maize gets stripped, even if the work goes on till three in the morning; and then there is a vast supper of some thick soup, *brôa* or maize bread, and lashings of the local wine, followed by a dance.

Beating and carding the flax is also made an occasion for gaiety, but of a more restrained nature, since it is a purely feminine occupation. A good deal of flax is grown in the north, and when it has been pulled and dried, and the precious linseed shaken out on to those same *liteiros* which are used for the olive-harvest, the stalks are first steeped in water for some days, then dried again, and roughly ground in the local mill—after this it is ready for beating or "scutching". On a biggish *quinta* a team of as many as six to ten women will come up to beat the flax, again in their best dresses: bright-blue blouses and aprons over dark skirts, maroon scarves draped over their heads and little flat round pork-pie hats of black plush or felt perched on top—walking in single file along the narrow field-paths, carrying their cork cylinders and their *espadas*, they look from a distance like a flock of blue and black ducks. Flax-beating is a dusty though not a dirty job, and is usually done on the *eira*, or threshing-floor; the women sit round on the low stone parapet, their cork cylinders, about ten inches in diameter and nearly two feet high, set up on end in front of them, and grasping a hank of flax stems in the left hand, they beat off the woody fragments of outer husk on the cylinder's edge with the *espada*, a kind of flat axe of chestnut-wood with a short handle and a shallow wooden blade, nine or ten inches long by four deep. It is skilled work, and they do it with great dexterity; talk and jokes fly with the silvery dust, as hank after hank of smooth linen stalks are deftly rolled and knotted and laid on one side. Meanwhile, within the open door of the barn or stable sit one or two old crones on low stools, a board with the points of nails sticking up through it hammered on to a low form or bench in front of them, and tease the beaten flax through the nails; to *sedare*, this is called—*seda* is the word for silk—and the coarser threads and scraps of husk are scraped off in a sort of fluff, till a much smaller hank of silk-smooth threads is left, ready for spinning. But the fluff is all gathered up—nothing is ever wasted in Portugal—and is also spun and woven into a rough off-white cloth called *estôpa*, used for dishcloths and other purposes; it is actually very pretty, wears forever and makes delightful chair-covers.

As far as its agriculture is concerned, Portugal in many places has still a biblical economy: reaping, gleaning, threshing the grain,

fetching the water—all are done as they are described in the Old
and New Testaments, and yet Portuguese agriculture is extremely
healthy, and highly productive. On the big estates and more open
country of the south it is possible to use the plough, though the fact
that cork-trees grow all through the fields make oxen on the whole
more economical for ploughing than tractors; but in the north,
with the tiny parcels of peasant-owned land and the small terraced
fields, ploughs are often impracticable, and the sloping ground is
dug by hand. Europe is sharply divided into countries where man
digs *away* from himself, as in the British Isles, and *towards* himself;
Portugal belongs in the second category, and the peasants use a sort
of magnified hoe with a blade as large as a normal spade, set at right
angles to the long handle, to dig their fields. They are good and also
highly intelligent cultivators; on sloping ground—and much of
Portugal is on a slope—they hack out transverse furrows so that the
torrential rains shall not carry the soil away downhill; they lay out
their irrigation ditches through the fields with a traditional skill
which is also highly scientific (as bees make their hexagonal honey-
combs, structurally the strongest and most space-saving form of con-
tiguous compartment that modern physics has been able to invent)
and along the sides of these ditches, because they are greedy and
thirsty plants, are planted the tall-growing bluish field cabbage,
whose leaves are cut and cut to feed the stock, while the patient
stalk pushes up and up, forever throwing out yet more leaves. In
early winter, when the newly-dug trenches still retain all their
sharpness of outline, the long narrow strips of field along some hillside, each with its drains in a slightly different pattern, look like
nothing so much as lengths of reddish-brown tweed of different
weaves, draped over the ridge. Ingenuity is in fact one of the key-
notes of the Portuguese countryman's character. The windmills, in
which many of the cereals are ground between great stones, are
usually owned by a little man who also has a plot of land of his own
to till; and once he has trimmed his cotton sails and adjusted the
wooden tickler which coaxes the grain out of the hopper, the mill
can be left to do its job alone. Unless the wind shifts; then there
must be readjustments. So he fits to the frames of his sails either
sets of wooden chocks, which make at each revolution a loud
cheerful clacking sound that can be heard half a mile away, or a sort
of clay whistle; any change, either in the direction or the force of

the wind alters this noise, so that the miller can hoe away without any backward glances, knowing that his ears will tell him if his mill needs attention.

Or this matter of *canas*, the tall blue-grey reed, *Arundo donax*, which borders all the little streams of Portugal with its thick woody stems, often twelve feet or more high. If the peasant lives on low ground, he plants these along the borders of his land as a barrier against stock; if not, he cuts them and makes fences of the stout stalks, and uses the leaves as bedding for his donkey or oxen; they will add humus to the manure for his fields. For this last purpose, too, he cuts the *mata*, the heathery furzy growth of the barren open heaths and the pine-woods; dried, done up in little bundles, his women-kind carry it home on their heads and stall their cattle on it and kindle their fires with it; *carqueja*, the less prickly sort, is sent and sold as kindling in the towns.

One of the striking things about Portugal in the 20th century is the contrast between these extremely primitive, though efficient, methods of agriculture and the highly up-to-date and scientific research into all agricultural matters undertaken by the Government. About all this the Portuguese show great wisdom. They do not mechanise for the sake of mechanisation, in a blind worship of the machine; if a method, primitive or not, suits the local conditions, and *works*, they leave it alone; if a more modern method is clearly better than the old, they apply it. Now the old biblical method of threshing very small quantities of grain, either by an ox tramping round dragging a log, or by man using a hinged long-handled wooden flail, does work—and where the smooth granite thrusts out through the soil in flat slabs forty feet across, why build a cement threshing-floor? But tying loose straw up in bales for transport is a slow and awkward job to do by hand—the pressure-baler is better; and so in central and northern Portugal one sees constantly the methods of 5000 B.C. and the present day side by side: the modern machine drawn up by the living rock, the neat bales beside the man with the flail.

The agricultural research stations at Sacavem, up the Tagus and Oeiras, investigate and introduce improved strains of cereals and disease-resisting potatoes and such things. Another, smaller and more specialised, the Laboratorio de Tecnologia at Alcobaça, deals with research into the propagation of cork-oak and olive trees, and into the disastrous disease latterly afflicting *Castanea sativa*, the edible chestnut; here too paper is made, on a minute experimental scale, from the wood of eucalyptus and pine and even some shrubby growths, to decide which combinations will produce the most valuable paper most economically. The method, here worked out, of propagating the olive by stock-shoots rather than by cuttings is coming into general use; it produces trees of a better shape, and more rapidly, than the old system.

Nothing exemplifies better the Portuguese combination of tradition, ingenuity, and scientific skill than their treatment of their forests. These are very important. The pine forests have a total area of 1,300,000 hectares, and represent twenty-eight per cent of the land surface. Within the last hundred years the beautiful Umbrella Pine, *Pinus pinea*, has been almost entirely replaced by the ugly but quicker-growing *P. pinaster*, which in its turn is now giving way in many places to Eucalyptus (*E. globulus*). In the privately-owned woodlands, large and small, the pines are tapped twice a year, spring and autumn, for resin, of which tens of thousands of tons are exported annually; but in the State forests, which comprise 400,000 hectares or about one-third of the whole, tapping is only allowed for the last two years before felling. The yellowish scars on the trunks above the little earthenware cups, the piles of white chips at the tree's foot, are one of the most familiar sights in Portugal. Tapping lasts for a month, and men with a curious long-bladed axe with a curl at the tip of the blade re-open the wound three times during this period, carefully covering the cup with a sort of wooden ping-pong bat so that the chips shall not fall into the resin; when the tapping is over, girls go through the woods scraping out the sticky contents of the cups with a sharp-bladed curved tool into metal cans, whence it is transferred to the barrels which lie about under the trees. *Pinus pinaster* is almost as much of a friend to man as the maize; the tree, always an ugly one, is made grotesque by being pruned to within a few feet of the leading shoot, but the prunings are an essential part of the national economy; they supply fuel for many bakeries, whether in town or country, and the cones and smaller scraps are used by the peasants for cooking—the needles are often used for stuffing mattresses.

The Portuguese Forestry Service has undertaken a tremendous task of late years in sand-dune fixation up and down the coast. The methods by which this is achieved will be described more fully in connection with the great State Forest of Leiria—but it is also carried on elsewhere, as for example between Figueira da Foz and Aveiro, where a sand-strip 25 kilometres long and 5 kilometres deep has been "fixed" and planted, in six years, at a cost of £300,000—a notable undertaking, as foresters will recognise. Counter-erosion work in the mountain districts, fish-hatcheries and the re-stocking of lakes and rivers all come within the purview of the Serviço Florestal; and experimental planting is being carried out on a considerable scale with a view to producing, in time, forests of hardwoods as well as conifers, and of finding more commercially valuable substitutes for the blood-sucking eucalyptus, and for *Pinus pinaster*, which seldom attains what foresters call "a first-class form", even in its eightieth year.

One of the enchantments of the Portuguese countryside is that there one can see life as it was lived in England when England was still merry, say in the 18th or early 19th centuries. Conditions are leisurely, since the country is only now being organised on an industrial basis, and if some of the villagers are illiterate, their standard of communal enjoyment is exceptionally high. (And if that is not a desirable "standard of living", what is?) Not only is work itself turned into an occasion for festivity and jollification, but jollifications pure and simple are freely undertaken. In the summer months, particularly in the northern provinces, there is an endless succession of fairs and pilgrimages, usually called *romarias*. A *Romaria* is literally a "going to Rome", but has it come to mean those popular religious festivals which draw the country folk from miles around.

Of course in Portugal the idea of a church festival is not in the least incompatible with dancing and junketing—in fact, it usually connotes them. The little whitewashed church is decorated with branches, banners and paper flowers; so is the square outside it, and there is the inevitable and ubiquitous bandstand, where in the evening rival "filarmonicas" (*anglice*, bands) will compete, the long day ending with a lavish display of fireworks. Mass is devoutly attended; the music is tuneful and lively—fiddles, double-bass and clarinet, as in the English country churches described by Thomas Hardy; and the sermon is usually of the powerful camp-meeting kind—so country tradition demands. The Portuguese peasant is as fond of sky-rockets as the Chinese is of fire-crackers, and as often as not the most solemn moments of the religious service are emphasised by a salvo of fireworks outside.

A procession usually follows. More rockets; village children dressed as little angels, and one as St. John the Baptist, with a wooden cross and a woolly lamb. The special saint who is being honoured is also represented—in a St. Sebastian procession, for instance, there are several tots in white satin tunics patterned with red wounds and splashes, and carrying silver arrows. The streets are strewn with rushes and herbs and the scent of the crushed wild mint and thyme fills the hot air as the procession goes by—the individual penitents arrayed in white sheets or walking on their knees in fulfil-ment of vows, the Brotherhoods, wearing their bright loose-sleeved silk robes over their Sunday suits, one or two invariably carrying a sleeping baby angel or an exhausted infant Saint. The heavy shrines, gay with flowers, are carried by robed church-wardens or more Brotherhoods, the poles of the canopies being held by the big farmers or perhaps the local nobleman. One or more bands are strung out through the procession, playing away in pious discord.

Some of these processions involve curious customs. There is one where the journey from the hill chapel to the village is so long that a halt is called halfway for lunch. The Monstrance is placed in a way-side chapel; a man leaps out from among the pilgrims—one wonders by what remote tradition he is chosen—and to the sound of bagpipe and drum begins a wild dance, gradually working him-self into a state of frenzy. He is King David dancing before the Ark of the Covenant!

In Ovar, on the eve of one such popular festival, as the groups from outlying villages are sighted in the distance, bearing their Saints shoulder high for the morrow's procession, the local Our Lady is borne out to the cross-roads to meet them, swaying and nodding above the heads of the crowd. The decorated shrine is left out there all night (in Portugal one can bank on fine weather in August), but since it is loaded with valuable gems and golden ornaments, a guard of little children is appointed to watch it! For hours they pray and dance and sing, but at last fall asleep round the feet of the image; and there is not a thief in the land who would dare to break through that charmed circle.

Every five years or so, or whenever they can afford it, takes place the most notable of all these processions, the famous Feast of the *Tabuleiros* at Tomar. These are elaborate pyramids or towers made of canes skewered through loaves of new bread and profusely decorated with paper flowers, and the delightful girls of Tomar carry them in procession on their heads, each attended by a swain who sees that the contraption does not topple over. Behind them walk the clergy, mysteriously bearing crowns of silver on black cushions; but they are there only to give Christian sanction to what is obviously a much older tradition—indeed the Romans when they came to Lusitania found the Tomar procession already an established custom. After the clergy comes a brass band and then, most astonishing of all, a number of bullocks, with gilded horns and garlands on their heads! These beasts are subsequently killed, not ceremonially, but in the municipal slaughter-house, and their flesh and the loaves of bread given freely to any who asks—so that the poor of the neighbourhood enjoy a gargantuan feast of beef.

In a class entirely by themselves, of course, are the pilgrimages to Nossa Senhora de Fatima, who appeared to three peasant children in 1917. The great pilgrimage, sometimes attended by hundreds of thousands of people from all over the world, is on May 13th, but lesser ones occur monthly through the summer, and that on August 13th is also very popular. In August there comes a break in the rhythm of the year's work on the land—the wheat and barley are reaped, the vintage and the maize harvest are yet to come; also the weather is sure to be fine. Factory hands pay into what may be called a "slate club" for months beforehand for this summer outing; charabancs are chartered, and off they go, the roof of each bus piled with hampers full of food for three or four days, for Fatima has few hotels and restaurants, and the pilgrims sleep and eat, mediaeval-wise, out on the open hillsides. At suitable intervals the buses pull up and everyone gets out to picnic—but song and dance are still living entities in Portugal, and to mouth-organ or flute or guitar, the by standers beating time with their hands, there is old-fashioned dancing round the ugly modern vehicles.

And oh, the beauty through which these pilgrims go, the full rich beauty of Portugal in high summer! In the hot hazy sunshine, blue in the distances, under the high silvery light, every olive-tree stands glittering like some individual delicate triumph of the metal-worker's art; the great heaps of grain and straw round the threshing-floors are palest gold; beside the streams the *canas*, at full height and in full summer leaf, are almost Cambridge blue, the peculiar dull metallic blue of verdigris, and so are the plumed lines of field cabbage along the irrigation ditches; the rich summer coats of the great oxen shine like burnished bronze in the sun as they placidly draw their creaking carts along the white dusty roads. The freshly turned soil on the distant slopes, between the silver shapes of the olives, has the pinkish tone of polished copper; the rice-fields of the valley-floors have lost their emerald brilliance, and are dusted over with the rusty brown of the full ears of grain, but the maize, not yet ripe, stands tall, lush and green, its polished leaves reflecting the pouring brilliant light. Rich the land is, rich and at rest—and through it the people go on their pious outdoor revels.

And what an enchanting and happy friendliness they show. If you pass the time of day with one of these family parties, gathered to eat in the shade, you are sure to be asked to sit down with them and share their picnic; whether you do so or not, you will be introduced to everyone, and the son home from the Americas will show off his Yankified English. The food alone makes it a temptation to accept: cold roast chickens or turkeys, whole hams, sucking-pigs boned and stuffed, fried salted herrings, piles of lettuces, vast loaves, country cheeses, and seven-litre wicker-covered *garrafões* of wine!—the mouth waters while the heart is warmed by such a spontaneous kindliness and courtesy.

It may be worth mentioning here that Portuguese standards of courtesy are both high and elaborate, picnics apart. The normal form of inscription on letters is "Most Excellent", for Mr. and Mrs. alike; you call the purser on a ship "Your Excellency"; in small shops all customers already present greet the new-comer as he comes in, and it is common form to shake hands with one's tailor or dressmaker, and inquire warmly after their health. It is not held against the foreigner if he fails to conform to this ceremonial, but it is much appreciated if he does.

The custom of merry-making and feasting over country operations extends to live-stock. The annual business of branding the young bulls on the great farms of the Ribatejo and Alentejo is a tremendous occasion. From a raised stand the owner and troops of his guests watch the operations, which are exciting and picturesque to a degree, men on splendid horses assembling, separating and eventually branding equally splendid and active bulls; there is a luncheon which normally lasts from 1.30 to 5 p.m., while the best local singers, men and women, pour out *fados*, the haunting, melancholy, monotonous, and yet strangely fascinating songs so beloved of the Portuguese. (You have to get your ear in to appreciate *fados*, but once you do they hold you for life.) A *Festa Brava*, a "wild" festa, these occasions are called; everything wild in Portugal is called either "brave", or "royal", in the case of game—the latter expression delightfully recalling the days when all wild game belonged to the Crown. *Pato Real*, you say, when ordering wild duck. There was a charming occasion some time ago when the City Fathers of Lisbon, having decided on a drive to rid the capital of its many ownerless cats, put a notice in the papers requesting the owners of *Gatos de Estimação*, Cats of Esteem, to put ribbons round their necks, in order that they might not be swept up with the unfortunate *Gatos Bravos*, the "brave cats", whom no one loved or fed. And the foreigner is startled to hear Portuguese friends with an imperfect command of English say of an over-lively young lady— "She is so brave!"—referring, not to her courage but to her wildness.

Country fairs, where cattle, horses, mules, sheep and pigs are bought and sold take place all over the country, much as they do at home; and as in Britain the traveller is warned of his approach to one by the fair traffic on the road: women perched on donkeys or afoot, in their gayest scarves and aprons, with baskets of produce on their heads, men driving small open carts, the seats draped in brightly-striped blankets, or leading calves or oxen. What is unfamiliar are many of the things exposed for sale—the coarse brown or green or yellow earthenware, gleaming like huge vegetables, the rows of mules with Arabic patterns clipped on their rumps, the gaily-coloured rope head-stalls, the soft-cured buff leather country boots, and, at the Alentejo fairs, the little waggonettes with curved wooden roofs, glossy with varnish and looking like sections of Canadian canoes turned upside down, in which the farmers of those parts drive about.

The most important and famous of these fairs is that held for the Feast of St. Martin, in mid-November, at Golegã. This is more than a local horse-fair; it is a national occasion. Here the great horse-breeders of the Alentejo and Ribatejo, dressed in their traditional costume (they wear it every day) of grey tight-fitting trousers, short grey Eton jacket, and wide flat-brimmed grey hat, bring their splendid animals for sale; and here comes the *cavaleiros*—bull-fighting is done on horse-back in Portugal—to purchase their mounts for the bull-ring, and the crack horsemen from the Army, the members of the international jumping teams, to see the finest selection of horse-flesh in Portugal parading round the ring in front of the little grand-stand, either led by gaily-dressed grooms, or ridden by members of the breeder's family, sometimes three generations at once. In the stand sits the *sociedade*, the high society of Lisbon, the diplomatic corps, visiting royalties—everyone. But Golegã is demo-cratic in the best sense; in the dusty open spaces beyond the arena, among rows of tethered mules and groups of lowing oxen and cows suckling their calves, the local farmers stump about, cigar in mouth, eyeing, criticising, exchanging comment and gossip with the local nobility, eventually buying with discretion; many of them have fine home-bred teams too, which they drive round the ring in old-fashioned low-hung surreys and curricles; and they often purchase, at high prices, new blood from the big breeders, over a glass of wine at one of the many refreshment stalls. Golegã may well be unique in the world, now that so much of Hungary's country life has been destroyed. Each big stud has its own stables, surrounding the fair-ground; delightful places, with whitewashed arched loggias in front of the neat stalls, geraniums in pots blooming everywhere, trim plots of grass on which one may sit while Arabs with Crabbet blood are trotted up and down the sanded paths by grooms in dark breeches, white stockings, frilled shirts under red or green sleeve-less boleros, and red-and-green tasselled caps hanging down their backs; there is always a dining-room, with wine on tap, where these great gentlemen-farmers entertain their guests, farmers or bull-fighters or kings. For the real aristocracy at Golegã are the horses, and before them all men are equal. And never more so than when, at dusk, the spirited creatures, excited almost to frenzy by all the noise and crowds, are being ridden back, often by immature grooms, to their stables—anything then is enough to make them bolt, and you may see beggars and kings, dukes and bull-fighters, Ambassadors and farmers, who a moment before were all chatting together on the dusty track, scattering headlong into the mule-lines as half a dozen stallions, entirely out of control come charging down on them, preceded by the warning shouts of their horrified riders.

Such a scene is typical of Portugal. They are an easy-going race, with a great naturalness and simplicity. The peasants work extremely hard, but there is no violent display of energy by anyone else, and absolutely none of the Anglo-Saxon idea of doing things to time. Time means nothing. It is perhaps significant that in a casual sojourn in Lisbon it is hard to discover more than four public clocks in the streets—and these are difficult to see. Women will sit serenely for an hour or more at the hair-dressers, waiting for an appointment. In the shops, there is no eagerness to sell—on the contrary it requires the utmost pertinacity on the part of the purchaser to be allowed to buy what he wants, and if it should be on an upper shelf, he probably will not get it at all. (A visiting American once said that he had never seen such "sales-resistance" as that put up by Portuguese shop-keepers.) In a way this casualness is rather restful, especially on a holiday; and more positively delightful is the gaiety that makes a *festa* of work, the happy spirit that bursts into song on every sort of occasion, the cheerful contentment with a life of labour, above all the warm-hearted friendliness, to one another or to the stranger. They treat animals well—there is none of the carelessness which too often makes travel in some countries a horror to northern Europeans. And on the whole the Portuguese are an honest race. They will very rarely actually steal. True, one must scrutinise one's bill in hotels, even in the Government-owned *pousadas*, unless one wishes to be seriously over-charged; and in even the best shops, if one has chosen, say, a pair of fine nylon stockings, and asks for five more pairs of the same quality and size, it is fatal not to examine each pair minutely, as the Portuguese themselves do, or one may find oneself landed with the same colour, indeed, but in any size, and with faults in the nylon. But that is less wilful dishonesty than because, in the second case, the shop-girl is too lazy to see what she is giving you—and in the first because the hotel clerk was talking to someone while he made out your bill, or gave you someone else's bill—as he will tell you, blandly, when challenged.

Another curious contrast in Portugal is between the extremely high level of *individual* scholarship and criticism in artistic matters, bearing fruit in a whole series of admirable books and monographs by such experts as Dr. João Couto, of the Art Museum, Dr. Reinaldo dos Santos, and Dr. João M. dos Santos Simões—to mention only a few out of many—and the tragic combination of energy and misguided architectual theory shown by the Portuguese Commission on Ancient Monuments, which is responsible for the care and maintenance of the national monuments. The Portuguese have a passion anyhow for pulling down and building up (which they do very well and at lightning speed), and the face of half the streets in Lisbon seems to change every few months. But applied to ancient buildings, this process is disastrous. Nearly every castle in the country which has been touched at all has been severely *over-restored*; and in how many churches have not the additions, the natural and normal accretions over the centuries since they were first built, within the last few years been ruthlessly torn away? Both historically and aesthetically, this is surely an error in conservation. All over Europe, churches have always received additions from the fresh impulses of genius or piety of succeeding generations; often the additions are as beautiful as the original building; and to remove these in order to reproduce, quite falsely and quite arbitrarily, the primitive structure is to deny history and to repudiate fact. It may seem unbecoming in a foreigner to intrude his or her opinion in such matters, but the artistic possessions of any country are not solely that country's own private concern, they form part of the common heritage of mankind; and the damage still being done is so grave, and the dismay and distress of the more travelled and educated Portuguese themselves is so acute that we have thought it proper to refer to this unhappy state of affairs. Many concrete instances must, in the interests of accuracy, be mentioned in later chapters; and perhaps, in any case, lovers both of art and of Portugal have the right to give utterance to their distress.

Where the national casualness is really rather heart-breaking is to the serious sight-seer with limited time at his disposal. Portuguese churches, strangely enough, do not stand open for private worship; perhaps because of the treasures they contain, except at certain hours of services they are kept locked. It does not in the least follow that the sacristan has the key—it may be any old crone, and she may live half-a-mile away. This business of getting hold of the key, the *chave*—"Ah shahve" are the operative syllables—ends by becoming a nightmare. Anything from ten minutes to an hour is required to produce it. (The record is one hour and fifty minutes, with total failure at the end!) The seasoned traveller, on entering a town, picks out the three or four churches of his choice, and while admiring the exterior of the first, sends his taximan or a series of runners off in pursuit of the *chaves* of the rest; by this means, though he may have to wait twenty minutes to get into church (*a*), churches (*b*), (*c*) and (*d*) will probably be ready for him. Plenty of small change should be carried; silver to give to the child or crone who actually brings the key, copper for the beggars and the swarm of children who assemble to see the fun. It is actually rather discourteous and unkind *not* to give to those who beg in Portugal, where voluntary Christian charity is more highly esteemed than governmentally organised relief. But it is not easy to carry enough change! In the case of the children, a good plan is to still their clamour and drill them into a row, making all brothers and sisters stand together, and then give a coin to the youngest member of each family; this amuses them highly, and prevents the noisiest and most active from getting tipped over and over again, as will certainly happen otherwise.

Many visitors to Portugal got something of a shock on first seeing a prison in a country town, with the inmates looking through the barred windows and holding out their hands for money. But although this may affect foreign susceptibilities, a little reflection shows that it must be very much more pleasant, if one is a prisoner, to be able to look out of a window on to the busy street, talk to one's friends, and receive money and ever-precious cigarettes from kind persons. In certain prisons, a lively trade was carried on in brushes, boxes and such-like, made by the prisoners, and much chaffering and bargaining could be seen going on between the housewife in the street and the maker of the goods behind the bars. But these small jails are fast being superseded by modern prisons.

For when all is said and done, what a lovable people is this, and what a happy one! The longer one lives among the Portuguese, the better one gets to know them, the country-folk especially, the more one is inclined to apply to them Robert Louis Stevenson's great praise of the simple laity, in every-day life:

> For those He loves who underprop
> With daily virtues Heaven's top

CENTRAL PANEL OF THE TRIPTYCH DO INFANTE BY NUNO GONÇALVES IN THE
LISBON ART GALLERY. (DOM HENRIQUE IS THE FIGURE IN A LARGE BLACK HAT)
By kind permission of the Museu Nacional de Arte Antiga

BELEM: GARDEN FRONT OF THE PORTUGUESE PRESIDENT'S PALACE

LISBON: CHURCH OF MADRE DE DEUS, SHOWING AZULEJOS PANELS ALLIED TO
BAROQUE WOODWORK

Support the falling sky with ease
Un-frowning caryatides;
Who with weak virtues, weaker hands
Sow joy upon the peopled lands—
And still with laughter, song and shout
Spin the great wheel of Earth about.

CHAPTER III

LISBON

LISBON is town with few buildings of real architectural note, though taken as a whole, it must be one of the most beautiful capital cities in the world. Built on a series of hills with deep valleys running down to the broad Tagus, the colour-washed houses attached like limpets to almost perpendicular cliffs, the unforgettable views from the many belvederes which have been opened up on every eminence, give perpetual delight to the visitor or the fortunate resident. The layout of the city looks simple on the map, but owing to the differing levels it is not an easy place for the stranger to find his way about. However, the Lisbon taxis, though driven like dirt-track racers, are numerous and cheap, and the extensive public transport system of trams and buses, both single and double-deckers, sometimes give a better view of the town than do the fast, shut-in taxis. There is also an underground railway. Particulars of the hotels of Lisbon and useful information will be found in the Appendix.

The centre of Lisbon is the rectangular square known as the Rossio, with the National Theatre filling up the north side and surrounded on the other three by the sober houses built by the Marquês de Pombal, trusted Minister of D. José I, after the great earthquake of 1755 which destroyed over half the city. It is remarkable that the general feature of Pombaline architecture is its simplicity, for at the same period numberless splendid rococo churches and buildings were being erected in other parts of Portugal. The colour-washed façades are broken only by regular lines of plain stone-framed windows, reminiscent of Adam's London, where Pombal had been the Portuguese envoy for some years, but there is a subtle difference in the proportions and the eaves of the tiled roofs turn up in an amusing Chinese manner.

The *Baixa*, between the Rossio and the river is divided by three main streets. That to the right, the Rua do Ouro, or Aurea, is where most of the banks and money-changers are and from it a lift ascends to the higher level of the Largo do Carmo. On the left of the Rossio is the Rua Augusta, and the Rua da Prata runs south from the Praça da Figueira, with its flower stalls and car-park, which lies behind the Rossio to the east. These main thoroughfares are crossed at regular intervals by side streets, so that in some ways this part of Lisbon looks like a tiny scale model of New York! The pavements of these streets, as well as many others in Lisbon, consist of mosaics of black and white stones in delightful patterns. A triumphal arch leads from the bottom of the Rua Augusta to the Praça do Comércio, always known as the Terreiro do Paço, which was nicknamed "Black Horse Square" by English travellers of the last century. This, designed by Eugenio dos Santos, is surely one of the really magnificent squares of the world, fit to rank with St. Mark's. To the south the huge open space is gently washed by the Tagus, with the long range of the Serra da Arrabida in the blue distance; the other three sides are bound by uniform arcaded buildings, flanked by two low square towers on the river, lovely in their similarity and perfect simplicity of proportion. In the centre of the square stands the huge bronze equestrian statue of D. José I, cast from eighty-four thousand lbs. of metal in eight minutes by Brigadier Bartolomeu da Costa in 1774, and designed by Machado de Castro, the greatest Portuguese sculptor of the 18th century, who, as this statue and his other work shows, should be much better known than he is to lovers of art in other countries. The King is clothed in breast-plate and plumed helmet and his splendid horse is trampling on writhing serpents. The whole thing is mounted on a gigantic pedestal which was dragged into Lisbon from a quarry some miles away by eighty yoke of oxen. On the front of the pedestal there is a bas-relief medallion of Pombal. When he was disgraced under D. José's successor, D. Maria I, this bas-relief was removed, and only in 1834, when the Liberals succeeded in establishing D. Maria II on the throne, was Pombal replaced. The medallion had been ordered to be destroyed, but the undertaking was entrusted to the man who had made it, and he could not bring himself to melt down his own work, so he bricked it up in a wall of the Arsenal and on his deathbed confided the secret to a nephew, who later told the story to Marshal Saldanha, who had it unearthed nearly sixty years after it was hidden.

It was at the north-west corner of the Terreiro do Paço, just in front of the General Post Office, that D. Carlos and his elder son,

D. Luiz Filipe, were assassinated by pistol shots on the 1st of February, 1908. This led to the ultimate exile of D. Manoel II, the younger son, who succeeded to the throne, and the proclamation of the Republic in 1910.

Up to the north-east of Black Horse Square stands the Cathedral or Sé, begun in 1150, in a part of Lisbon which almost entirely escaped the great earthquake of 1755. The heavy façade has great dignity, but the interior has been so much restored that it has lost much character, though there still exists the font where St. Anthony of Padua was christened in 1195, and in the little chapel at right angles to it is a Crib by Machado de Castro. The lovely renaissance chancel has not been touched, though every now and then proposals are made to have it replaced by a modern Gothic one! The High Altar, like that in St. Peter's in Rome, faces the congregation, for the Metropolitan of Lisbon says Mass facing the congregation, because in the 18th century King John V obtained from Rome the liturgical privileges of the Papal court, and since then the Archbishop of Lisbon has been one of the three Patriarchs of the West. The chapels set star-wise behind the High Altar are almost unused though with beautiful crucifixes on most of the altars, and some of them contain fine Gothic tombs. The cloister behind can be visited, but that also has been very much restored.

On the opposite side of the road stands a little church, Santo António da Sé, which is of interest to hagiologists as it is built over the room in which St. Anthony of Padua was born, now turned into a chapel and entered through the sacristy. The present church, lovely in its proportions, was built in the 18th century by Mateus Vicente, the architect who designed the Estrêla Church, on the other side of the city, and it was paid for with money collected by the children of Lisbon, who made little altars with an image of the Saint on the doorsteps of their houses. This custom still survives, and children's altars can be seen all over the town in the month of June, round about the time of St. Anthony's feast on the 13th. Past the Sé, a public garden lies to the right of the street, with a splendid view over the Tagus and the roofs of the houses of Alfama, a quarter of Lisbon that was not destroyed by the earthquake since like the Sé it stands on solid rock, and has been little touched since mediaeval days. In this garden there is a case with books, which people can take out on a small deposit and read sitting in the sun. Similar bookcases with an attendant are to be found in summertime in most of the public gardens of Lisbon.

Further up the road to the left the Espirito Santo Foundation in an old palace exhibits fine furniture and pictures and incorporates a school of craftsmanship.

The Castle of St. George rises above this part of the town. The golden-white battlements stands high, and from them there is perhaps the best of all views over the city, stretching right out to the bar of the Tagus, with the pinnacled Sintra hills as the backcloth to what is a most dramatic sight. Within the outer wall of the castle still stands a little mediaeval village grouped round an exquisite tiny, formal square, with benches and plane trees and a church at one side reminiscent of a French village "place". Between the castle and the river, the narrow 16th- and 17th-century streets and alleys are the scene of great festivities on the feast days of the three Patrons of Lisbon, St. Anthony, St. John and St. Peter, on June 13th, 24th and 29th. During these nights no one goes to bed. *Ranchos* or the members of the parish orchestras roam about dancing and playing on their musical instruments, all dressed up in gay country costumes, Bonfires are lit in the streets, and people old and young dance round them or jump through the flames, an unforgettably Hogarthian sight. Dances are held in all the markets of Lisbon and here also the fun goes on all night, the stalls are turned into little eating places where fresh sardines roasted over open charcoal stoves, or a glass of wine can be bought.

Up the river the great Italianate church of S. Vicente stands out on a wide terrace. The interior has a notable baldacchino over the High Altar and good choir stalls behind. In St. Anthony's chapel to the right, there is an inscription stating that the Saint's mother, Tereza Taveira, is buried there. In the cloisters of the old Patriarchal Palace next door are a splendid series of azulejos picturing the fables of La Fontaine; these cloisters lead to the Bragança Pantheon where the stone coffins of all the later Kings and Queens of Portugal are assembled, from Dr. João IV (d. 1656) and Queen Catherine of Bragança, to D. Manoel II, the last King of Portugal.

The Feira da Ladra, Lisbon's Caledonian Market, takes place on Tuesdays and Saturdays in the Campo de S. Clara behind this church.

Not far away stand two other churches, each with terraces in front and splendid views. The Augustinian convent of Graça, now a barracks, is one of the largest in Lisbon. The High Altar of the great church, a splendid baroque piece, encloses two silver angels who hold in their hands the coffer given by the King of Ormuz to the Archbishop of Goa, and is topped by a marble statue looking like the younger Pitt. The sacristy contains a good early 18th-century tomb and fine decorations.

The second, the little church of N. S. do Monte on the next eminence, is a very ancient place of pilgrimage, consecrated to S. Gens, one of the first Archbishops of Lisbon, who was martyred on this spot. The stone chair on which the Saint sat is preserved in the church, and expectant mothers go and sit in it to obtain what in Portugal is called a *boa hora*, or rapid and safe delivery.

. . . . . .

From Terreiro do Paço, where the car ferries leave for the south side of the Tagus, a road with trams runs parallel to the river-side road to Poço do Bispo. On the left the Manueline doorway of the church of Conceiçao Velha stands out most strangely from the Pombaline offices on either side. In the second chapel on the right stands the statue of Our Lady of Rastelo, brought from the little chapel at Belem where the great 15th-century Portuguese navigators, like King Arthur's knights, spent the last night in prayer before they sailed.

A little farther along, up the Rua dos Bacalhoeiros, is the Casa dos Bicos, an architectural curiosity built in the 16th century, the façade consisting entirely of pointed stones cut diamond-wise. The road soon makes a loop to pass the Artillery Museum, installed in an old palace, which is of interest to all students of arms and is open, like most other museums in Portugal, every day except Mondays. Further up the river the vast pink early 18th-century buildings of Santos-o-Novo stand out to the left. This convent, which originally belonged to the order of S. Tiago, has the largest cloister in Lisbon and is now used as an alms-house for great numbers of elderly ladies of small means, who each have two or three rooms.

The road then passes the church and convent of Madre de Deus (shut on Mondays) with a lovely rather plain late Manueline exterior which gives no indication of the splendid 18th-century interior. The nave is lined with enormous very bright blue azulejos panels representing formal landscapes and gardens with Piranesi-like buildings and figures, and in the chancel is a trick one of an avenue of trees. Above, beautiful gold baroque woodwork surrounds delightful 18th-century canvases of the life of St. Francis, and the ceiling consists of twenty paintings set in wide ribs with gold shell motifs between.

It is always worth visiting the sacristies of Portuguese churches, as they frequently contain exceedingly fine pictures and furniture. The tiny sacristy of Madre de Deus is quite exquisite, with 18th-century pictures of Joseph and his Brethren beautifully grouped, by André Gonçalves, above good polychrome decorative tile panels. Behind the splendid vestment chest, which has a gold back with reliquaries inset, are three very good 16th-century Portuguese panels. The ceiling is by Pedro Alexandrino, an indefatigable but very competent 18th-century painter, whose work especially ceilings, is to be found all over Lisbon.

The lower choir contains good boiseries and under one of the altars lies a statue of the dead Christ, an image to be seen in many Portuguese churches, from which they are carried in procession through the streets on Good Friday. A door leads to a charming round-arched cloister and then to a tiny double Gothic one lined with patterned tiles. The custodian takes the visitor upstairs through the ante-choir, with more canvases by André Gonçalves, to the upper choir, which is like a large and richly jewelled box. The painted panels in the ceiling are all set in gold, behind the stalls are wonderful gold baroque reliquaries and on either side of the window into the church are a pair of very lovely portraits of King John III and his Queen, Catherine of Austria. There are also Portuguese Primitives, mostly restored, and a strange early German panel, in very bad condition, of all the scenes in the Passion set round and about the city of Jerusalem. It is so unusual and so architectural, yet with a multitude of people, that in some ways it reminds one of those 17th- and 18th-century Portuguese cribs with a crowd of painted terracotta figures in an architectural landscape; these may possibly have been inspired by this picture. A museum of azulejos is being installed in the dependencies of the convent, which will show the evolution of this decorative form of art.

The 18th-century Palacio da Mitra, now the Lisbon Museum, is on the left, just before Poço do Bispo. In it are some good topographical paintings and a small collection of prints and china.

Behind are the buildings of the Mitra or Lisbon Workhouse, which houses over a thousand men, women and children.

· · · · · ·

At the north-west corner of the Rossio is one of the most grotesque railway stations in the world, with enormous Moorish horseshoe-shaped entrances, decorated in the Manueline style. It rather reminds one of the station façade at Kiev, which is built like a Russian crown. Once inside, the passenger must either ascend in a lift, or climb up several flights of stairs to the main departure platforms. These can also be approached by a road with several hairpin bends in it, from behind the west side of the Rossio. As the trains leave the station they enter a tunnel over two miles in length, which emerges into open country at Campolide, rewarding the traveller with a splendid view of the great Lisbon aqueduct.

In the centre of the Restauradores, an open space to the north of the Rossio, is an obelisk (a favourite monumental form in Portugal) commemorating the Restoration of 1640 when the country threw off the hated Spanish yoke. On the west side stands the Palacio Foz, constructed by an Italian architect, Fabri, and now the offices of the Secretariado Nacional de Informação, with a good Tourist Section. Beside it ascends one of the semi-funicular trams peculiar to Lisbon, where transport from one level to another is necessary, owing to the extreme steepness of many of the streets.

On the other side of the Restauradores another funicular leads up from the Largo da Anunciada to near the Campo dos Martires da Patria, usually known as the Campo de Santana. Surrounding this garden are the old Medical Schools and two big hospitals, S. José, the largest in Lisbon, installed since 1769 in the old convent of S. Antão, and the Hospital of Capuchos are near. On the east side of the Campo de Santana stands the Palace of Bemposta, now a military college. Catherine of Bragança, widow of Charles II, lived in this palace on her return to Portugal.

From the Restauradores, the Avenida da Liberdade ascends for about a mile to the Praça Marquês de Pombal with a modern statue of the statesman. The Avenida is bordered by wide gardens where there are pleasant open-air cafés in the summer. At the top the Parque Eduardo VII is a large open space; in it is the Estufa Fria, for those interested in horticulture one of the sights of Lisbon.

Several acres have been transformed into an enormous cool-house, in which flourish innumerable plants, bushes and ferns, protected from the sun by horizontal lattices of wood; paths wind in and out of the beds, water flows under little bridges, and the whole thing makes a most enchanting place in which to wander on a hot summer's day. The church of São Sebastião de Pedreira, behind the north-west corner of the park, is a curious example of floriated 17th-century work. All the interior walls are covered with carved wooden foliage and cherubs in high-relief, painted Wedgwood-blue and white.

Farther north along the Bemfica tram-route is the splendid 17th-century Palacio de Palhavã, now the Spanish Embassy. This was the abode of the "Meninos de Palhavã" (Palhavã means worthless straw), the three natural sons of D. João V—their lovely little carriage can be seen in the Coach Museum at Belem. The Palhavã Palace is astonishingly haunted by the ghosts of these young men, who ring non-existent bells in the main bedrooms to summon their servants of two hundred years ago. This palace is an exceptionally good example of Portuguese architecture of that date, and has a formal garden with good statuary, a private manège and an exquisite courtyard with azulejos, containing the stables, opposite the front door.

The Zoological Gardens are farther along the Estrada de Bemfica in the park of Laranjeiras, with its lovely pink palace; at one side stands the highly picturesque ruined theatre built by the Conde de Farroba. The Lisbon Zoo is remarkable in that to it the words "Zoological Gardens" do most strictly apply: it contains some of the finest formal rose beds in Europe, several Dutch gardens, and superb trees and shrubberies, among which the dwellings of monkeys, badgers, giraffes and other *ferae naturae* are disposed in a manner at once the most natural and the most artistic possible. One of the most amusing features of the place is the Children's Zoo. which is exceptionally well planned. Miniature houses in little gardens, with tiny bantams in the chicken runs, can be hired for the afternoon, and the cages are filled with baby animals. Feeding-bottles with milk in them can often be hired at the entrance with which to feed the baby pigs, though at one time they swallowed so many of the rubber teats that this practice was suspended.

·   ·   ·   ·   ·   ·

To the west of the Rossio lie many of the shopping and residential quarters of the city. The Rua Garrett or Chiado (almost every well-known thoroughfare in Lisbon has a nickname in common use) contains the best shops. On the left going up, the Martires Church, with a lovely ceiling painted on a green ground, is dedicated to the English and Frankish Crusaders who eight hundred years ago fell during the re-taking of Lisbon from the Moors, and at the top two churches face each other, to the north Loreto, the Italian church, and to the south N. S. da Encarnação, which has a formal painted ceiling with architectural details in sepia by Pedro Alexandrino. The entire side of this church giving on to the Rua do Alecrim is covered with pale blue pattterned tiles.

Between the Chiado and the river is the Biblioteca Publica, in the same building as the Contemporary Art Museum, which contains good 19th-century as well as modern pictures; nearby the 18th-century S. Carlos Opera House, the most elegant in Europe, has lately been very well restored, and good foreign companies as well as the National Orchestra constantly perform in it.

A steep street, the Rua do Alecrim, goes down from the Praça de Camões at the top of the Chiado, past the palace where Junot stayed when he was French Ambassador, which is just opposite the fantastic statue of Eça de Queiroz, Portugal's greatest 19th-century novelist. The writer in full panoply of frock coat and cravat is being ardently worshipped by the almost naked figure of Truth, with extended arms. This street leads to Cais do Sodré, the station for Estoril, and starting-point for some of the ferries to the other side of the Tagus. Near here in the Largo do Corpo Santo stands the pleasant octagonal church of the Irish Dominicans, who have been in this same place for three hundred years.

To the north of the Chiado, the Gothic ruins of the Carmo Convent, now an Archaeological Museum, stand in the Largo do Carmo. It was here that the Holy Constable of Portugal, Blessed Nuno Alvares, who fought at the Battle of Aljubarrota, entered in old age the Carmelite Order as a lay brother. His relics lie in a chapel on the first floor of an old palace at right angles to the ruins.

The most interesting building in this western part of Lisbon, the Church of S. Roque by the Misericordia headquarters, is up the Rua da Misericordia, a continuation of the Rua do Alecrim. It was built by Felipe Terzi at the end of the 16th century, and it was in this church that Padre Antonio Vieira preached in 1642 a sermon that went on for two days and a night! The last chapel on the left, dedicated to St. John the Baptist, was built exactly a century later by order of Dom João V, and is said to have cost two hundred and twenty-five thousand English pounds of that day; more than any chapel of its size has ever done. It was constructed in Rome by Vanvittelli the architect, of Caserta near Naples, of agate, lapis lazuli, alabaster and verde antica, with mosaics and paintings, and then taken to pieces and sent to Lisbon in three ships. On the same side is the tomb of a Cornish nobleman. Sir Francis Tregian, who is buried upright near the pulpit. Having been imprisoned for his Catholicism under Queen Elizabeth, he came to Portugal, lived here for twenty years, and after his death was regarded as a saint, and numerous pilgrimages used to take place to the tomb where his incorrupt body was found a century later. It is known that a great number of 18th-century and earlier manuscripts relating to his Cause at Rome were in Lisbon, but they have been lost for many years, though several historians have searched for them in the National Archives. However, there are so many private libraries which have not been examined that the papers relating to this unofficial English saint may well turn up some day. The church has a most beautiful late 16th-century painted ceiling of the Exaltation of the Cross, rococo side altars of the utmost richness and great glass-fronted relic cupboards surrounding the High Altar. In the sacristy there is a magnificent series of painted panels on the life of Saint Francis Xavier, attributed to André Gonçalves, whose work is also in Madre de Deus, and decorative furniture of the same period. On the other side of the nave is the entrance to the Museum, which is filled with Church ornaments and vestments of the most splendid rococo period, still used on great feast days. There are also very interesting 17th- and 18th-century portraits and furniture. In the Misericordia next door the weekly lottery, in aid of many Portuguese hospitals, is drawn publicly on Fridays at mid-day; the proceeds of the tickets or *cautelas*, for the purchase of which all pedestrians in the main streets of Lisbon are pestered daily, go to support this excellent cause.

The Rua D. Pedro V rises from S. Roque, first past the *miradouro* or viewpoint of S. Pedro de Alcântara and then through the

Praça Principe Real to where, some distance along, the Botanical Gardens lie at the other end of an avenue of palms to the right; they contain a superb labelled collection of Portuguese and exotic trees and plants. In the Rua de S. Marçal, almost opposite, the British Institute has an excellent library of English books and a Reading Room with all the English papers and magazines. Temporary membership can be taken up by visitors.

Behind the pink palace to the north of the Praça do Brasil or Rato lies the Amoreiras Garden. On one side are the arches of an aqueduct, which terminate in the Casa das Aguas Livres, or Mãe das Aguas, a huge 18th-century water cistern which can be seen on an order to view obtainable from the Water Board, 24 Avenida da Liberdade. Under the middle arch of the aqueduct is a little chapel dedicated to Our Lady of Monserrate. The octagonal interior has some splendid azulejos from the 18th-century Rato factory, which also made so many of the delightful commercial tiles still to be seen outside old shops all over Lisbon, illustrating the wares inside. The Praça das Amoreiras and the little streets round are filled with pretty houses and long low Pombaline buildings which were originally factories for the Rato ware and for silk, watches, buttons, fans and other industries, though many huge blocks of flats have been built in this quarter.

At the top of the Praça das Amoreiras there is a lovely Doric archway, over which the aqueduct flows. The Lisbon Aqueduct was built between 1729 and 1748 and crosses the wide valley at Campolide about a mile farther north. This astonishing and splendid piece of engineering, one of the glories of Lisbon, consists of thirty-five great pointed arches, the centre one is sixty-five and a half metres high and nearly twenty-nine metres wide.

.   .   .   .   .   .

From the Praça Principe Real, the Rua do Seculo, one of the most picturesque streets in Lisbon, cuts through to the Calçada do Combro, past an enchanting semi-circular Place with trees and a fountain designed by Carlos Mardel, who embellished 18th-century Lisbon so greatly with his palaces and fountains.

Farther on is another semi-circular Place, with classical details, from which rises the Calçada dos Caetanos, leading directly to the Bairro Alto, one of the 17th-century quarters of Lisbon little affected by the earthquake. The narrow streets are filled with beautiful houses, now mostly tenements, where gay washing hangs out of the windows. Indeed, through all the side streets of Lisbon washing is hung out, even at ground floor level, on triangular lines supported on pieces of wood, so that the sheets and underclothing of the inhabitants flap freely and delightfully in the faces of the passer-by. Lisbon is one of the cleanest cities of the world. Lorries empty dustbins daily, even in the poorest quarters; and this matter of drying the washing in the sun and sweet air at all levels is symptomatic of the innate wisdom of a nation which loves cleanliness. The air is filled with the peculiar cries of the street hawkers: the musical voices of the women who sell oranges, the flute notes of the knife-grinder, and the curious expectorant, or even retching accents of the man who wishes to purchase old iron, "Carapaus frescos"—fresh smelts—is the cry of the handsome barefooted "varinhas" or fish-wives, who prudently and economically only wear their slippers in fine weather, and balance the flat baskets containing their wares so majestically on their heads. Nor must one forget the patient donkeys of the vegetable sellers, laden with delicious vitamins in panniers, who stick their little dark noses across the pavement into the open doorways, while the housewives lower baskets with the money for their orders on a string from the upper floors.

At the top of the Calçada dos Caetanos is the English College, or "Colegio dos Inglesinhos", founded over three centuries ago for the education of English seminarists during penal times when the first students actually walked to Lisbon from Douai in northern France. The College is staffed by English priests and still educates students from the English dioceses. Visitors can be shown over the building, which has some good historical pictures and tapestries and a nice Chapel. Richard Russell, one of the College Professors, taught English to Catherine of Bragança, and played an active part in the negotiations about her marriage with Charles II. When the bride sailed for England with all her suite from Black Horse Square in 1662 Father Russell accompanied her as Almoner. He later returned to Portugal, became Bishop of Portalegre and then Bishop of Viseu, where he died.

In the Calçada do Combro at the south end of the Rua do Seculo stands the finest rococo Church in Lisbon, that of the Paulistas or Santa Catarina, which is now open all day. It was re-built after the earthquake and is a riot of astonishing gilding, lightened by the lovely plaster ceiling with pastel shaded reliefs of saints enclosed in Rex Whistlerish cartouches and swags. The chancel is lined with superb boiseries on which recline golden female figures of heroic size; in the centre the high altar retable soars up in steps like a great throne to the roof, and the gilded organ at one side is most beautiful. The exterior of this marvel is quite plain and usually has a sentinel standing outside, as the adjoining convent is now a barracks.

The Calçada do Combro goes on downhill passing the palace of S. Bento, the new and imposing Houses of Parliament, on the right and ascends again to the Largo da Estrêla in which stands the magnificent Basilica of the Sacred Heart, usually called the Estrêla Church, built at the end of the 18th century in fulfilment of a vow made by Queen Maria I, if she had a son. Though smaller and not so splendid as the basilica at Mafra, the Estrêla Church is incomparably more beautiful externally; and the interior in addition to containing exceedingly fine statues and good paintings, has a luminous quality that is entirely its own. The great, pale, exquisitely shapely dome, that can be seen from all over Lisbon poised in the air behind a pair of tall open belfries, is an extraordinary feat of architecture, for unlike the dome of St. Paul's which is made of lead, this is solid stone, and the basic problem of the weight was solved by building two domes, one inside the other. The façade combines all the good qualities of the Renaissance with baroque ingenuity in the arrangement of the splendid statues by Machado de Castro, which demonstrate how much he owed to Bernini.

The first impression of the interior of the church is of great height combined with a rarified lightness of atmosphere, owing to the delicate pink, yellow and pale blue-grey marbles with which it is lined, reflecting the strong light pouring down from the much-pierced dome. The nave is not cluttered up with seats, so that a clear view can be got of the spring of the walls and the marble floor. The picture in the high altar retable is by Pompeo Batoni, that 18th-century Italian whose work is now arousing such interest; it is very effective in the vastness of its conception and the use of a brilliant red in the garments of the figures.

The tomb of the foundress on the left of the High Altar is a delicious example of the fashions of the First Empire applied to memorial art. It was made in 1816 and consists of a black marble coffer resting on lions couchant with a serpent wreathed round a winged hour-glass on the front, two life-size mourning angels perch on the top and marble skulls at the corners are crowned with ormolu ivy leaves. In the sacristy stands the great black marble tomb of Inacio de S. Caetano, who rose spectacularly from being a clown to the Archbishopric of Evora and Confessor to the Queen. Behind the vestment chests are quite lovely late 18th-century mirrors with the original glass set in gold, red and brown frames. Up a dark narrow staircase behind the sacristy is one of the glories of the church, an enormous painted terracotta Christmas crib, or *Presepio*, by Machado de Castro, in a great glass case about ten by fourteen feet, framed in grey, red and gilt Adam-like decoration. Portugal is famous for the splendour and ingenuity of these 17th- and 18th-century *Presepios*, Many churches possess them and they come out at Christmas and remain till the Epiphany; but none is better or more delightful than this one. The crib itself is a welter of scenes and figures, with angels perching on broken pediments, for Machado de Castro was a true son of his age in feeling that art always improves on nature; and the procession of the Three Magi winds slowly down the hills behind, accompanied by a wise elephant and some contemptuous camels. At either side of the case we see the people of Bethlehem, or indeed of Lisbon, for they stand for every race and time, going about their ordinary avocations, working, cooking, playing cards, and idling, while in the centre is the Holy Family. so beautifully and touchingly modelled.

The English Church and Cemetery is up the Rua da Estrêla at one end of the Estrêla Gardens. The cemetery, in which the Dutch have equal rights with the English, is famous as the burial place of Henry Fielding, and lovely in spring with Judas trees and flowering shrubs. The registers of marriages, baptisms and burials of the British Colony in Lisbon began in 1721, but were transmitted to London until 1808. There is a gap from 1754 to 1762 which covers the period of the earthquake. In 1815 a church dedicated to St. George was built in the cemetery, this was burnt down and rebuilt in 1885 when the Royal Arms were removed and placed over the gate.

The parsonage house at 4 Rua da Estrêla, a plain 18th-century building, was erected by the millionaire Englishman Gerard de Visme and used as a British Hospital till about 1843, when it was converted into the chaplain's house. The present excellent British Hospital is in a building to the north of the cemetery just above the old Jewish graveyard—with its outlook over the bird-haunted cypresses and open space it is in an ideal situation.

Many of the foreign Embassies and Legations are in the Lapa district below the Estrêla church, sloping down to the "Janelas Verdes", or Lisbon Art Gallery, originally installed in Pombal's own palace, to which a large new addition has lately been built. The ceramics section is particularly fine in armorial *Compagnie des Indes*, the Portuguese equivalent of Chinese Lowestoft, and there is a good collection of European porcelain cups and saucers and early examples of the Portuguese factories of Rato and Vista Alegre, as well as glass from Marinha Grande. The 18th-century figures, both in wood and terra-cotta, by Machado de Castro and his contemporaries are worth seeing, but the most notable exhibit is the enormous silver table service made by the Germain Brothers for Dom João V.

The picture galleries upstairs are almost all hung with Portuguese Primitives of the first half of the 16th century. These are of interest to all students of painting, for they are a century later than those of other countries, and little is known outside Portugal of this productive and flourishing school that existed, obviously under strong Flemish influence, in the two main centres of Viseu, where Grão Vasco had his studio, and Evora, where Frei Carlos was the leading painter. The most notable of these Primitives is the great triptych "do Infante" by Nuno Gonçalves, with vivid serious-faced full-length figures, including the big black-hatted Infante Dom Henrique, grouped round Dom Afonso V who is kneeling at the feet of St. Vincent, the patron Saint of Lisbon. It is a most strange and quite unforgettable picture, unlike anything else and conveying deeply the greatness of both the portrayer and the portrayed. It is also worth looking at the pictures by Domingos de Sequeira, who might be called the Portuguese Ingres, which have a curious and individual charm. When the Peninsular War ended in 1814 the Portuguese Government had to decide what they proposed to give to the Duke of Wellington, who had been in sole command of the united armies. The Portuguese titles of Duke of Vitoria and Count of Vimeiro were conferred on him, as well as the Marquisate of Torres Vedras. But the Government, who were then in Rio de Janeiro, also decided

BELEM: INTERIOR OF THE JERONIMOS

LISBON: PRAÇA DO COMERCIO ("BLACK HORSE SQUARE")

to present to the Duke a great silver-gilt Empire table garniture, consisting of candelabra, centre piece, dishes of all sizes and spoons and forks. Domingos de Sequeira was commissioned to design this. He took four years over the work and the detailed drawings are in this museum. The service is now on view with the other Wellington treasures at Apsley House at Hyde Park Corner in London. The gallery possesses many pictures of all the European schools, though the English school is sadly under-represented. There is a room full of Zubarans and a small Isenbrandt, whose work, outside Bruges, is so rare. Another of his pictures, a tiny round one of the Virgin and Child in a landscape, hangs in the museum at Coimbra. The carpets, tapestries and church furniture are also worth seeing. This Museum, like most others in Portugal, is open daily from 10 a.m. to 5 p.m., excepting Mondays and public holidays, when it is closed. It is also open on Saturday evenings from 9.30 to 11.30 p.m.

The Largo das Necessidades, some way to the west of the Janelas Verdes, has a garden on a terrace overlooking the Tagus with an obelisked fountain put up in 1747 by D. João V in front of the Necessidades Palace, now the Foreign Office, one of the loveliest of the many lovely palaces of Lisbon. It was built as a royal residence between 1745 and 1750 and among the foreign princes who stayed there was the Prince Regent. The long low terracotta pink façade of the Palace, with a slight angle in the centre, terminates in a Church, and shows exceptionally well the Portuguese genius for proportion allied to originality in architecture, which reached its zenith in the 18th century. The Palace and the Church are not generally shown to the public, but the whole ensemble of the little garden with its view over the river, the pale red and white Palace behind and the great fountain in front are most beautiful.

. . . . . .

The suburb of BELEM, Portuguese for Bethlehem, is on the extreme west of the city and can be reached by trams which start from the Terreiro do Paço and go along the Rua da Junqueira, under the great bridge over the Tagus.

At Belem is the magnificent Coach Museum or Museu dos Côches, even better than the collection in Vienna, and of the greatest interest and beauty. The vehicles are all placed in two long lines down the 18th-century riding school (built by an Italian,

E

Jacomo Azzolini) adjoining the enchanting pink 18th-century palace, one of the official residences of the Portuguese President. The coaches are astonishing in their splendour. The earliest, in which Philip II of Spain travelled to Portugal, is late 16th-century (the only other of this period which survives is in the Kremlin) and there are three magnificent gilded baroque coaches on huge wheels which brought the Portuguese Ambassador and his suite from Rome in 1716. Many of the vehicles are beautifully painted, and there are charming late 18th-century and Peninsular War examples. A large gallery at the side shows more exhibits including the little pony-chaises, like Queen Victoria's, which were used by the Princesses in the Royal Parks. Upstairs there are dresses, uniforms, harness, pictures, prints and cases of bibelots connected with Lisbon or with the Royal Family.

A few hundred yards further on past the square in front of the Coach Museum is another big public garden; in the spring the cod-fishing fleet of three- and four-masted schooners lie in the Tagus off this garden before sailing on their eight months' trip to the fishing grounds of Newfoundland and Greenland. At the opposite end rises the Jeronimos Church, begun in 1502, one of the most original and beautiful places of worship in the world. The great South doorway, looking towards the river and rising the full height of the building, is an extraordinary example of highly-decorated Manueline work, that late flowery Gothic seen only in Portugal, unique in its vitality and originality. The fine West End has, alas, been ruined by the addition of a completely modern arch-way connecting the West front with the Ethnological Museum next door, so concealing a good renaissance doorway, as well as the Manueline West door. But it is the interior of S. Jeronimos that is so truly astounding. The effect is of a vast space with the enormously high fan tracery of the roof springing with effortless ease from six great octagonal columns covered with decorations of an incredible closeness and richness. The ornate roof over the wide transept is apparently unsupported by human agency and that also gives a unique impression of space. On either side of the transept are good altar-pieces, and the strange marble tombs of the Cardinal-King and D. Sebastião supported on the backs of elephants. The high altar and chancel are a lovely example of classical work, later than the rest of the Church. The 16th-century High Altar retable, of the

Passion in five painted panels, is attributed to Cristovão Lopes and the tabernacle is a good example of Portuguese silver work of a century later. The square sacristy, entered by a small door to the left of the transept, has a beautifully proportioned roof supported by a central stone column in the form of a palm-tree. Behind the vestment chests is an interesting series of 17th-century panels of the life of Saint Jerome. Long ago there was good stained glass in this sacristy but it has disappeared, as has most of the glass in the country, for strangely enough Portuguese churches are extremely poor in stained glass.

Portugal is a land of cloisters; every convent, every monastery has one, if not two or more, and of the many original and beautiful examples, those at Jeronimos are so wonderful that they are unique even in Portugal. In two storeys, with lovely fan tracery in each, the windows on to the garth are all different, and the Manueline carving and decoration on every inch of stone is extraordinary. Stairs lead up to the first floor and then again on to the broad open terrace which runs right round the top. The whole Church and the cloisters are the apotheosis of the Manueline, born of an exuberant age when the Portuguese navigators were enlarging the known world; much of the decoration is nautical and ropes, anchors, seabeasts and astronomical instruments prevail.

Adjoining the great church is the Ethnological Museum occupying what was the Monastery Refectory, with fine Roman mosaics. The Marine Museum, with a fascinating collection, is nearby. Near the river is the Museu de Arte Popular with a full collection of Portuguese country exhibits, earthenware, models and clothes, and examples of some rural arts and pursuits that are no longer practised as well as the many which remain.

Behind Jeronimos, the early 19th-century Ajuda Palace, which stands out boldly on the hill-side, contains amusing portraits of royal personages, tapestries and a room filled with furniture made out of Saxe porcelain, which was a wedding present to D. Maria Pia from the King of Saxony, a fantastic yet delightful example of Victorian taste. It may be said the great rooms and the furniture are so mid-Victorian that they are now of deep interest to the student of that period of interior decoration. There is a famous library which can be consulted by students. The palace is not open to the public, but an order to view can be obtained from the

Secretariado Nacional de Informação, Palacio Foz, Restauradores, Lisbon. The huge Tapada da Ajuda nearby is a semi-public park with a motor road running round it.

The tiny, domed church of Memoria at Belem, conspicuous on a hill both from the river and the road to Estoril, was built in 1760 by João Bibiano in thanksgiving for the escape from assassination of D. José I, when Pombal took his fearful revenge on the Tavora and Aveiro families and had them all executed with terrible savagery near by. This church, which was permanently closed, has now been restored and re-opened. The interior, like a pocket edition of a Roman Basilica, is charming, the lovely pierced dome letting in a translucent light on the pale pink and cream-coloured marble and painted wooden galleries with which the placed is lined. In 1923 Pombal's coffin was moved here and above his tomb hangs a carved wooden arm pierced by shot wounds. This is the votive offering presented by the King in gratitude for his safety. Close by is one of Lisbon's new housing estates, in which the tenants automatically become the owners of the property after paying a moderate rent for twenty years.

Rather farther down the river, rising dramatically—and literally —from the waters of the Tagus, stands the Torre de Belem, constructed about 1515 by Francisco de Arruda, one of the many Portuguese architects who was sent to Morocco to restore the fortifications there: it betrays strongly the Moorish influence on this brilliant builder. It stands on the spot from which many of the navigators, including Vasco da Gama, sailed. The Manueline architecture is interesting though much restored, and there are some fine stone ceilings; a room in one of the upper storeys has a curious whispering-gallery quality like that in the dome of St. Paul's.

The church and Irish Dominican Convent of Bom Sucesso in the Rua de Pedrouços was founded in 1639 by an Irishman, Father Dominic O'Daly, who also started the church and community of Corpo Santo in Lisbon, already referred to. In 1652, this priest negotiated the treaty defining the relations between the newly-restored Portugal and France, and was Bishop-elect of Coimbra at the time of his death. The Community have been in these premises at Belem for three hundred years, since the original house was given by a pious lady, the Condessa da Atalia. As the convent was always under the strong protection of the British Embassy, the nuns were not expelled in the suppressions of 1834 nor in 1911, though they did have to leave for a month during the Peninsular War.

Lisbon, and indeed the whole of Portugal is full of these enchantingly odd links between the two countries, and here a vivid sense of the historical past is of even greater importance for a heightened pleasure in the present than in many other countries, whose beauty and interest leap to the eye without the subtle undertones so often to be found in Portugal by the inquiring traveller.

CHAPTER IV

THE FAMOUS ENVIRONS OF LISBON:
QUELUZ, SINTRA AND MAFRA

LISBON has within easy reach two 18th-century palaces, each superb in their very different ways, and a little town which is an almost perfect piece of romantic beauty. Queluz and Mafra were built within forty-five years of each other, but Sintra has grown up from Moorish times and seems now to have remained fixed in the most exuberant moment of Strawberry Hill Gothic.

QUELUZ is about fifteen kilometres north-west of Lisbon on the way to Sintra. It can be reached by train from the Rossio station, or by buses starting from the Restauradores in Lisbon.

Started in 1758, the palace stands in a wide and shallow hollow among low rolling downland. It is an exquisite small example of the rococo period, colour -washed pale pink, with most beautiful semi-circular wings, not unlike those at Wardour in Wiltshire, springing out from the main block on to a great open gravelled square which has in the centre a good Regency statue of D. Maria I. On the other side of this huge space are contemporary houses, which with the Town Hall and clock tower make a perfect ensemble, like a very lovely 18th-century picture.

The palace was built by the second son of D. João V, D. Pedro, who afterwards married his own niece, later Queen Maria I, who in years to come would lie demented behind the closed shutters in this very place. The original architect was Mateus Vicente de Oliveira, and later, the French sculptor and architect, Jean Baptiste Robillon, who also laid out the gardens, was called in. The building has been admirably restored after a fire which took place in 1934. It may justifiably be said that, apart from Bacalhoa, which is on a comparatively small scale, Queluz is the most sympathetic piece of restoration in Portugal.

The interior consists of a series of charming, often quite small rooms, with beautifully painted walls and ceilings, leading out of each other. The Sala das Mangas has yellow azulejos and very fine 18th-century Hepplewhite armchairs. The Sala dos Embaixadores was the chief victim in the fire, and is the only room where the restoration is over-obvious though the Chinoiserie panels above the long looking-glasses are most original and quite delightful. The Queen's dressing-room is lined by heavenly panels of children playing and dressing themselves up in formal clothes. These are by João Valentin and José Corado Rosa, whose work deserves to be better known; it can also be seen in the lovely Sala das Merendas where there are four panels of groups of 18th-century figures picnicking in sylvan scenes.

The music-room has a wonderful Empire grand piano with great gilded paterae, and some good furniture. Beyond the throne-room, which is also used as a ball-room, with superb crystal chandeliers, are two or three small rooms, one with a fine equestrian portrait of D. João VI and a picture of a child playing with a bird and cards thrown carelessly on a table by her side which is quite delightful; there is also a curious canvas, possibly by Sequeira, of a Madonna with the Holy Child who is clasping a little red-clad wooden Peninsular War soldier in his tiny fist! At the end is the gun-room, surely unlike any gun-room built before or since, for the walls are frescoed with painted trees and foliage in the same manner and possibly by the same painter as the great dining-room at Ramalhão, while the ceiling is adorned with hunting scenes. In the former kitchen of the palace there is a very good restaurant which serves teas as well as luncheons.

The topiary gardens are delightful, with formal balustrades and exquisite statuary. It was along these hedged alleys that Carlota Joaquina ordered Beckford, on his first visit there, to run races with her Maids of Honour, and here in hot weather the Queen would sit on the edge of a fountain with her legs plunged in the water. The garden façade is most beautiful in its artful irregularity, the reclining figures on the left of the main building and the statues on the pediment of the lower garden front are all quite lovely. A great staircase, which breaks into two half-way down, leads from the far corner of the palace to this lower garden, where there is a Dutch canal lined with blue and white azulejos panels representing shipping scenes, which seem to rise out of the water in the most fantastic way. On the little formal bridge are statues and good polychrome tiles. On this canal Lord Kinnoul, then Envoy Extraordinary to D. José, saw three splendid galleys with allegorical personages on board, after a great exhibition of fireworks at one of the Royal parties.

Later, when the King and Queen had departed for Brazil and the French were in Lisbon, Junot, with his unfailing eye for good settings, lived for a time at Queluz and improved the gardens. And even now they are not desolate like so many beautiful places, for the Government uses Queluz for official entertaining. Queen Elizabeth II and Prince Philip stayed here on the occasion of their State Visit to Portugal.

. . . .

To many Englishmen SINTRA is the most famous place in Portugal, largely owing to the passion expressed by a long line of poets and men of letters for the damp and luxuriant flora and the fantastic follies and gazebos, which crown every hill and line the roads. The sudden complete change in vegetation and climate is most strikingly shown to the motorist from Lisbon, who within a hundred yards passes from barren stony pastures to this fertile Eden, the first station in Childe Harold's Pilgrimage, the opening scene of the Trail of the Bleeding Heart; "Horrid crags, by toppling convent crowned". For Sintra lies at the east end of a rocky range of mountains about 26 kilometres from Lisbon; it is reached by train from Rossio Station, and there are buses from Estoril and Cascais which go by the long route round the west end of the Serra de Sintra, taking about an hour and a half and going through superb scenery, or the short direct road from Estoril. (Times can be ascertained at the Turismo office in the Arcade at Estoril.) Sintra station is about ten minutes' walk from the village, but buses or trams labelled "Vila" run between the two; they do not, however, always meet the trains, so inquiry should be made as to whether they are going off at once or not. To the right of the station, other buses start on a long country run to Praia das Maças, a seaside village, through Galamares and Colares, and there are trams as well in the summer.

There are three Sintra villages: that of São Pedro de Sintra, which is the highest: Santa Maria, half-way up the hills, and Sintra, the lowest of the three, but all are on escarpments at one end of the Serra or mountain range which, because it rises straight up from the plain that stretches to the sea, gives an extraordinary impression of wild and romantic grandeur and even of height, though nowhere do these hills exceed two thousand feet. Each eminence seems to be crowned with a castle or a palace, floriated towers emerge from seas of foliage, ferns droop from gnarled branches and every sunny wall in the summer is a sheet of purple bougainvillea, pink geranium or blue plumbago. In the spring, the mimosa is in flower, the geckos and lizards emerge, and at night countless fireflies hover about the dark stony lanes.

The central square is bounded on one side by the Royal Palace, now a museum, standing at the top of a great flight of steps, with its two huge oast-house chimneys which can be seen from every point; and by the little pink chapel and buildings of the Misericordia Hospital. The battlemented walls of the Moorish Castle stand out against the blue sky high above, and on the other side is the Hotel Central, where meals are served on a terrace looking over the great square, with its sleepy movement and busy-idle people. The other hotels of Sintra, are just off this square and the luxurious Hotel Palacio de Seteais is about a mile away on the Monserrate road.

An archway to the left of Sintra palace leads to a formal terraced garden, open to the public though few seem to know of it, an ideal place for a picnic lunch. The interior of the palace should be visited for it is Moorish in origin, and one of the earliest buildings in Portugal, though largely added to in succeeding centuries; it has always from earliest times been a royal residence. It was here in 1429 that the Embassy of Philip the Good was received, of which John Van Eyck was a member, whose visit so largely influenced Portuguese painting. The greater part of the palace is shown, and contains some lovely pictures, furniture and porcelain, and the place is filled with azulejos of all dates from the 15th century onwards, including the very rare early black ones which are round the door in the Sala das Sereias. The huge kitchen with its great conical chimneys has pale grey tiles half-way up the walls, unlike the pale blue tiles at Alcobaça which go right up to the kitchen roof. The Moorish dining-room at Sintra is surrounded by very early blue, green and white azulejos and the chapel, which was lamentably re-decorated in the last century, has a lovely large-tiled floor in various shades of green and white. The next room has some good Oriental porcelain and a pair of most amusing Chinese pagodas in a painted marbled glass case which were presented to Queen Carlota Joaquina by the Emperor of China in 1806. The great state bedroom with a huge Italian 17th-century bed with fine miniatures set in the back, is lined with extraordinary 15th-century tiles on each of which is a raised green vine leaf, not unlike Victorian Wedgwood plates. In the little room next door, the Sala das Sereias with the black tiles, there is a delightful ceiling, with a ship in the centre and mermaids rising up from the sea in cartouches on a green ground.

Most of the rooms have good painted ceilings, especially the Sala dos Brasões, almost square in shape, the walls lined with 17th-century azulejos of country scenes, where the ceiling is composed of a number of panels with the arms of seventy-two noble families of Portugal, painted in 1515, Those of the Tavoras were erased by order of the Marquês de Pombal, after the execution of the whole family, following their alleged attempt on the life of D. José I. The Sala das Pêgas is one of the earliest in the palace. The ceiling is crudely painted with a multitude of magpies, each in its own panel. Legend says that this was done after an incident in which D. João I, caught kissing one of his English Queen's ladies, adroitly quoted his own motto "Por Bem", so each of the birds holds these words in its beak. The Sala dos Cisnes is enormous in size and has curious green and white diamond Arabic azulejos on the walls, reminiscent of Persian work; on the ceiling are depicted numbers of swans, each in a different position. There is a good full-length portrait of D. Sebastião and an interesting half-length of Catherine of Bragança, presumably painted when she was a widow and had returned to Portugal, and on the tables are a number of delightful Chinese porcelain dishes in the shape of birds, fishes, and animals.

The parish church of S. Martinho, behind the Hotel Central and the Post Office, has three good Primitives in the chancel, but is not otherwise of interest. At the west end a terrace with stone wall-seats hangs above the clustering roofs and little gardens of the lower town and overlooks the plain to the sea; in the distance under the hills an extraordinary Manueline erection emerges from the greenery —this house was built in the last century and everything is in the same exuberant style, house, chapel, and even the stables.

Leading upwards from the north side of the parish church are many pretty little alley-ways and steps. Along one of them, rather bearing to the right, is an exquisite fountain, the Fonte da Pipa, with a weeping pepper tree above it. There is a long Latin inscription dated 1788, and most beautiful azulejos of life-size classical figures. The former Hotel Lawrence, where Byron stayed in 1810, on the Monserrate and Seteais road is now a restaurant and guest-house.

Higher than Sintra itself, up a turning to the left off the main square, are the two villages of SANTA MARIA and São Pedro. The former is perfectly delightful, with colour-washed houses clinging to the mountain side. A lane leads from the Sabuga Fountain to the well-restored church of Santa Maria, which is one of the few Gothic churches near Lisbon, though it has a façade and bell tower added in the 17th century. On St. John's night in June the village boys and girls build a huge bonfire outside and jump through the flames, as is done all over Portugal. A tree-embowered lane passes the Trindade Convent, and winds on to SÃO PEDRO de Sintra, where in the great space beyond the church, which has Manueline details inside, a huge fair is held every second and fourth Sunday of the month. This is one of the few genuine country fairs remaining near Lisbon. You can buy live fowls, donkeys or pigs, country boots, goats-hair blankets, pottery and haberdashery, and there are always a number of stalls for antique and second-hand objects where good things can still occasionally be picked up.

Returning to Sintra on the main road down the hill from São Pedro, a road forking off to the right should be taken, from which a quite lovely view can be seen of Santa Maria and the hills behind it, with the Moorish Castle and a more modern folly, which remains a ruin, to the left.

Sintra is full of good walks, though many of the properties are walled. A footpath leads up from the extreme end of the fair-ground at São Pedro, along the south-east side of the Sintra range with marvellous views towards Cascais and Estoril and the estuary of the Tagus. This ultimately comes out at the Lagoa Azul, a pretty little tree-embowered lake beyond Penha Longa, which is a large, restored convent with a big church, the scene of a *romaria* or religious festival on Whit Monday. About a kilometre along the Lisbon road from São Pedro, at the cross-roads where the Estoril and Lisbon roads meet, is the 18th-century palace of Ramalhão, lately admirably restored and now a convent school. William Beck-ford spent some months here in 1787, and many of his fantastic letters were written from this house. He brought with him an English gardener and English plants, which, he reported, shot up to strange heights. In 1794 the property was bought by Carlota Joaquina, later to be Queen of Portugal, who subsequently spent much time here plotting against the husband she loathed. After many years the property fell into semi-ruin, and one could wander all over the great deserted rooms, haunted by Carlota Joaquina and her rustic lovers, until one reached the enormous dining-room, painted with Brazilian trees reaching to the ceiling, with cork-encrusted grottoes in the corners and in the centre a gigantic cork dining-table, which has now been taken away, though the frescoes remain. Now young voices banish the sinister memories of this great rambling house with its wide terrace below the long formal garden façade.

Pena Palace on the very top of the mountain above Sintra is best reached by car, for although quite near as the crow flies, it is a very steep climb up. The palace was re-built in 1840 in the Scottish Baronial style, but with strong Moorish feeling, on the site of an early monastery, by the then King-Consort of Portugal, Fernando II, cousin of our Prince Albert. The interior is left much as it was when the last Kings of Portugal inhabited it, and the rather pathetic discomfort of so many royal palaces, with the bedrooms all leading out of each other, is here fully shown. It is strange that as late as 1840, royal builders should still have clung to this tradition of earlier palaces, which can be seen all over Europe. But the views from the gardens and terraces of Pena are unforgettable. At one point, the whole estuary of the Tagus is visible in the distance with, on exceptionally clear days, Cape Espichel standing out on the far southern horizon; on the north-west the plain stretches to where Mafra, looking like "the enchanted palace of a giant" rears its minaret-like belfries against the lines of Torres Vedras, and to the south-west is the whole top of the Sintra range with its bosky many-coloured woods, the Alhambra-like dome of Monserrate beneath and the land falling to the sea.

A small double cloister and parts of the chapel are all that is left of the original monastery, in which the finest thing is the High Altar made in 1532 by the French Master, Nicolas Chanterene, in sculptured alabaster and black marble. On the Gospel side of the altar is a good Nottingham alabaster of the crucifixion, with some traces of the original colour remaining.

One of the royal apartments is made of cement worked to look like wood, an extraordinary conceit, and D. Carlos's Empire bed and the room furnished throughout in Saxe porcelain, like that at Ajuda, have their individual quality. Another room is filled with *papier maché* furniture. It is an odd fact that so many good and unusual pieces in this material are to be found in Portugal, though there is no record of any having ever been made in the country.

The park surrounding the palace is wild and splendid and contains one of the most important silvicultural collections in Europe. On an escarpment of rock, slightly below, but towering above the three Sintra villages, is the Moorish Castle, also restored by D. Fernando; it is pleasant to climb about the castellated walls and see the wide views over the plain. At the beginning of the 12th century, King Sigurd of Norway led a Crusade in the course of which he took this castle from the Moors, according to Snorre Sturlason, the Norwegian historian who wrote a century later.

The road down from Pena passes several quintas or country properties, but for the walker there is a little-known overgrown footpath which leads straight down the mountain side and comes out opposite the exquisite faded façade of Seteais. This, one of the loveliest palaces near Lisbon, is reputed erroneously to be the scene of the signing of the Convention of Sintra in the Peninsular war, but now it is considered more likely that this was signed in Lisbon in Junot's palace in the Rua do Alecrim, opposite the statue to Eça de Queiroz. Seteais was built at the end of the 18th century by a Dutchman, and the triumphal arch with its busts and inscription was made in 1802. This splendid house with its long, low wings on either side of the arch, is now a most luxurious hotel. The rooms with their frescoed walls have been beautifully restored, and furnished. The long drawing-room, overlooking the great plain and the sea in the distance, was painted by Pillement. The originality of the design with different trees painted between the high windows, their foliage meeting overhead, is a delight to the eye. There is a good restaurant open to non-residents.

Beyond Seteais, past a square water-tank and sunken orange grove, the quinta of Penha Verde lies to the right. The fourth Portuguese Viceroy of India, D. João de Castro, lived here, and built the many little chapels that are scattered over the property, in one of which his heart is buried near the pine trees that he planted. Many of these chapels are of extreme interest, with fine azulejos, and they can be seen on application at the house. The graven stones before the gate, brought by the Viceroy from Goa, have Sanscrit rhymes from the Vedas on them.

About 3 kilometres farther along the road, a lane leads down to the right to the Quintas of São Bento and São Tiago, now both in English hands. Tradition says that S. Bento is a Templars' foundation dating back to the 12th century, and that its chapel is built on the site of a Roman temple. The Templars' Hall has a fine roof and the Chapel has been lovingly restored.

Continuing along the main road the Quinta de Monserrate is soon reached on the right. This property, for long owned by the English family of Cook, of Doughty House at Richmond, has been sold to the State. The park contains a very fine botanical collection which is shown to the public in aid of local charities; it was laid out in the middle of the last century by Scottish landscape gardeners. Rare trees, shrubs and plants are to be seen everywhere, and there are lovely vistas with waterfalls and lakes. The house itself is a strange example of the Moorish taste and used to be filled with fine objects of art, which were sold by auction in 1946.

Opposite the entrance, a footpath leads up the close-wooded hills to the Cork Convent or Capuchos—which can also be reached by road from Sintra. This strange place, on the very top of the Serra, encircled in mist for many days of the year, was founded in 1560 as a small convent of reformed Franciscans of the rule of St. Peter of Alcantara, and is so remote and odd that it is well worth a visit. The twelve minute cells, cut out of the living rock, with their tiny doors, have in each a rough stone bench covered with cork and some have cork cupboards and other fittings in them, and even the passages and cells used to be floored as well as roofed with cork. The Chapter House is exceptionally curious, with its cork benches, so are the tiny refectory and kitchen. In the grounds a little way from the convent is the cave in which lived for many years St. Honorius, a hermit, who died in 1596, and later became the subject of some of Byron's gloomier lines about Sintra. The convent is set just above a lovely wooded dell, and in the spring and early summer wild flowers carpet the grass-grown ground, lizards dart about, the water tinkles endlessly into the little basin set in the middle of what in more conventional monasteries would be the cloister garth, birds sing, and there is a great peace over the whole place.

The road from Capuchos goes on over the top of the Serra to PENINHA, at the western end of the range. The little pilgrimage chapel there has good azulejos dated 1711, and numbers of *Ex votos*.

The little village of EUGARIA, beyond Monserrate and the Duke of Cadaval's Palace, has many formal houses in terraced gardens and up a steep lane to the left is the enchanting quinta of Rio de Milho, built by an Italian diplomat early in the 18th century and famous for its camellias and agapanthus. Farther on up the same lane stands the Quinta do Carmo, a former convent, now in private hands. It has enormous quiet beauty, with huge umbrella pines leaning over the church and the buildings. Admission is by no means certain, but occasionally the owners can be persuaded to show the place to a foreign visitor. The sacristy is interesting as it contains fine 18th-century paintings of Carmelite saints, including one of the Englishman, St. Stephen Harding, and some of the choir stalls from the church are also there with exceedingly good late 17th-century painted panels of the life of St. Francis. The unused church is in such a state of decay and desolation that it is quite painful to see. In the *coro alto* are more stalls like those in the sacristy, but the sun pouring in on them all day has almost destroyed the paintings on the backs, which would have well repaid careful restoration.

Beyond Colares, which is a great wine centre, there are lovely beaches and the two little seaside villages of PRAIA DAS MAÇÃS and AZENHAS DO MAR. But the bathing hereabouts is extremely dangerous, as the great Atlantic rollers come straight in, and there is a very strong undertow. To return to COLARES, the parish church is of interest, owing to the early patterned azulejos which line the nave, right up to the plain ceiling. In the square outside there are some lovely low 17th- and 18th-century houses, where the key of the church can be obtained in the barber's shop. Outside the West door is a good pillory, though that at one side of the Misercordia chapel farther up the village is of much greater interest, with a twisted decorated column. This chapel, built in 1623, contains a plain gold renaissance retable, enclosing 17th-century panels. The Estalagem do Conde near Colares, is very well spoken of.

A lane leads up behind the Misericordia through mounting country under three archways, one of which is pure Chinese with a kind of flat *pailou* on the top, to the seemingly lost and almost unknown village of PENEDO, where at Whitsun there still takes place a most unusual survival from Roman times. An ox is driven through the streets in procession on Whit Saturday and then killed. On Whit Sunday there is another great procession and *romaria* to the church, meat from the ox is given to all the poor people round, and the children get cakes. The village church looks like a small modern chapel, but the interior of the little building is of extreme interest. There is a most rare renaissance barrel roof with carved stone secular motifs, consisting of whorls, starfish, shells, and bow-like ribbon ornaments. The walls right up to the ceilings are lined with plain patterned tiles in which are set six quite large rectangular polychrome azulejos panels, about four feet by three, of the life of St. Anthony. They are obviously country made, but 17th-century work, and most unusual in their colouring, which is yellow, purple, blue, green, brown and white. The date 1647 is given on a tablet in the chancel. The space above the chancel arch is also filled with patterned azulejos, and a tile panel of the Crucifixion is in the centre. From outside a lovely view can be seen of the Sintra mountain tops and the curious remote village with its 16th- and 17th-century houses below, and splendid quintas round about, among them being the Quinta Mazziotti with its 18th-century gardens; but every lane in this part of the country, so near to Lisbon, leads to some beautiful building or beautiful view, and are well worth exploring on foot, as most of them are not suitable for cars.

Two tracks lead out of Penedo, and both meet the main coast road from Colares to Cascais, just below PÉ DA SERRA, a village consisting entirely of most exquisite 18th-century country houses; not far is CABO DA ROCA with its lighthouse, the most westerly point of Europe.

·   ·   ·   ·   ·   ·

Apropos of *romarias*, a most singular one takes place in the tiny village of JANUS, between Sintra and Praia das Maçãs, where there is an extremely old, mosque-like circular church in a field a little distance away from the houses, to which on the 17th of August each year the country people bring their beasts and drive them slowly three times round the church. (Not very long ago the animals were formally blessed, but now this blessing no longer takes place.) All

QUELUZ: BRIDGE OVER DUTCH CANAL ORNAMENTED WITH AZULEJOS

MAFRA: ATRIUM TO BASILICA

SINTRA: MOORISH TILES ROUND A DOORWAY IN THE PALACE, SHOWING VERY RARE BLACK TILES IN SALA DAS SEREIAS

SINTRA: VIEW OF MOORISH CASTLE FROM THE PALACE (ON SKY-LINE)

kinds of animals are brought, oxen, pigs, goats, sheep. The church is filled with wax ex-votos of lambs, pigs and cows, as all the local country people come here when they have a sick beast. Outside, a little fair is held with things laid out on the grass, sometimes strange pottery objects can still be bought, such as rough images of the Phoenician Ashtaroth, globe-breasted, narrow-waisted, snake-entwined, the whole disguised as a toothpick holder (often with a whistle as well) or in the form of a jug.

. . . . . .

MAFRA is within easy distance of Sintra by bus or car and can also be reached from Lisbon by bus; travellers by rail are warned that the station is some miles from the town itself. The vast monastery and palace, which overwhelm the little place, were started in 1713 by D. João V in fulfilment of a vow made if his wife Maria Anna of Austria should have a child; John Frederic Ludwig of Ratisbon was appointed architect after the plans of Juvara had been rejected. This colossal building was actually finished in thirteen years, between 1717, the date of the laying of the foundation stone, and 1730. The dimensions of the whole place, two hundred and ninety thousand square feet, are almost as great as those of the Escorial, which it was intended to rival. Huge sums of money were poured out and extraordinary tales are told of the forty-five thousand men who worked through the summer of 1730 to complete the building. Over a thousand oxen hauled the stone, and a special hospital, costing £20,000, was built for the sick workmen. It is curious to speculate whether the employment of so many men on one building affected the economy of Portugal in other ways, for at that time the population was considerably less than it is now, and yet presumably the crops were harvested and life continued, even though so great a proportion of the man-power of the nation was concentrated in that one place.

Sitting in a café opposite the façade—over eight hundred feet in length, from which the yellow and green lichen has now been stripped—one cannot feel that it is really great architecture, and yet there is an extraordinary balance about it that is curiously satisfying. The minaret-like carillon towers of the church with its ornate central façade, the light and beautifully proportioned dome just showing beyond them, and the squat square pavilions at either end, crowned with flattened onion-shaped cupolas relieve the almost puritan simplicity of the wings and rows of windows. The façade of the church, with semi-circular shallow steps leading up to it, is a lovely example of Italianate work, with enormous baroque statues, their marble hair and clothes billowing in the wind; the interior of the church has splendid pink, grey and white marbles from every quarry in Portugal, and is of immense size, though so well proportioned that this is hardly noticeable. Some of the iron grilles are of exceptional beauty, as are the sanctuary lamps; and the organs made in 1807 for D. João VI, husband of Carlota Joaquina, are splendid. But the chief glory of Mafra is the grisaille rococo library, which with the great library at Coimbra gives to Portugal two of the most beautiful rooms in the world.

A museum of church and monastic furniture occupies several galleries, but those who have little time to spare would do well to leave this to the last, as the exhibits are mostly highly restored and in some cases re-painted. The chief thing of interest in the museum is the unusual isolation ward chapel of the monks, with an altar at one end and cells on either side of the central aisle.

On the first floor an endless range of rooms along the front and east side of the palace must be traversed to reach the library; these are the former royal apartments, where poor D. João VI took refuge from the wife who hated him, and spun her unceasing plots at Queluz and at Ramalhão. Some of these rooms have charming painted walls and ceilings, with fine Empire consoles and delightful early Victorian furniture, and from one of them windows look down into the church; at last the foot-weary visitor turns to the left through the King's oratory, and soon comes to an extraordinary room, entirely furnished with the heads and skins of stags shot in the forest behind the palace. The tables, the chairs, the very chandeliers are all made of antlers, and the sofas are upholstered in deerskin. An immensely tall long-case clock, made by W. Trippett of London, which used to stand in the sacristy of the church, is now upstairs in one of these rooms. It is a curious fact that almost every church sacristy in Portugal possesses an English grandfather clock. It has been suggested that at some time in the 18th century a whole ship's cargo must have been sent by some early speculator to Portugal, and Pombal himself is known to have ordered two hundred for public offices after the great earthquake.

Walking through these galleries it is worth looking out of the windows at either side, as lovely foreshortened views of the dome and the towers of the church can be seen, as well as the four great courtyards round which the palace is built. Oddly enough, there are no cloisters at Mafra, though Portugal in general is so rich in them.

At last one reaches the library, containing over thirty thousand volumes. It is two hundred feet long and very narrow, with a lovely white plaster barrel roof and a flat central dome surrounding a rayed sun; the windows look out on one side to the great chase, and on the other to a knott garden surrounding a large basin of water in one of the courtyards. All the way down the library are little alcoves for students, lighted by outside windows, the bookcases and the gallery above them are decorated in carved wood, all painted in grisaille and white. A common conception of libraries is of dark, gloomy places, but this one at Mafra is one of the lightest rooms in the world, with its clear pale colours, its delicate gilding, and its innumerable windows, Incidentally, a trained staff keep the bindings of the books in a most unusual state of perfection.

In the church towers are two huge sets of carillons made in Antwerp in 1730. It is said that the King ordered one, and they wrote back asking if he was aware of the cost. In answer, the King sent the money for a pair. Carillon concerts are held on Sunday afternoons in the summer, but it is well to make sure of the time from the daily papers. It is a most curious sensation to get out of a car some distance from Mafra and to hear these giant musical boxes sending forth their tinkling notes through the clear air over the surrounding fields.

King Manoel II and the Queen-Mother spent their last night on Portuguese soil at Mafra before leaving in 1910 for exile in England. They actually embarked from the Praia das Ribas at ERICEIRA, a little town on the coast about 10 kilometres away, famous for its lobsters, kept in nurseries in the rocks, and the strong Atlantic air. The Hotel de Turismo is excellent, there are three or four good estalagems, and some fine churches. That of the Misericordia has interesting 17th- and 18th-century paintings and gilded baroque woodwork. There is a museum attached, which contains a small collection of local curiosities.

At the edge of the town, to the north, is the odd little mosque-like chapel of S. Sebastião, with beyond it wild, deserted beaches stretching right up to the great headland of Peniche, thirty miles away, a forgotten and unvisited part of Portugal, wonderful for the walker, with its wild flowers, beautiful views and sense of space.

CHAPTER V

THE LESSER-KNOWN SURROUNDINGS
OF LISBON

THE suburbs of Lisbon are not at all like the picture which the word calls up in English minds. There are buses—but they often run between pink or creamy walls overhung with blossoming trees, past the formal gardens and baroque façades, many also pink, of 18th-century quintas and palaces; little roads or walled lanes lead off into open country where the wheat is green, and olive trees decorate the skyline with silver shapes; sheep straggle along over the cobbles, from one patch of surviving pasture to another. BEMFICA, Lumiar, Luz, out to the north-east, are all like this, behind the main roads, which are now lined with tall, new blocks of apartments.

The church and convent of S. Domingos de Bemfica and the adjoining Palace of Fronteira, belonging to the Condes da Torre, are typical. The palace is a magnificent house, and can some-times be seen when the family is away, but the really splendid gardens are usually shown at any time if permission is asked at the front door. These are the great glory of the place—the formal knott garden, with box-bordered walks and statuary, flanked by a great oblong tank a hundred feet or more across, with stone steps on either side leading up to a terrace walk above, with pyramidal pavilions at either end roofed with lustrous copper-glazed tiles. Set in the wall below this terrace, and reflected in the green waters of the tank are twelve huge 17th-century tile panels of soldiers on horse-back, curiously reminiscent of the Velasquez equestrian portraits in the Prado; they are said to represent the Doze de Inglaterra, the twelve knights who, according to a favourite legend, went to England in the Middle Ages to fight for the honour of twelve fair English ladies. In the private chapel of this palace St. Francis Xavier said his last Mass on European soil before sailing for India.

Opposite Fronteira is the church and convent of S. Domingos de Bemfica, now a school. The church has interesting tombs, and off the cloister is the classical early 17th-century Capela dos Castros, in which are buried D. João de Castro, Viceroy of Portuguese India, whose heart lies at Penha Verde, and many of his family. The large Pombaline house at the side of the convent was built by the English millionaire Gerard de Visme, whose name occurs so often in the history of 18th-century Portugal. A delightful walk of about four or five miles can be taken from Bemfica to the heights behind Ajuda, over Monsanto hill and through the new national park; it is rough but pretty.

.   .   .   .

Behind the Zoological Gardens, in the LARGO DA LUZ, where a big annual fair is held early in September, is a very curious church, largely ruined in the earthquake of 1755; the only part that now remains is the High Altar and the sanctuary, which are still used. It is a good example of late 16th-century classical work, with some pleasing statues, fine wood-carving and 17th- and 18th-century pictures both in the church and the sacristy. Close by is the Military School for the sons of officers.

A little way beyond Luz, the tramline ends at the delightful village of CARNIDE, set in real country, and but little altered in the last hundred years. The Carmelite Convent in the Rua do Norte, founded by a natural daughter of the Emperor Mathias in 1642, is now a home for old ladies, run by the Sisters of Charity, who will gladly show the highly-decorated church, which has a good painted ceiling, and the cloisters on request.

.   .   .   .   .   .

The Lumiar buses start from the Restauradores, and soon pass the great red brick bull-ring, for some curious reason called the Campo Pequeno, built in 1892, where bull-fights are held almost every Sunday in the summer. In Portugal bull-fighting is very different from in Spain, as neither the bull nor the horses are killed; the bull's horns are padded, and the superb horses, usually stallions, are as highly trained as polo ponies, and splendidly ridden. At the end of each round, a number of oxen come trotting into the ring, and lead the bull out.

The road goes on through the Campo Grande, a long narrow public park. To the west are the new buildings of Lisbon University, spare, functional and modernistic, and the huge Teaching Hospital of Santa Maria is nearby. The airport is not far away.

In the centre of the village of LUMIAR a turning to the left leads in a few moments to the enchanting Largo da Duquesa, with a fountain surmounted by an 18th-century figure of a boy. Farther on one comes to an open village green, on which stands the Church of St. John the Baptist, famous because it is alleged to house the Head of St. Bridget. (St. Bridget must have had three heads, as two other churches in Europe make the same claim.) Anyhow it reposes in a silver-gilt reliquary made in 1780, and in the same chapel is an inscription, dated January 1283, stating that the three Irish knights who brought the Saint's head to Lisbon are also buried here.

The immense house with the superb façade, just across the open space from the church, is the 18th-century Quinta Palmela, where Alemeida Garrett the writer met Sheridan's daughter, Mrs. Norton. Indeed, this part of Lumiar is a sort of Palmela family suburb, full of exquisite houses, large and small, all belonging to various members of the great ducal family—a bit farther on, towards Paço do Lumiar, one of the loveliest of all stands on the right, the Quinta do Monteiro Mor, a perfect little rose-pink 18th-century palace in another formal clipped-box garden.

In about a mile this same road reaches PAÇO DO LUMIAR itself, with yet more lovely country-houses, among which is the Quinta dos Azulejos, now a school and shown on request; the 18th-century formal garden is filled with tiled panels of every type.

From Lumiar itself the main road to Odivelas passes over a little stream, along the left bank of which runs the old military road which goes right round Lisbon. Civilian vehicles are prohibited, so delightful walks, with good views and wild flowers under foot, can be taken along this little-known way. Before reaching Odivelas, the road passes the shrine of Senhor Roubado, which was built after the church of Odivelas was robbed in 1671; azulejos panels describe the sacrilege.

The church of ODIVELAS was originally built in 1295; the Gothic apse and two side chapels still remain, with their slender lancet windows and graceful groining; the nave is 18th century, but contains the gigantesque tomb of Dom Diniz, husband of S. Elizabeth of Portugal. He looks, from his effigy, a nice benevolent man. The adjoining convent has two rather desolate cloisters, one Gothic, one Renaissance. It was here that Philippa of Lancaster, the English Queen, died surrounded by three of her sons, including D. Henrique, better known as Prince Henry the Navigator; and here as a nun lived that Paula Teresa da Silva (1701 to 1768) who was called Madre Paula, and was loved by D. João V.

Some miles out in the open country, near the town of LOURES, is the splendid Quinta do Correio-Mor (the Postmaster General), one of the most famous of the 18th-century quintas round Lisbon, Unlike many Portuguese country-houses, this one seems to crouch in a fold of the hills; it is built round three sides of a great court-yard, and in some way is subtly depressing. The overgrown formal gardens, the skinniness of the very fowls and dogs in the courtyard, the derelict air of the buildings, which so often enhances the beauty of 18th-century architecture, here seems somehow sordid and slightly sinister, and the low overhanging hills on every side shut in the gradual dissolution of the great off-white building. The property has recently changed hands, but the casual visitor is almost always shown round the rambling house and the gardens by one of the ancient crones who sit in the untidy courtyard concocting strange messes. Inside there is an extraordinary kitchen with azulejos plaques of hanging joints, venison, poultry and game on the walls—more ingenious than beautiful. On the same floor as the uninteresting chapel is a side door, which leads straight into a formal garden with four immense yews, so unusual in Portugal; the long, low façade of the upper storey of the palace which gives on to this has Classical medallions let into the walls. The great water tank, such a feature of Portuguese gardens, is backed by fine mythological panels of azulejos, but alas, these are in a terrible condition, broken and defaced so that the original beauty of the place is very marred and even the statues stand desolately about in the neglected formal gardens.

. . . . . .

The suburbs on the opposite side of Lisbon, down the Tagus Estuary towards Estoril, are much more suburban in the English sense; but they have their beauties. Electric trains run frequently from Cais do Sodre station in Lisbon to Estoril and the terminus at Cascais. The fast trains take thirty-five minutes, and those that stop everywhere on the way, just under an hour. There is also a wide motor road that follows the Tagus along to Cascais, past a number of little yellow forts, built by King John IV, father of Catherine of Bragança.

The first building of interest on the route is the immensely long 18th-century Rope Factory, part of which is still in use; one end is part of the Institute of Tropical Medicine, which is seen to the right of the railway before coming to Belem, where the great group of buildings and the Coach Museum have already been described in Chapter III.

About a mile behind CRUZ QUEBRADA, in the hills near the auto-strada, is the Stadium, which was constructed for international football matches and sports meetings. It is a beautiful piece of functional architecture, with all the seats and walls made of real stone, so it should weather well and never get the painfully decayed look of ageing cement.

There is a good restaurant at CAXIAS called Monaco with a terrace looking over the river. In this village are some splendid houses, amongst them a lovely palace, now used as a Staff College, which was built by a son of D. Pedro II. The gardens and gazebos are enchanting examples of 18th-century work. About a mile inland stands the Carthusian monastery, founded about 1595 by a negress, D. Simoa Godinho, and now used as a reformatory school. This and the Charterhouse at Evora were the only two in Portugal; it was at Caxias that Domingos Sequeira, the painter, lived for some time as a novice. The church and cloisters are of little interest.

OEIRAS is one of the most interesting places near Lisbon, for it contains a quite lovely 18th-century country palace built for the Marquês of Pombal by Carlos Mardel, who designed so many of the fountains of Lisbon. The immense property is now an Agricultural Institute. The palace with its curious Chinese eaves, semi-circular wings, arches over the road and dependencies, all painted a delicate rose-pink in colour, has extraordinary charm. The formal gardens are famous for their statuary and azulejos, and stretch right up the valley to the waterfall of the Poets, bordered with tiles and marbles of Homer, Virgil, Tasso and Camões, sculptured by Machado de Castro; here is also the waterfall of the Mina de Oiro, where the water drops from a great height into a series of semi-circular basins. But one of the loveliest things in this great property, filled with curiosities, is the Casa da Pesca, or fishing pavilion, a little way along a drive leading inland off the old road past the palace; its great walls, surrounding a huge water tank, have splendid azulejos panels with a lovely tiny 18th-century lodge at one end. The palace is now the property of the Calouste Gulbenkian Foundation, and fine examples of their collections are on view to the public in the beautifully shaped rooms.

The Fort of S. Julião at CARCAVELOS, where so many political prisoners languished during the Miguelite wars, is a graceful example of Vauban-type fortifications. The beach is lovely and there are two hotels. Opposite, high on a reef in the Tagus, stands the round lighthouse of BUGIO, marking the bar where the white crests of the waves toss endlessly against the horizon. A couple of miles inland, and visible for miles, is the little village of S. DOMIN-GOS DE RANA, whose enormous church has a ceiling painted by Pedro Alexandrino, and a very unusual 18th-century canvas of St. Francis Xavier, painted in the Chinese manner by a European.

Both the railway line and the road go on through Parede, S. Pedro and S. João do Estoril to ESTORIL, a modern watering-place with a number of good hotels and pensions, listed in the Appendix, and an 18-hole golf course. The Casino, where roulette and baccarat can be played, opens at 3 o'clock every afternoon. There are fresh sea-water swimming pools, a pleasant English library and Bridge Club, and a small sandy beach with a good restaurant. Like other *plages* the place is filled with gardens, good shops and luxurious villas.

On the beach at MONT' ESTORIL, just beyond, Alva's army feigned a landing before capturing Cascais, when in 1580 he advanced on Lisbon to enforce the Spanish claim to the crown of Portugal. Nine years later Queen Elizabeth sent an English contingent to the support of the Prior do Crato, one of the Portuguese pretenders to the throne; these worthies, when forced to retreat to Cascais, light-heartedly sacked it.

Sacked or no CASCAIS, the little town at the end of the line, remains a genuine fishing-village in spite of the recent pulling-down of so many of the older houses, and the construction of hotels, and blocks of flats—it still has its old fish-market, where the day's catch is sold to the dealers and the bare-footed fishwives; one must confess that during the sales these latter *sound* as if they were talking very much in character! There are some excellent restaurants, and hotels including the Baia, the enchanting Estalagem Albatroz and the Solar D. Carlos. The Parish Church is full of interest; it not only contains exceptionally good gold baroque woodwork, but has, in the nave, a whole series of signed paintings by Josefa of Obidos, the late 17th-century woman painter, who had her studio in the little walled town near Caldas da Rainha from which she takes her name. Just opposite the church is the entrance to the delightfully wild and unexpected park, which has a small zoo at one end. The Castro Guimarães Museum in this park has good furniture and porcelain and a library with a foreign section, from which books can be borrowed.

A road leads out of Cascais past the Museum to the BOCA DO INFERNO, a huge cavity in the rocks, into which the sea comes roaring through a natural arch, making a sinister whirlpool or cauldron in rough weather. The road goes on past a lighthouse, with several good sea-food restaurants and lobster nurseries, to PRAIA DO GUINCHO, an immense stretch of splendid sand, very danger-ous for swimming owing to the strong undertow. Here also there are some excellent restaurants, and luxury hotels.

· · · · · ·

A good expedition, taking in some little-known country, is from Mafra to Torres Vedras and then across by by-roads to Alenquer. A turning about half a kilometre up the Mafra-Ericeira road, sign-posted "Torres Vedras", leads to a new road which goes straight to Torres Vedras through splendid country. To the right under the great wall of Mafra Chase is GRADIL, a prosperous little place with a most lovely small manor-house set sideways on to the church. It is 18th century, yellow-washed, with beautifully shaped windows and decorative panes, and now used as a school; it is a delightful sight to see numbers of little girls in bright yellow pinafores and boys in white, sitting round the steps of the church having their sandwich lunch in the mid-day break. Past Gradil, on the main Lisbon-Torres Vedras road, VILA FRANCA DO ROSARIO lies about 2 kilometres to the south. In this village a narrow side-turning to the east goes through ENXARA DO BISPO to PERO NEGRO. The road is rough though metalled, but quite possible by car if taken slowly. The road soon passes on the right what appears to be a ruined Classical narthex to a church on a high terrace; actually, this strange building was started but never finished. It is curiously beautiful, with flat pilasters decorated with foliated capitals and three empty windows above the arched entrance, through which at certain angles the distant country-side is most exquisitely framed. Near the Convento do Barro at Enxara do Bispo, there is a prehistoric burying-ground on MONTE DA PENA with a large circular Neolithic tomb attributed to the 12th or 11th century B.C.

But to return to the main road, about 10 kilometres before reaching Torres Vedras is the village of TURCIFAL, which has an exceptionally fine late 18th-century church on a terrace at the top of a flight of steps, with a huge façade not unlike that of S. Maria at Estremoz; inside it is lined with pink and cream marble in rather simply patterned swags right up to the plain whitewashed ceiling. There is a singular dark wood salomonic-columned High Altar retable, very much in the Grinling Gibbons manner, as is the screen behind the main door, of natural wood picked out in gold; a pair of confessionals are decorated in the same way. In the sacristy there are very pale fruit-wood vestment chests, and an extremely fine Queen Anne Chinoiserie black and gold lacquered long-case clock with the original works, and on the face the legend, "Wm. Trippett, Jacob Garon, London".

There are country-houses on either side of the road to Torres Vedras, and the land is mostly vineyards, so that in the autumn a strong smell of wine permeates the air, and men and women, their arms and legs stained dark with grape juice, can be seen in groups along the road. At the harvest there are big *romarias* in almost every village near here. On the right a rounded basalt mountain with a pilgrimage chapel on the top stands out boldly for many miles.

. . . . . .

TORRES VEDRAS, a small, busy, prosperous town with a countrified museum, is full of Portuguese Primitives. It is a great centre of the wine trade and has big fairs on the 22nd of January, 29th of June and the third Sunday of August. The Lines of Torres Vedras start here and end at Alhandra on the Tagus, south of Vila Franca de Xira. These fortifications, built during the Peninsular War, helped at one time to save Lisbon from the French, and can with some trouble be traced to-day, with their redoubts at all strategic points.

In the main square of Torres Vedras, the Praça da Republica, stands the now restored 16th-century Graça church; the key and those of the other churches in the town are to be obtained from the sacristan, whose whereabouts may be discovered in the town council offices next door. A side door in the narthex of Graça leads to a room in which are some fine tiled panels of the life of S. Gonçalo of Lagos, whose shrine is on the first altar on the Gospel side of the church. He was Archbishop of Braga, and there are still more panels about him in the cloisters and the sacristy, which contains fourteen Primitive paintings from the church of S. Maria do Castelo, the best of which is of the Adoration of the Magi. The renaissance gilt wood retable of the High Altar is very fine and most unusual, with a pair of wonderful polychrome statues on either side, one of St. Frances of Rome with her two children, the other of St. Gertrude. The pale watery gold ambones with their Prince-of-Wales-feathered tops are also singularly lovely.

Those who are interested in ecclesiastical architecture and decoration—and a high proportion of the major architecture of Portugal is ecclesiastical—should always make a point of visiting the Misericordias in the various towns. These originated as hospitals with chapels attached, run by a lay body of local citizens, and in most places continue their original function. One of the earliest Misericordia foundations is that at Bragança started in 1418, but all through the centuries they were founded by public-spirited men and usually have exceptionally interesting chapels or churches, often untouched since they were originally built, and frequently containing good pictures and fine furnishings.

The Misericordia church in Torres Vedras is in the Rua Serpa Pinto and is an attractive building; the High Altar and the two flanking ones are on a kind of stage at one end, set in a polychrome marble surround which covers the whole upper wall of the church. The nave is surrounded by 18th-century paintings of angels, and there is a lovely gallery and fine wooden stalls for the *Mesa*, or Board of Guardians. The early 18th-century sacristy has an exceptionally fine carved gilt and wood back to the vestment chest, rising to a central point with formal gold vases placed at intervals along the plinth. The parish church of S. Pedro in the Rua Miguel Bombarda contains unusual medallion-like azulejos, with emblems such as a cock and a ship; there is also a lovely little organ, painted blue, green, red and gold, and an enchanting grisaille-and-gold gallery. Over the chancel arch is a re-painted early panel of St. Peter, and in the side chapels are rococo altars and pictorial tiles. Near by is the singular Chafariz dos Canos—a fountain, semi-circular in shape, with Gothic arches and a Gothic wall at the back, dated 1561, not unlike an English market cross. The little castle on a green mound at one side of the town is unrestored, and by it is the church of Sta. Maria do Castelo, containing still more Primitives.

About 4 kilometres outside Torres Vedras towards the coast, on the S. Cruz road, a rough but quite passable lane, signposted "VARATOJO", leads to this forgotten village, where there is an enormous convent, like a factory, one of the first Franciscan Friaries in Portugal, which has now been returned to the original owners. Above the monastery is a lovely uneven space with trees, from which a formal double staircase leads down to the pedimented porch. Within the friary is a Gothic cloister with a cultivated garth and a much later upper storey. The church is quite small, long and narrow, with a row of polychrome statues of Franciscan saints in a side chapel. The first chapel to the right has a most amusing early Victorian altar with a white marble frill simulating, a gathered linen cloth, hanging above the black marble base, which has a coat of arms inset. This odd conceit is usually hidden under the real altar cloth.

Half a kilometre beyond Maceira, north-west of Torres Vedras, is the site of the Battle of VIMEIRO, where on August the 21st, 1808, the future Duke of Wellington in command of English and Portuguese troops beat the French commanded by Junot. A monument was erected on the site a century later. North of Vimeiro, on the old coast road to Peniche, is the town of LOURINHÃ, built beside a little stream. The restored Gothic parish church stands out on a hill close by, with a good view over the vineyards in the valley. The actual Igreja Matriz or parish church in the Praça da Republica is lined with azulejos of vases of flowers on a balustrade and has a lovely tiny cloister behind. The Misericordia possesses some well-preserved Primitives, one of which, of St. Anne standing, with Our Lady and the Holy Child in her arms, is most uncommon.

A road from Lourinhã leads through Bombarral to CADAVAL, a

village on the slopes of the Serra de Monte Junto; in the church are two paintings by Josefa de Obidos, and from this village the Serra, which is singularly beautiful in its plain, tree-less, desolate form, can be explored. Towards the top of the hill are the strange semi-underground Ice Houses, or *Pocos de Neve*, which were built in the last century to store the winter ice and preserve it through the summer. Blocks of ice were taken down to Lisbon, first on mule-back to the railway and then by train or river boat to the Café Martinho da Arcada, which still exists in the corner of the Praça do Comercio; it was then the only place in Lisbon where ice-cream could be obtained in summer. This extraordinary industry ended about 1885.

. . . . . .

Near CUCOS, a spa with hot mud baths, just outside Torres Vedras, there is a 17th-century aqueduct nearly 3 kilometres in length. South of RUNA, in which is the big Military Home for Incurables, the parish church of S. Pedro in DOIS PORTOS has a pleasing single-columned porch to the side door; inside there is a most unusual carved wooden ceiling in a type of carpet pattern that might well have been inspired by Moorish tiles, and particularly lovely gold wood retables to a pair of side altars. In the chancel are four extremely good 17th-century painted panels set in quite lovely washed gold and pink rococo frames. The three naves have gold painted decorations on the columns and the architraves of the arches, but the church has undergone serious restoration.

The road goes on south from Dois Portos near PERO NEGRO, where the landscape turns red with lovely rich soil smelling of the harvest and of growth, to the little church at SAPATARIA, which is along a narrow road and is only of interest to azulejos fans, as the nave is lined with good early patterned tiles up to the roof, and three 17th-century polychrome panels of the Evangelists, earlier than those in the chapel at Penedo near Sintra. There were four, but one was pulled out when a side chapel was made. The altar fronts are of the very rare early Moorish raised tiles.

Between Sapataria and Dois Portos a turning leads east to SOBRAL, from which, about 5 kilometres away, the very singular church of S. Quintino in the village of the same name can be seen. A good road leads from the little village to the church, which

is a large wide three-naved 16th-century building, with exceptionally fine early 17th-century azulejos right up to the ceiling, in huge
Persian-carpet-like polychrome squares, each with a different
pattern. The church was drastically restored several years ago, when
all the polychrome baroque retables were taken out but the
interesting Manueline chapel of S. Quintino was left. Most of
the early stone statues have been re-painted, and even the Primitives
hanging on the walls have been badly restored. In spite of these facts,
the building is still deeply impressive.

It is strange that while so much was taken out of the church
during the restoration some particularly hideous Edwardian azulejos
of scriptural subjects should have been left on either side of the
chancel, whose Manueline arch is peculiarly lovely, like that at
Caldas da Rainha, with a kind of star-shaped centre decoration
which of course has also been re-painted; above it is an early
crucifix with statues on either side. But one of the curiosities of the
place is the semi-circular baptistery, sticking out from one corner
like a little temple within the church. A small cupola, covered with
azulejos and signed and dated "Simão Correia, 1592", rests on
columns, and on the low ceiling there are circular terracotta
plaques with curious heads engraved on them in white outline.

The situation of the church is quite lovely, set on a rise in beautiful
country with little copses breaking up the fields and rolling pastures.
The Manueline West doorway is highly decorated, each side having
different carvings; it is dated 1530, and on the left is a most strange
face with a basket of fruit on its head. There is an 18th-century
house at one side, once the village school, and just opposite the
West door an unusual cottage with a Tuscan-looking columned
verandah, where the key can be obtained.

A road north from Sobral leads to the extremely interesting town
of MERCEANA, which contains the best late-renaissance building
near Lisbon; the road is bordered at intervals by curious large
ecclesiastical buildings, looking like very shallow vertical sand-
wiches!—these are the 18th-century Stations of the Cross, wooden-
shuttered shrines like the façade of a chapel, with height and breadth
but no depth, which are opened during the Holy Week processions.

The church of N. S. da Piedade in the centre of Merceana contains
such remarkable work that the details are most probably by a pupil
of Nicolas Chanterene for much of it is reminiscent of the work of

LISBON: THE SPORTS STADIUM

TORRES VEDRAS: WITH INVISIBLE "LINES" BEHIND

SETUBAL: INTERIOR OF THE JESUS CHURCH

the master in the chapel of the Reis Magos at São Marcos near Coimbra. The exterior has a dull three-arched narthex which gives no hint of the beauty and richness within. There is an exquisitely beautiful renaissance chancel arch, dated 1535, with gilded cherubs' heads in high relief and medallions, possibly of Queen Leonor and John II. On either side of the aisles are lovely 18th-century azulejos panels of religious symbols held up by pairs of cherubim, with unusual polychrome architectural surrounds. The windows have gold and white garnitures and the capitals to the columns are painted, as are the architraves of the arches; the ceilings of the side aisles are also painted. There is a quite perfect little gold-and-white rococo organ-loft and a good pair of 18th-century pictures in rococo frames in the chancel. In the centre of the High Altar retable is a most unusual kind of turntable contraption, with on one side the statue of Our Lady of Pity, and on the other cherubs surrounding a tabernacle. The whole church is so lovely and so unspoilt, though in very good order, that it should be seen by anyone who is interested in the later manifestations of renaissance architecture. The sacristy has good vestment chests and a fine ceiling.

A short way beyond the town, a turning to the right off the main road leads to ALDEIA GALEGA DA MERCEANA, a little village whose white-washed houses are outlined in royal blue, in a fashion formerly common but now dying out. In the church of Our Lady of Pleasures, which is singularly unspoiled, there is a charming light gold-and-white organ-loft, and a pair of delightful somewhat similar ambones, with cherubs sitting, their little legs dangling, on the sounding-boards above; the corners are supported by pairs of female caryatides, reminiscent of those supporting the choir stalls at Braga.

Farther along the Alenquer road, a turning to the left is sign-posted MECA, which is a quite lovely village, with a most beautiful very formal 18th-century church. The road, good like most country roads now, leads up a valley through an avenue of big white poplar trees to the church, which is built of honey-coloured sandstone and dedicated to Sta. Quiteria, who gives protection against mad dogs. The façade, tall and narrow, has two belfries and a high narthex with green grilles to the windows, and the Bragança coat of arms in the centre. Inside it is all of marble, reminiscent in some odd way of the interior of the Estrêla in Lisbon, and even of the great church at Milagres, near Leira, though it is less original than the latter. There is a good painted ceiling by Pedro Alexandrino, and altars with 18th-century statues between pairs of plain grey marble columns. The whole church has a severe and restrained richness, and is all of a piece architecturally and decoratively. A big *romaria* takes place here from May 23rd to 25th each year.

The main road goes on into the delightfully situated and most elegantly industrialised town of ALENQUER, piled up on the hill above the river which supplies water to several exquisite 19th-century brick-built factories; the rest of the town looks completely Moorish, as its name implies. From the main road from Lisbon to Oporto, it presents one of the most startlingly beautiful pictures of a town in the whole of Portugal. In the upper town, the convent of S. Francisco has a delightful, very large double cloister.

Between Azambuja and Cartaxo a track to the right leads off the main road, near the Horticultural Institute, to the ruined monastery of SANTA MARIA DAS VIRTUDES, of which the little that now remains is incorporated in some farm buildings. But this was the spot where Christopher Columbus came to visit King John II, to discuss possible explorations.

A little past the bridge of Sta. Ana, before reaching Cartaxo, is the CASA DOS CHAVÕES. The quinta is known to have existed in the 14th century, though the original palace has been constantly rebuilt. There are fine azulejos in the chapel, and some painted rooms remain. The gardens are exceptionally lovely, with ornamental terraces, statues and tiled panels, some of which relate to the history of the owners; many are very rococo in feeling, and the whole collection is most comprehensive, and should be seen by anyone interested in this unfamiliar branch of art.

The rich, low-lying lands by the river near VILA FRANCA DE XIRA give pasture for herds of horses and of the famous black bulls; for Vila Franca is the bull-fighting centre of Portugal, and every spring a bull-run takes place through the main street of the town, the side roads being barricaded off with vans; then anybody can try their luck with the bulls, which gallop freely up and down the street and often injure foolhardy amateurs.

The very comfortable Estalagem da Leziria is much used by bull fanciers as is the Estalagem do Gado Bravo, on the road to Samora Correia over the great British-built bridge which spans the Tagus here. This hotel has a private bullring. The kennels of the St. Hubert

Foxhunt are near Samora Correia and the Hunt often meets there. The autostrada which starts near Lisbon Airport ends at Vila Franca.

One end of the Lines of Torres Vedras terminates at ALHANDRA about 5 kilometres south of Vila Franca, and a column commenorates the fact. Lovely walks can be taken over the hills hereabouts, which remind one of the Border Country. The old road and railway going south from Santarem to Lisbon follow the line of the river through the fertile lands bordered by the *lezirias* or low-lying meadows which are often flooded in winter. Halfway between Alhandra and Lisbon there are two obelisks commemorating the meeting of D. Miguel and his father after the former's abortive attempt to seize the crown in 1823.

CHAPTER VI

THE SOUTH SIDE OF THE TAGUS

ALONG the south side of the Tagus or *Outra Banda* there are many delightful riverside towns and villages, and beyond, the splendid range of the Serra da Arrabida can be seen on clear days from all over Lisbon, with the castle of Palmela standing up on an isolated hill at the east end.

There are ferry boats taking motor-cars from Terreiro do Paço to certain of the towns which are too far up-river to be adequately served by the Tagus bridge, and small passenger ferries go to the nearest point on the other side, CACILHAS. This town is of little interest, but it is a starting point for buses to the whole south of Portugal, and to the Serra da Arrabida, or cars can be hired there; on the river front there are a number of sea-food restaurants, perhaps the best of which is the Floresta, with a big room upstairs and a balcony with tables overlooking the really lovely view of Lisbon piled up on its wreath of nine hills across the water. This restaurant is a favourite place for dining on hot summer evenings, when the lights come out, one by one, all over the city; the wide river darkens, and night suddenly falls. A pleasant walk can be taken along the river-wall, past the restaurants and then bearing up to Almada, skirting the Seminary and the huge monument to Christ the King, and continuing through footpaths over the low hills rising from the river, as far as Porto Brandão or Trafaria, a total of eight to ten miles, though the bridge over the Tagus is already leading to all this part being developed.

PORTO BRANDÃO is a fishing village with an interesting Social Centre founded many years ago by a priest from the English College, housed in an old palace. Above on the cliff are the huge buildings of the former Lazareto, or quarantine station, at which all passengers arriving in Lisbon by boat up to the eighties of the last century had to stay for five days. The Lazareto could lodge about eight hundred people at that time.

At TRAFARIA one of the most terrible acts of Pombal's dictatorship took place on the 23rd of January, 1777, when he ordered the village to be set on fire because the fishermen had resented the press-gangs and roughly handled a sergeant. It is the starting-point of a bus that goes along the coast through a forest of mimosas to COSTA DE CAPARICA, a favourite watering-place for Lisbonians, where there are several hotels, pensions and restaurants. At Caparica there is an immense stretch of sandy shore running south for several miles, with the fishing boats often drawn up on the beach, their high prows, below which an eye is painted, standing up like needles.

From the top of the cliffs behind this little seaside place there is a most wonderful view of the blue Sintra hills, the mouth of the Tagus and the great white curve of coast stretching south for 30 kilometres almost to Cape Espichel. Close to the edge of the cliff stands a restored Capuchin Friary founded in 1558.

.   .   .   .   .   .

Up the Tagus from Cacilhas there is a naval base at ALFEITE, and near by is the lovely Quinta do Alfeite, which belonged to D. Nuno Alvares Pereira, the Holy Constable of Portugal. Small passenger ferries go from Terreiro do Paço to Cacilhas and big boats to Seixal, Barreiro, Montijo—formerly called Aldeia Galega—and Alcochete.

SEIXAL, looking delightful from the bay with its many semi-ruined tidal mills, is disappointing on landing. BARREIRO is the terminus of the railway system to southern Portugal and the boats connect with the trains. MONTIJO, about an hour by ferry, is a very pleasant town, with a three-naved parish church containing good columns and fine azulejos. To the east there is an 18th-century pilgrimage church dedicated to Our Lady of Atalaia, the scene of a big *romaria* during the last week-end of August.

ALCOCHETE, farther up the river, is also reached by ferry, but it is not always possible to return the same day, owing to the tides and the weather. The voyage is delightful, right up past mediaeval Lisbon and the quays as far as Poço do Bispo and the sea-plane base at Cabo Ruivo. Alcochete is most attractive. In the Instituto Samora Correia there is a superb Lucas Van Leyden of the Virgin and Child. About 8 kilometres to the east in the marshy land by the Rio das Enguias is BARROCA DE ALVA, formerly the property of a French merchant, Jacome Ratton, who in 1767 built a farm house, now much restored; near by on a tiny islet is the very small early circular chapel of S. Antonio da Ussa, possibly once a mosque, which except at very low water can only be reached by boat. It is surrounded by a semi-ruined crenellated wall and two huge umbrella pines overhang the strange little edifice.

The main road from Cacilhas to Setubal goes through COINA (the first station of the military road which the Romans built from Lisbon to the south), to AZEITÃO, where stands the great lassical Tavora palace, with the coat of arms erased by order of the Marquês of Pombal when the then Duke of Aveiro was arrested in this very house for his alleged complicity in the plot to assassinate King José at Belem, and subsequently executed. There are iron rings for the donkeys and mules on the huge fair-ground, which forms the forecourt to the palace, where a big fair is held on the first Sunday of each month. Azeitão is a charming place with its little country palaces, narrow alleys and numbers of fountains. The palace of Nogueira, built by the real wife of D. Pedro I, up a lane opposite the Misericordia, is notable but semi-ruined, and now let out as tenements. The parish church of S. Lorenço which you come to, to the west of the fair ground, has undergone drastic restoration, but it is still a delightful building with fine rococo altars, large 18th-century canvases in the chancel and azulejos panels on the walls.

A short way along the Setubal road, to the right, lies the Quinta das Torres, with a good restaurant; one can also stay in the comfortable bedrooms. The house—built round a courtyard—contains some splendid azulejos, including two huge panels of the Siege of Troy and the Death of Dido. In the centre of the great water-tank, which washes one side of the house, is a lovely little pavilion with a cupola supported on twelve columns.

VILA FRESCA DE AZEITÃO has a curious church in beautiful surroundings, with very early patterned azulejos covering all the inside walls; some polychrome panels are inserted, one of them, dated 1648, being of St. John the Baptist and another of St. Michael. There are two good "bust reliquaries", and the Four Evangelists in silvered wood on the High Altar, also an amusing statue of S. Aloysius dressed in a real cotta and cassock.

A little way out of the village stands the marvellous palace of Bacalhoa, one of the earliest inhabited houses in Portugal, It is known to have been bought in 1528 by the son of Afonso de Albuquerque. Found almost in ruins by an American lady, who acquired it about 1930, the palace has been superbly restored under her loving care. The extraordinary pavilions, crowned with grooved melon-like cupolas, are one of the most original features. Renaissance windows and loggias give on to wonderful views over the olive-silvered countryside as far as Lisbon thirty miles away. On one side are formal gardens of clipped box planted with orange and lemon trees, and a great water-tank backed by an exquisite pavilion with three pyramided towers, where there are many remarkable azulejos including the earliest dated panel in Portugal, that of Susanna and the Elders, 1565. When Watson saw Bacalhoa in 1907, there were genuine Della Robbia medallions set in the walls, but these, as well as many of the tiles, were lost when the palace was left abandoned for so long.

The excellent road to Setubal goes on through quite lovely country; the red earth, with olive trees and vineyards, stretches away to the Serra da Arrabida on the right. PALMELA, whose gigantic castle lies to the left of the main road, is a splendid ruin, but much of the mediaeval system can still be traced. The earthquake of 1755 started its dissolution and the Knights of the Military Order of S. Tiago abandoned it soon afterwards; indeed most of the village is built with fragments of the castle and of the monastery near by. Nowhere is there a roof, except over a part of the Knight's church, decorated with their symbolic sword-cross and which contains the tomb of D. Jorge de Lencastre, the last Grand Master of the Order. The cloister garth has a beautiful wisteria and everywhere there are great stone embrasures in the walls, through which can be seen glimpses of the deep red valleys, Lisbon far away to the north and the wide estuary of the Sado to the south.

SETUBAL, the big fishing and sardine canning town on the Sado, has a splendid *pousada* (inn) in the Castle of S. Felipe with superb views. The Clube Naval is a good restaurant. (In the last century the town used to be called "St. Ubes" by English sailors.) It is one of the most ancient cities in Portugal, and existed before the time of D. Afonso Henriques; the expedition which finally drove the Moors from Alcacer do Sal set out from here. Orders can be obtained to go through the canning factories, but it needs a strong stomach and an insensibility to fishy smells to enjoy this experience.

Just outside the city, the pyramids of salt left to dry in the sun on the banks of the river are a curious feature of the landscape, as they are round Aveiro. Rice is largely grown up the Sado valley; the paddy-fields make some of the towns and villages unsafe during the summer, owing to the prevalence of the malaria mosquito, though much research (in part financed by the Rockefeller Trust) has been conducted on how to overcome this danger.

Setubal looks curiously unfinished as a town, and cannot be called attractive, though it is surrounded by magnificent country and has in it singularly beautiful things. There are enormous dusty open spaces, and by the river yet more desolate acres, from which the remarkable promontory of TROIA can be seen, jutting into the wide river from the opposite bank. This strange, very long, narrow, sandy spit was the site in Roman and possibly in Phoenician times of a flourishing community. The place has been little excavated, at low tide the foundations of the Roman villas can be seen sticking up through the sand, and every now and then, notable finds of Roman coins and pottery are made by chance. A ferry boat goes in the afternoon to Troia from the little dock on the water front at Setubal, taking about twenty minutes over the crossing and returns after giving the visitor half-an-hour in that extraordinary place. Portugal is one of the few Latin countries that boasts of a good many well-authenticated ghosts. Poltergeist manifestations are fairly frequent, and this buried town of Troia is felt by many people to be singularly haunted, even on a hot and sunny day.

There are numbers of convents, monasteries and churches in Setubal, and delightful country-houses and quintas surround the town. The largest church is that of Santa Maria da Graça in the Praça do Exercito, built in the 16th century. At one side of it, in the Terreiro da Santa Maria, are three Gothic arches, all that remain of a mediaeval country-house. The church has a good façade with a pair of double belfries linked by an open gallery. Inside the three naves are magnificent, with four pairs of huge round columns, up which are painted 17th-century gold and polychrome decorations. The church also possessed a most beautiful and unique set of six large oblong grisaille canvases of the Passion, painted in the Chinese style, with 18th-century Chinese figures, and false frames of red velvet painted on the actual canvas. These astonishing objects were hung high on the walls, unglazed and unframed, above bright blue 18th-century azulejos panels. They are now housed in the local Museum next to the Jesus Church. There is a charming light choir gallery and the ceiling is amusingly painted with a balustrade on which stand pots of decorative flowers. The High Altar is unusually wide, with steps leading up to it of inlaid black on red marble, and the *boiseries* are very fine. On either side of the chancel stand two Puginesque Gothic confessionals, which look strangely grotesque and incongruous as if they had come out of the Pena Palace at Sintra.

At one end of the public garden of Boa Hora stands the church and convent of the Grilos. The buildings make a delightful ensemble round three sides of a stone-paved space, on which the crickets or *grilos* actually sing in the summer. Inside, the church is quite perfect 18th-century rococo, like an exquisite drawing-room. The decoration is in Wedgwood blue and pale green, and the altars are pink and white. There are lovely powder-blue azulejos panels of scenes from the life of S. Augustine, in polychrome architectural tiled surrounds, so the whole church gives a delicious effect of lightness and grace.

The Campo de Bomfim is now a well-laid-out public park with shady walks and fine trees. The chapel at one end, dedicated to Senhor de Bomfim, is lovely and untouched. The key can be obtained at the little cottage next door. There is a most beautiful painted ceiling with flowers and classical *motifs* enclosing panels of golden dogs and golden men. Fine 18th-century canvases hang in this chapel, which is *very* tiny, and the gilded rococo woodwork is of extremely good quality. In the chancel is a tablet saying that a Padre Diego Mendes built the High Altar in 1667. The sacristy has delightful pictorial *ex votos*.

One of the most famous churches of Setubal and indeed of Portugal has, alas, been so stripped by restoration that it now has the strange appearance of an embalmed thing. This is the Church of Jesus, founded by King Manoel I's nurse in 1494, a fantastic Manueline building with writhing, twisting stone pillars, and a beautiful main doorway. There is a most peculiar High Altar, set up on a kind of shallow balcony, with a mean little staircase at one side. All the gilded woodwork has been taken out, but strangely enough the rather ugly 18th-century blue-and-white tile panels remain, as do, more fortunately, the charming pair of Directoire gilt corner consoles on either side of the High Altar. The notable series of fifteen paintings by the "Master of Setubal", which used to hang in the nave in splendid gold baroque frames were all taken out and restored for an exhibition of Portuguese Primitives in Lisbon. They are now in the very attractive Museum next door to the church, which contains not only the grisaille Chinoiserie canvases from Santa Maria da Graça, but also a good selection of polychrome statues. The archaeological finds from Troia have a section to themselves and there are quantities of Roman coins from the vicinity. The "Master of Setubal's" paintings are of great interest to all students of European Primitives; they can be closely examined and compared with those in the Janelas Verdes in Lisbon.

The cloister behind the Jesus Church is quite charming and now forms part of the Museum, where the original nun's choir looking down into the church, should not be missed. There is a painted wooden door over the grille on which are fine pictures of saints, by far the best is that of the foundress of the convent, which belonged to the Poor Clares, and there are immense numbers of amusing bust reliquaries and good rococo decoration.

The façade of St. Julião, in the Praça de Bocage, has been relieved of the chocolate-brown tiles which formerly covered it, so that its lovely early lines and Manueline doorway can now be seen properly. Inside there are 18th-century azulejos of fishermen and fishing scenes from the Gospels.

The new road from Setubal to Portinho over the Serra da Arrabida is very lovely, and gives the walker or motorist the sensation of being in an aeroplane, for the sea and the spit of land on which is Troia, jutting out into the estuary of the Sado, are so far below that the waves look like ripples, and often clouds hide the surface of the water. The road goes through wonderful carpets of wild flowers in the spring, to where the CONVENTO NOVO lies just below the road almost at its highest point. This was founded in 1542 by St. Peter of Alcantara, the friend of St. Teresa, who spent some years of his religious life here. The convent is a charming group of white-washed buildings, decorated with unpretentious mosaics of stones and shells, with little hermitages and chapels scattered over the property, which now belongs (as does most of the Serra da Arrabida) to the Palmela family. An order to view the convent should be obtained beforehand at 116 Rua da Escola Politecnica in Lisbon. Rough tracks lead higher still to the little chapels of the Convento Velho, where those monks who wished to lead a more solitary life could retire and live in the tiny hermitages. And what a place for the eremitical life, even today so remote; in the 16th century the only distraction could have been the amazing beauty of the hills and the distant sea below, and the sky which seems so very near; but the wise hermit would know how to use all these gifts to help and not hinder him in his chosen life.

Apart from its magnificent views, the SERRA DA ARRABIDA is remarkable for its vegetation. The great limestone ridge, rising to a height of over two thousand feet and running almost due east and west has as it were two climates, one for its northern aspect, another for its southern, looking out over the great estuary. In two or three places the moist north slope is still covered with the untouched original forest of the Peninsula—oaks (*sessilifolia* and *Toza*), bay, ilex and gigantic specimens of the tree-heath, *Erica arborea*, some of them over thirty feet high, with an undergrowth of smaller heaths, ferns and aromatic bushes. Here grow the wild peony and the Iberian bluebell, with its upright head and widely open bells, *Hyacinthus orientalis*, and here in spring the charcoal-burners catch baby badgers, take them home and fatten them for meat—by autumn they will fetch a good sum.

Out on the sunbaked southern slopes is a more shrubby growth—seldom more than fifteen feet high and often less, mainly of evergreens: *Viburnum tinus*, the Laurestinus of English gardens, with its flat heads of pink buds and white flowers; more bay and heaths; *Pistachio lentiscus* with its neat tiny close-set serrated leaves, its reddish stalks and flower-catkins, and a few scrubby oaks. Here are the cistuses of the rocks—the whitish woolly *albidus* with its sickly mauve flowers, the smaller *salvaefolia* with creamy-yellow blossoms, and with them the rare, tiny treasure, their cousin, *Helianthemum cordifolia*—all mixed up with one of the many wild lavenders, *Lavendula Stoechas*, and the spurges, especially the tall, woody, handsome *Euphorbia characas*. In March and April the careful searcher will find the only wild tulip of the Peninsula, *Tulipa australis*, so slender and fine, its narrow petals bronze without and yellow within, and with great luck, the very rare *Linaria melanantha*, with silvery-blue foliage and dark wine-coloured flowers. These are the flowers of early spring, late March or April, and with them comes the yellow ophrys with its brownish tongue, *O. fusca*. But a few weeks later come fresh beauties. Now the sandy margins of the road are glorified with great flat masses of a brilliant gentian blue, as much as two feet across, of the low-growing blue pimpernels—*Anagallis coerulea*, with very large flowers on long peduncles, and the small-flowered *A. latifolia*, with broader leaves and smaller flowers; above them among the rusty-green scrub rise the great drooping white heads of the wild opium poppy, *Papaver somnifera*, on long graceful stalks set with blueish-silvery leaves. When two or three of these happen to stand close to one of the blue cushions of the pimpernels, even the least botanically-minded stands ravished at the sight—the vivid mass of small blue flowers, so perfectly shaped, so humbly placed, and the immense pearl-white cup of the drooping poppy with its golden heart.

There are lovely things on the way, too. The road from Cacilhas to Santana runs across heathy ground and through sparse pinewoods where the great white-flowered gum-cistus, *C. ladanifera*, opens its fragile blooms, three inches or more across, to the sun; in March the silvery sand under the trees bears a sort of tiny snowstorm, two or three inches above the ground, of the exquisite green-tipped white bells of *Leucojum trichophyllum*, minute cousin of our English Summer Snowflake; and more in the open are the small violet-blue stars of *Romulea bulbocodium* on their fragile stalks, and the big white or yellow flowers of *Anemone palmata*, its bronzed leaves, with their strange subterranean stalks, pressed flat against the soil. To wander about gathering all these in the hot sun, while the air is full of the drone of bees and the scent of the wild lavender, is a strange enchantment, especially in what should be the chilly days of March, to English people.

About 3 kilometres beyond the Convento Novo a turning leads down to the left to Portinho da Arrabida, and the fantastic grotto of SANTA MARGARIDA, an enormous cave with stalactites, into which the sea comes at exceptionally high tides. At one end is a chapel, and on the 20th of July there is a popular local *festa*. When Hans Andersen visited Portugal, he was enchanted with this extraordinary cave and its natural columns and fantastic domes; he mentions it in his Diaries.

PORTINHO DA ARRABIDA has an excellent small Estalagem in an old fort. There is a lovely bathing beach with warm, soft, translucent water, through which every pebble on the sandy sea-bed can be seen, and a strange variety of local fowls pick up a living by pecking away on the shore and occasionally even venture into the ripples for an especially succulent shrimp.

The wide road goes on round the end of the Arrabida ridge, passing below the little shooting-lodge and chapel of El Carmen, up on the hillside with a most superb view looking over Calhariz and Sesimbra right out to the distant Atlantic.

Before reaching Sesimbra, a drive through the pine woods to the left leads to the beautiful 17th-century palace of CALHARIZ, belonging to the Duke of Palmela, which rises out of the meadows with the great hills in the distance. The exterior of the house, surrounded by formal gardens and Dutch canals, is extraordinarily satisfying with its strangely small rectangular first-floor windows, but inside, like so many Portuguese houses, it is a complete contrast. The walls are lined with fine azulejos which nevertheless give a cold feeling to the living-rooms, in which hang some interesting family portraits and there is lovely furniture.

SESIMBRA is an enchanting little fishing town, squashed in under steep cliffs, and reached by a pass between the hills, with a castle, now almost entirely rebuilt, crowning a summit on the right; the town itself has some lovely buildings: an early fort, a Misericordia chapel with a good Primitive in the hospital, and the parish church, with a courtyard in front, which contains unusual painted decoration, not unlike that in the Graça church in Setubal and at Dois Portos, on the pulpit and the heavy stone columns supporting the low rounded arches that separate the three naves; these are variously dated 1643, 1644 and 1649. The beach, crammed with fishing boats, lies to the right of the 17th-century fort of St. Teodosio, which was built against the pirates which infested this coast at that time. Practically every man in this town of eight thousand souls lives either by fishing, boat-building, or sail-making. There are two good hotels in Sesimbra, the Mar and the Espadarte.

About 12 kilometres beyond Sesimbra, right out on the high promontory of CABO DO ESPICHEL, stands the extraordinary shrine of Nossa Senhora do Cabo. A rough road leads over desolate heathy country, bright in spring with the tiny hoop-petticoat daffodils, to the derelict-looking group of buildings. A vast sandy space is closed at one end by the church; on both sides are the lovely long low semi-ruined pilgrims' houses with little rounded squat-arched arcades supporting the first floors. D. José I built these two wings of rest-houses for the innumerable pilgrims who came to the shrine, and granted the precincts the right of sanctuary. Even now many of the Lisbon parishes send parties here during the summer. Inside the church there is a quantity of rather poor white and gold painted woodwork; just below the ceiling hang a series of presumably 18th-century pictures in black frames, so darkened with time that it is difficult to see if they are good or not, and there are some delightful *ex votos*.

The image of N. S. do Cabo goes on a yearly visit to twenty-five churches round Lisbon, and is carried each year in procession from one to the other. Beyond the church at the edge of the high cliffs, looking out to sea, is a tiny domed chapel dated 1756, while inland from the church is yet another little round chapel. But the whole place is so beautiful and so poignant in its semi-ruined desolation, with wild flowers underfoot and birds crying overhead, that no one should miss Cabo do Espichel.

The road from Sesimbra to Cacilhas passes about 4 kilometres from one end of the lagoon of ALBUFEIRA, a brackish lake with excellent rough duck-shooting and fishing, which are strictly preserved. The old Royal shooting-lodge at the sea end bears the arms of the Braganças and was a favourite resort of D. Pedro V. Every five years or so a channel is ploughed with oxen through the sand barrier to the sea, so that the lake can be cleaned out by the tide; the breach silts up in about a month. The lake is so full of *tainha* or grey mullet that an active swimmer in the warm shallow water can catch them, it is said, in his hands. The little colony round the shooting lodge only consists of the head gamekeeper, two or three revenue officers, and their wives and children, who are linked to the world by sandy lanes. At the main road end of the lagoon there is a marshy valley, which is the home of millions of bull-frogs who bellow even in broad daylight, and of herons and cranes, coots and all manner of wild duck.

CHAPTER VII

THE ALENTEJO

THE great rolling plain of Portugal which stretches south of the Tagus right up to the mountains on the Spanish border is sparsely populated; the land is poor and chiefly noteworthy for great forests of cork oak, *Quercus suber*. The endless heaths, sweet with gum-cistus in the spring, with distant grey-blue masses rising from the desolate plain, denoting Evora or Montemor-o-Novo in the distance, cannot but be considered peculiarly lovely by the modern traveller, who should be sure to read his Borrow before venturing into these parts.

However, the country east from Cacilhas is not very interesting at first. VENDAS NOVAS, on the road to Montemor-o-Novo, was where D. João V built a palace in which to lodge, for only two nights, the royal parties for the double marriage, in 1729, of his daughter to the eldest son of King Philip V of Spain, and of the Spanish Princess to his own heir-apparent. The palace, of little architectural interest, was built in nine months by two thousand workmen and is now an Artillery school.

MONTEMOR-O-NOVO was the birthplace of St. John of God (1495–1550), who devoted his life to the care of lunatics, and is the scene of a great fair on May 1st each year. The castle dominates the little town, and the walls enclose a 17th-century convent, now a school, and a public park. The Parish Church was originally part of the old Convent of St. John of God, built in 1625 on the site of the house where the saint was born.

The most important city in the Alentejo and one of the most interesting architectural towns in Portugal is EVORA, which has a good hotel, the Planície in the Largo de Alvaro Velho and the superb Pousada dos Loios by the Museum and Cathedral. Evora is like a toy city in that it has the grand ingenuity of a child's construction. There are arches and arcades, aqueducts and squares, little spoilt and still surrounded by the greater part of the mediaeval walls, and it is this ensemble which gives the town its peculiar character. Evora may be said to be the cradle of the Portuguese classical movement, and the architecture shows traces of influence from many European countries including a lovely little Roman building, one of the very few in the Peninsula. This is commonly called the Temple of Diana, it stands next to the Cathedral and is quite entrancing in its grace and lightness; it has been attributed to the end of the second or early part of the third century. The delicate pillars are of granite while the bosses and capitals are in Estremoz marble.

One of the most extraordinary examples of a battlemented church is that of S. Bras, just outside the city walls in the Rua da Republica, built in 1482 (*romaria* on February 2nd). On either side six plastered pepperpot turrets stand out, with battlements in between, and there is a large square porch at the west end. Unhappily the church is now surrounded by an ugly public garden which makes it look like a pantomime scene. The interior is strange rather than beautiful, with a rounded ceiling and green and white 16th-century diamond azulejos covering the nave. In the same street, but inside the walls, stands the granite church of S. Francisco, a good example of Moorish-Gothic architecture. The interior has a very wide single nave, and contains some fine Gothic tombs; the High Altar retable is 18th century and on the Epistle side are two charming renaissance tribunes. Good Primitive paintings hang in some of the side chapels. Off the church is the curious "Capela dos Ossos" or Charnel House, with a good painted ceiling; similar collections of patterned skeletons are common in Capuchin churches all over southern Europe.

The semi-ruined Graça church, between S. Francisco and the Misericordia, should on no account be missed, as the façade, though not large, is a most magnificent example of what might be called classical baroque. It is Michael-Angelesque in its imaginative power. The granite façade is supported by four Corinthian pillars enclosing the narthex, and above is a window with two enormous stone rosettes on either side; on the pediment, sitting like Simon Stylites on the tops of the side pillars are four figures of heroic size, their legs dangling, and behind are two great globes from which rise granite flames. On either side of the tympanum are two similar but somewhat smaller figures. The roofless and ruined interior has an armorial arch to the High Altar, and the date 1537 on one of the windows. The Palladian double cloister to the right should also be seen.

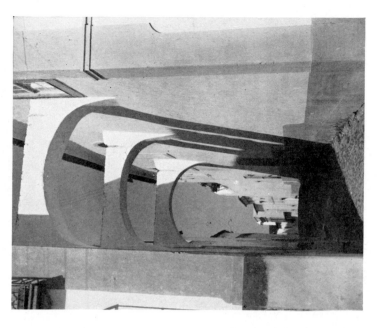

EVORA: ARCHES OVER A ROAD

CAMPO MAIOR: WROUGHT-IRON BALCONIES

ALTER DO CHÃO: RENAISSANCE WATER-FOUNTAIN

ALTER DO CHÃO: CASTLE AND MOSAIC PAVEMENT IN SQUARE

The Praça do Geraldo in the centre of Evora surrounds a vase-shaped fountain, built in 1570 by Afonso Alvares. Not, I fear, that at which Borrow sat and spoke to at least two hundred of the children of Portugal upon matters relating to their eternal welfare, though he omits to state in what language he spoke. This square is composed of pleasant buildings above charming arched arcades. To the north stands the Parish Church of S. Antão with three naves and a lovely high groined roof above noble columns.

The Cathedral or Sé was consecrated in 1204 and is more interesting than beautiful. The façade has two dissimilar towers over an arched porch and the large central lantern with its pepperpot effect is extremely unusual in Portugal. The huge building is a strange conglomeration of periods, compressed, unlike those at Tomar, into a small space. The cloister is 14th, the great retable (now in the museum) 15th, the choir and the pulpit 16th, the sacristy and the lateral chapels 17th, and the chancel and High Altar 18th century, the last two built by Ludwig, the architect of Mafra. The interior is three-naved, with new white cement pointing to the granite columns, which gives an unpleasing niggling effect. The North transept is good renaissance work, dated 1529, and there is lovely early gold wood-work in the church and very interesting statues. The 16th-century stalls in the upper choir and the 18th-century organ should be noticed.

The 17th-century sacristy is lovely. Another room contains church vestments and ornaments, including an astonishing French 13th-century ivory statue of the Blessed Virgin seated on a chair with the Holy Child in her lap, which is strangely Byzantine in feeling. The statue opens to reveal a triptych with tiny scenes of the life of the Virgin, carved in high relief. The present painted wooden head was put on in the 16th century, but there is a tradition that the original head is in Moura.

Evora's great Library contains over fifty-five thousand volumes and an immense number of MSS, some of which, relating to the English in Portugal, have been examined by members of the Lisbon Branch of the Historical Association, who publish their findings in most interesting Annual Reports.

Beyond the Library in the Rua Oriental de Diana stands the monastery of the Loios now the perfectly arranged *pousada*, built between 1485 and 1491. The church contains good Gothic tombs, as well as two delightful renaissance ones in Estremoz marble. The big classical tomb of D. Francisco de Melo is thought to be by Nicolas Chanterene, who is known to have worked in Evora. The walls are lined with large azulejos panels of the life of St. Lawrence Justinian, some of them signed Antonius A. B. Oliva and dated 1711. The 15th-century cloister and the chapter house with its interesting doorway of two Moorish arches divided by a Manueline column are incorporated into the *pousada*.

Beside the Loios is the strange Palacio Cadaval, flanked by two high towers topped with pyramids. Near by, the Museum contains an interesting and important collection of pictures, among them being the great retable of the Virgin in Glory Crowned by Angels, originally forming the high altar of the Sé. It may be by Gerard David, is obviously of the Bruges school and is one of the best Flemish pictures in the country. There are also good Primitives, among them being some by Frei Carlos, who worked in Evora.

The curious Romanesque arch of Dona Isabel in the road of the same name leads to the Largo de Alexandre Herculano, which is surrounded by splendid palaces and houses; here is the church of S. Tiago (the key can be obtained from the sacristan of the Cathedral) which was rebuilt in the 17th century. The interior is completely lined with blue and white azulejos panels signed and dated, Gabriel del Barco 1699. The painted ceiling (1700) is exceptionally good, as is the chancel arch.

In the Largo de Joaquim António de Aguiar stands the convent and church of Calvario founded by the Poor Clares in 1570, with a good refectory and two-storeyed cloister. Here was immured the "Sempre Noiva", Dona Isabel Juliana de Sousa Coutinho, after her forced marriage with the son of the Marquês de Pombal. She later married the father of Pedro, first Duke of Palmela, D. Alexandre de Sousa Holstein, who as a boy had had an English tutor, Mr. Billingham, and fell in love with this Dona Isabel, who did lessons with him as a child. But she was an heiress, and Pombal arranged a marriage between her and his second son. The girl, who was then only thirteen years old, refused, but shortly after her fourteenth birthday she was forced into a wedding to the young count; however the marriage was never consummated and for three whole years she remained silent. After this successful defiance of the great statesman by a girl in her early teens the marriage was annulled, and she spent some years in this Convent at Evora. When Pombal was disgraced after the death of D. José I, Dona Isabel was released and D. Alexandre came back from Italy, where he then was, to marry her. He had been brought up in the European diplomatic world and later entered on a sentimental friendship with Mme. de Stäel; he became Portuguese Minister in London between 1812 and 1819, and represented his country at the Congress of Vienna.

In the Largo do Colegio, the Liceu and a seminary occupy the former Jesuit University, which was suppressed by Pombal when he turned the Jesuits out of Portugal. The College was visited by St. Francis Borgia, the companion of St. Ignatius, who abandoned his dukedom to become a Jesuit; his room is still shown. The vast classical cloister is magnificent with a splendid double row of arches and in the centre of one side rises a great pediment surmounted by sceptred statues of heroic size, and a bronze sun. The whole place is profusely ornamented with azulejos, and some of the rooms have enormous panels of them, representing scenes from the lives of various saints, forming one of the most remarkable collections of 16th-, 17th- and 18th-century tiles even in Evora, which is particularly rich in them; invaluable to students of this art which the Portuguese have made so peculiarly their own. Many of the rooms also have good painted ceilings, and the little theatre with its charming renaissance decoration is most unusual. The church attached to the college has good boiseries and interesting canvases, which came from the now ruined Graça in 1844, and the sacristy ceiling has a fine barrel roof.

The palace of the Condes de Basto in the Pátio de S. Miguel was where Queen Catherine of Bragança stayed after her return to Portugal as a widow. It has an unusual partly Romanesque tower and late 16th-century frescoes, possibly Italian, in the ground floor rooms.

At one side of the Portas de Moura is the lovely palace of the Cordovils; but every street in Evora contains good 16th- and 17th-century buildings—in the Rua da Misericordia stands another very fine palace called the Casa Soure, with a delightful balcony and the conical dome so often to be seen in Evora, and in the same street is the Misericordia church, lined with good azulejos panels of the Life of Christ, dated 1716; there are exceptionally beautiful early

18th-century canvases by Francisco Xavier in splendid rococo frames and golden caryatides wearing Red Indian feather head-dresses.

In the Travessa da Milheira the convent of S. Clara, founded in 1452, has a curious bell tower and most unusual brick-work. The church contains a fine 17th-century painted ceiling in poor condition, some baroque work, and in the *coro alto*, various interesting paintings. The convent, now a barracks, has a beautiful double renaissance cloister, the upper doric columns made of marble, the lower of granite. The Rua da Carta Velha nearby is known to have borne the same name since 1375, a delightful sidelight on the city of Evora.

Near Evora there are many extremely interesting buildings. The Charterhouse or Cartuxa, one of the only two in Portugal, the other being at Caxias near Lisbon, is just outside the Porto da Lagoa, past a charming little rococo palace, with granite windows and a fine panel of azulejos on the façade. This Charterhouse was begun by Felipe Terzi, the architect of S. Roque in Lisbon. The Carthusians have now returned after a lapse of over a hundred years. The huge black and white marble façade of the church rises from the top of a wide flight of steps; the lower part consists of a five-arched narthex with a much narrower three-windowed storey above, surmounted by a formal pediment enclosing three statues.

Three kilometres farther on stands the Monastery of S. Bento de Castris, with a 16th-century Manueline two-storeyed cloister. It is now a Salesian Trade School for boys. In the church are picturesque 18th-century azulejos of the life of S. Bernard. There is a *romaria* on Ascension Day.

About 5 kilometres to the north-west of Evora stands the little-visited Convent of Espinheiro founded in 1458 but re-built a century later (*romaria* on April 14th). It is now a strange, almost fortified-looking building, in which D. John of Austria was quartered during the Spanish domination of Portugal; the painter Frei Carlos, whose work is in the Evora Museum, lived and painted here, and it is even said that D. Manoel I received the news of the discovery of the Cape route to India in this place. The church has lovely renaissance and baroque details. Splendid magnolias grow in the garth of the little 15th-century two-storeyed cloister, of which the upper floor has marble columns, while in the lower are octagonal granite pillars.

Near Evora are a great wealth of neolithic remains, including many dolmens, some of the most noteworthy being: Paço da Vinha, Valadas and Pinheiro do Campo.

.　.　.　.　.　.

ARRAIOLOS is a little town noted since the middle ages for its carpet-making, which still goes on. The designs are like cross-stitched samplers, made with natural dyes. In the centre of the town the Misericordia contains various canvases of merit. Like most towns in the Alentejo, Arraiolos has a castle, though little of the original now remains. On the highest point inside the walls stands Senhor dos Passos, formerly the parish church, with a fine ceiling. Half a kilometre outside the town the QUINTA DOS LOIOS, formerly a convent founded in 1527, has a 16th-century two-storeyed cloister with a marble fountain in the garth, and a church of which the exterior is fortified. The interior is completely lined with blue pictorial azulejos right up to the high vaulted roof. There is a panel of St. Edward the Confessor inscribed as "Rey de Inglaterra".

Ten kilometres south-west of Evora along the Alcaçovas road is the QUINTA DE VALVERDE or MITRA, formerly a Capuchin convent but now an Agricultural College. The 18th-century build-ings are charming and the round chapel has a cupola supported by columns of Estremoz marble and four semi-circular chapels sur-rounding the central space. The little two-storeyed cloister with Doric columns is also delightful. Indeed the whole quinta is excep-tionally beautiful with formal gardens, a great water-tank and fountains and gazebos scattered about the property.

.　.　.　.　.　.

On the Vila Viçosa road, 34 kilometres due east of Evora, stands REDONDO, a cheerful little town with a castle and good ironwork, particularly on the houses in the Rua São Miguel; indeed one of the striking and delightful things about these small Alentejo towns is the great wealth of balconies and window-boxes in the most exquisitely graceful and elegant wrought-iron. The Parish Church, built at the end of the 16th and beginning of the 17th century, was restored in 1818. There are still good baroque altars, and in the first chapel to the left there is an ivory statue of Christ nearly eighteen inches in height. The retable of the High Altar contains an interesting early

17th-century picture of the Annunciation signed Jozephus Xancrius, and a pair of contemporary images stand on either side. The convent church of S. António has a classical façade; the interior is lined with 18th-century azulejos, and there is a little cloister at the side with good statues. The Misericordia Hospital, founded at the end of the 15th century, has an attractive church with a Manueline choir, a painted groined roof, a pulpit in Estremoz marble and fine baroque gold retables; there is also a Primitive painting in the chancel.

On the slopes of the Alto de São Gens in the Serra de Ossa to the north of Redondo lies the convent of S. Paulo, again very little known, which can be seen in the distance from Redondo. On Ascension Day there is a popular *romaria*. It was rebuilt at the end of the 18th century, and is in a most beautiful situation. It was to this remote spot that the Marquês de Pombal exiled the bastard half brothers of D. José, the "Meninos de Palhavã".

Just outside TERENA, which is half-way between Redondo and the Spanish frontier, stands the extraordinary 14th-century church of Sa. da Boa Nova, fortified like a castle with a great coat of arms on the exterior. The High Altar retable encloses lovely 16th-century paintings and in the chancel hang a number of pictures of uneven merit, some quite delightful.

MONSARAS, also near the Spanish frontier, east of Reguengos, was taken from the Moors in 1167 by D. Afonso Henriques, who gave the city in that year to the Templars. It is a very strange, tiny town at the top of a hill and crowned with a castle. The entrance is through an ogival archway, and the keep, very high, overlooks a marvellous stretch of the south of Portugal. The Largo de D. Nuno Alvares Pereira is surrounded with lovely houses. Nearby stands the parish church of Santa Maria de Lagoa. It is almost square with four great pillars supporting the roof. It contains fine rococo work, good canvases and a small museum in an upper room.

. . . . . .

ESTREMOZ, 50 kilometres north-east of Evora, on the direct road from Setubal to Elvas, is a good place in which to stay for a few days while exploring the very interesting towns and convents of the Upper Alentejo—the Hotel Alentejano is adequate. The castle stands boldly on a hill above the flattish surrounding plain, and the town is deeply interesting both architecturally and historically; it is surrounded by 17th-century fortifications, vast earthen ramparts faced with brick, and there are some very lovely gateways, one of the most beautiful being the Porta de S. Caterina. Estremoz is famous for its earthenware, made in lovely Roman and, it is said, even Etruscan shapes, on sale in the shops and markets; little painted earthenware figures for Christmas cribs are also made here. Just outside the town are great quarries which supplied the marble for the Escorial—all this part of the Alentejo is full of marble.

In the great castle on the very summit of the hill, built by D. Diniz in 1281, his widow, St. Elizabeth of Portugal, died in 1336; the room in which she died was later transformed by the mother of our Queen Catharine of Bragança into a tiny chapel, with delightful frescoes of the Saint's life on the walls. Part of this castle is now a *pousada* and behind it is a village within the outer walls. King John V rebuilt much of the palace and castle, but left practically untouched the magnificent keep; from its top a really amazing view can be had, from Palmela near Lisbon on the west to Marvão, over-looking the Spanish frontier to the east, and even to the Serra da Estrêla away to the north, beyond the Tagus. The cottages round about are gay with flowers. At the foot of the keep is a beautiful little *largo* with two churches—the great walls of one of them, S. Maria, of bare stone and whitewash, stand starkly up; this church was once a mosque, and inside it one can still imagine the Mussulman civilisation as it were seeping through the Christian trappings and additions.

In the centre of the town is the Rossio, surrounded by trees and palaces; the Town Hall is in a beautiful old convent, built in 1698, with a splendid staircase and azulejos panels. A country museum is next door. The Misericordia Church and Hospital are also in this square, occupying a former convent of the Knights of Malta founded in 1539; there are two cloisters, a double one with a lovely Gothic lower storey, and another smaller one. The church is unfortunately badly restored. In the Largo de D. José I is the 17th-century Palacio Tocha, famous for its great azulejos panels of the War of Independence.

The traveller should make an effort to get into the former Convent of S. Francisco, now the Cavalry barracks; it was founded in the 13th century, and its great square, surrounded by low yellow-washed buildings, is very noble. An inner cloister, bright with flowers, has been partly built in to make more accommodation, but is still beautiful. The great corridor upstairs has been quite delightfully arranged, with shields recording the Division's battles on the walls between contemporary arms, sabres, muskets, etc.—as these battles are in many cases those in which British troops also took part, it is peculiarly interesting to the English tourist. But the whole place is a shining example of how well a religious foundation can be treated, when in lay hands.

Leading up to this corridor is the famous staircase with its frieze of most unusual tiles, in delicate pinks and yellows and greens, with ribbons and garlands looped between slender vases and small panels. The visitor fresh from Evora cannot fail to be reminded of the designs frescoed on the walls of the old Inquisition Palace there, near the Cathedral. But there is an even more interesting resemblance, possibly an actual relationship, to the remarkable multi-coloured tiles in the great Bragança Palace at Vila Viçosa, only 17 kilometres away, which for so long puzzled students; they are now known to have been designed by a Dutchman in the 16th century and the fascinating story of how this discovery was made will be told in its place. But Vila Viçosa was far the biggest, most important and richest residence in that whole region, and if a foreign artist produced a wholly new type of design there, what more natural than that local decorators should copy it? It even seems at least possible that the characteristic wreaths and flowers on the pretty painted "Alentejo" furniture, still being made today, originated in the Vila Viçosa tiles.

The Convent Church of S. Francisco can be entered from the street—it is Gothic, with three naves, and contains a splendid 17th-century Tree of Jesse, and the remarkable tomb of Vasco Esteves Gato, whose bearded head rests on three pillows and his feet on two dogs!

The Alentejo, owing to its savage and quite un-Portuguese climate of icy winters and intensely, Spanishly-hot summers has several curious features of peasant dress and peasant architecture. The brilliantly white-washed cottages are sometimes built without windows, the doors and wide chimneys letting in, in summer, quite sufficient of the blinding sunlight. In winter the shepherds tend their flocks draped in long fustian cloaks with three-tiered capes over the shoulders, and fur collars. For work, however, such a garment is inconvenient, and the labourers wear sheepskin chaps, with the fleece outside, strapped to their legs, and above, a curious sheepskin garment like a stole, covering the back and shoulders and coming down in two pieces in front, leaving the arms free—most practical, and highly picturesque. For their work in the stiff clayey soil of the fields the women fasten their skirts between their legs, producing a curious effect of tight knickers above their home-knit stockings, and always wear a man's felt hat clamped over their kerchiefs. All carry their food afield in *Taros*, small cork buckets with wooden handles and tight-fitting cork lids; cork is non-conducting, and this local thermos keeps the food either cold or hot, as required.

BORBA on the Elvas road is known for its excellent wine and for the fact that even the doorsteps of the humblest cottage, as well as the lintels and frames of all the windows and doorways, are made of the local marble. In the main square stands the Town Hall, built in 1797, and the Parish Church dedicated to Our Lady of the Snows, with good marble details. On the south-east side is the Fonte das Bicas, a lovely fountain erected in 1781 in white marble with a medallion of D. Maria I, and busts of the Queen and her husband on either side. The church of S. António is filled with marble work and the High Altar is by the same craftsman who designed the Fonte das Bicas. The church of S. Bartolomeu, built in the second half of the 16th century, contains Zubaran-like canvases with an exceptionally good vaulted ceiling. The altars and doorways and most of the church furniture are all of marble and in the splendid chancel arch black marble is introduced to contrast with the white. The Convento das Servas has a remarkable double renaissance cloister, one of the largest in the country, with a central fountain covered in azulejos, and the walls lined with polychrome 17th-century tiles.

VILA VIÇOSA, with a good pension, the Lisboeta, was the first town in Alentejo to declare against the French in 1808. It seems to be set down suddenly in a plain. It was here that the King of Portugal dedicated his crown and his realm to the Immaculate Conception of the Blessed Virgin in 1646, after which the kings were never actually crowned again. There is a large ruined castle, part Moorish, part mediaeval, on Roman foundations, and with splendid views; but the real reason for visiting this town is to see the great palace of the Dukes of Bragança, which takes up the whole of one side of an immense open square, the Terreiro do Paço, where in old days bull-fights took place, watched by the ladies over the wall of the formal garden which bounds the square on the right. Most intelligent guides take visitors through the long range of rooms. The present building was started in 1501 and only finished a century later, but it replaced a much earlier structure, probably Moorish, for in the basement near the great water-tank at the back are several rooms communicating through slender twin arches supported on a central column, as in the Alcazar at Seville. There are not many of these in Portugal, and the visitor should ask to see them. The garden too is particularly pretty. The great plain façade of creamy marble, gently coloured by time to a warm gold, with three rows of twenty-three windows, is extraordinarily satisfying in the beauty of its proportions. It was in this building that John IV, during the Spanish usurpation, received the overtures from the Portuguese noblemen which finally led him to the throne; and from here he set out in December 1640 to take possession of that throne, having heard of the successful rising in Lisbon. And now in this palace are kept most of the personal possessions of the last King of Portugal, Dom Manoel II, who when he died in exile in England in 1932 left all his estates and belongings back to his own country. They make a most curious collection of the good and of the bad. Among the furniture are many mid-Victorian pieces, and a bedroom which might have come out of Inveraray before the fire. There is a fine library, and a great deal of splendid Napoleonic china with whole services of "Paris", "Naste" and "Naples". There are also good Brussels, Aubusson and Gobelins tapestries in the palace, some badly in need of repair. The interior decorations were only finished by D. João V who employed the French painter Quillard, a pupil of Watteau, for them and for the portraits of the various Dukes of Bragança which are set in the ceiling of one of the galleries.

Several of the tiled panels from Vila Viçosa, with biblical scenes and the peculiar colouring and form of decoration already referred to, have been removed to the Ajuda Palace in Lisbon—one remains, behind a brass bed upstairs, and all about are quantities of the plain blue and white ones, very Dutch-looking, which led to the discovery of their authorship. Some years ago the Curator found in a drawer a single tile with a snail on it, signed "I.A.B. 1558". Later, looking through the Burlington Magazine, he came on a picture of a majolica vase designed by the Dutch artist Ian van Bogaerts, on which was a panel with a Bible scene; and the figures in this scene were identical with those in one of the Vila Viçosa tiled panels! Further research established the fact that this artist had designed the tile work at the palace—work whose colouring in fact strongly recalls the majolica of that date.

To the left of the palace is the Convent of Chagas or Poor Clares, with a fine classical doorway. The buildings look extremely attractive with their roofs at many different levels. The octagonal pavilion and beautiful mirador were built in 1530 and re-decorated in the 18th century; and the charming cloister has pleasing chapels in it. The interior of the church contains an interesting early 16th-century triptych at the side of the High Altar.

Opposite the palace stands the church of the Agostinhos, a lovely sober building filled with the extraordinary and splendid 17th-century Bragança tombs, all alike—great black and white marble coffers resting on the backs of coal-black lions couchant.

A delightful museum of ecclesiastical art is situated in the old church of Santa Cruz, and is well worth a visit.

Nearby is one of the entrances to the great Bragança Chase or Tapada which is now under cultivation. It is the largest enclosed space in the country; the wall surrounding it is 18 kilometres long.

Near the station is the huge Campo da Restauração where the Lapa church was built in 1756, which is a good example of its period with a pair of high rococo belfries. The south side of the Praça Nova is taken up by the Town Hall, a charming building built between 1754 and 1757 by the same architect who built the Lapa church, José Francisco de Abreu.

One of the finest pillories in the country stands up near the castle; it is made of granite, tall and slender, and is surmounted by a decorated sphere with a cross on top. Inside the castle walls is the Conceição, now the Parish Church, a renaissance building which has been constantly added to and restored. The interior has three naves, 17th-century polychrome azulejos, and some interesting Primitives in fine frames.

. . . .

The fortified city of ELVAS, where the plums come from, stands on a vast mound jutting up from the plain, with the hills of Spain and the smoke cloud above Badajoz in the distance. Approaching the town the first thing to be seen is the quite extraordinary five-tiered aqueduct that takes water across the plain to the city; this was built on Roman foundations between 1498 and 1622 and actually paid for by the people of Elvas themselves. It took nearly fifty years for the water to reach the walls of the city and another eighty for it to run into the lovely Misericordia fountain, built by Diogo Marques in 1622, which still stands, with its cupola on six marble columns, surmounted by an equestrian statue of D. Sancho II.

Elvas is rather sinister, for the mere number of human souls confined in the comparatively small space within its ramparts is oppressive. The narrow streets wind up and down, and the place is filled with soldiers, for it is one of the chief garrisons of Portugal. The houses, which are difficult to see because the streets are so narrow, some only six feet wide, have fine chimneys and curious Arab-like terraces and verandahs with good ironwork; but narrow and dark as they are, the inhabitants contrive to have flowers blooming in pots on their window-sills, and cages with singing-birds hanging at their doors—often a minute cage with a *grilo* or cricket in it is perched on the bird's cage; the loud jolly trills of the cricket inspire the goldfinch or linnet to fresh bursts of song.

In Elvas there are several very interesting churches, certain of which have notable baroque features. Not far from the Porta de S. Vicente, which is the usual way into the town, is the church of the Ordem Terceira de S. Francisco built in the first half of the 18th century. The High Altar is a riot of baroque wood-work and the nave has large azulejos panels on the life of the patron saint. The sacristy is also pleasing. In the Largo do Marquês de Pombal stands the former monastery of the Dominican friars, now a barracks, but the church is of interest. The exterior has Gothic features and a marble baroque doorway. Inside there are three large naves, the roof supported on black and white marble columns with gilded capitals. The side altars are of marble, but the High Altar is exceptionally richly gilded and on the walls are huge pictures in noble baroque frames; the organ should be noted. The Rua de Olivença, which is known to have born the same name in 1435, when it was the main street of the city, leads ultimately to the Largo de Vasco da Gama near the Museum. This houses an extraordinary mixture. Portraits, church plate, doll's houses, early typewriters and sewing machines, penny farthings and sedan chairs are all on view.

The Sé, or Cathedral, when the town had a Bishop, is now the Parish Church of the city. It is a Manueline building much altered in the 17th century, with a delightful black and white chequer-board pavement to the square in front. The interior is well proportioned, with fine rounded arches and pillars with gilded capitals. There is a great organ made in 1762 by an Italian, Pasqual Caetano Oldoni; and the side altars are also 18th century and built of Estremoz marble. The High Altar is the work of José Francisco de Abreu, who worked at Mafra, and built the Lapa church at Vila Viçosa; in it is a panel painted in 1749 by an Italian painter, Lorenzo Gramiera. The sacristy is finely proportioned with good church ornaments.

A little farther up than the cathedral is the most interesting and exciting church in Elvas, that of the Freiras de S. Domingos, built in 1543. It is an octagon and the interior, unlike that of most octagonal churches, is extremely beautiful and original, with good proportions and lovely decoration. The cupola is supported on eight elegant marble columns with Tuscan capitals; gold and coloured formal painting adorns the columns and transomed bays, and the whole church is lined, right up to the lantern of the cupola, with polychrome azulejos, dating from 1659. As the building is only lit by the lantern and two windows, the great height and the glittering tiles give a most curious mosque-like feeling to the whole place. There is a good renaissance doorway, and fair boiseries on the altars.

Outside the walls of the city there are few buildings of interest, but near the aqueduct is the church of Senhor Jesus da Piedade, built in 1753; it is full of rather touching *ex-votos*, for there is a big *romaria* here from the 20th to the 23rd September each year.

Just outside the main gate of Elvas, with a fine view of the aqueduct, is one of the nicest of the Government *pousadas* or inns, that of Santa Luzia. A road leads south from Elvas to JUROMENHA, a tiny unspoiled walled town on the frontier.

To the north-east of Elvas stands the frontier walled town of CAMPO MAIOR, with a castle which played a great part in the many wars between Portugal and Spain, as it did in the Peninsular War, when it was besieged at various times. General Beresford was given the castle when he was made Marquis of Campo Maior. The Parish Church has a Bone Chapel, not unlike that in S. Francisco in Evora, and St. John the Baptist Church, built in the 18th century, contains good marble work.

.   .   .   .   .

PORTALEGRE was the Roman Amoea; the whole district was then exceedingly populous, as is shown by the many Roman roads and bridges which still remain. It is a large and gay town standing high on the foothills of the Serra de Portalegre which divides Portugal from Spain, with the huge wide 18th-century façade of the Cathedral standing up from the surrounding houses, and is one of the few towns in Portugal which does not seem to have any historical interest, but is worth a visit on account of the cathedral, the museum, certain of the churches and the lovely baroque palaces with bulbous balconies which line the streets, and the perfect 18th-century azulejos to be found in almost every house. The monastery of S. Bernardo, now a military barracks, has a good baroque doorway and a curious patio surrounded by great azulejos panels, with a marble fountain in the centre. The interior of the church has other azulejos dated 1739 on the life of St. Bernard, an 18th-century choir and the very fine Estremoz marble renaissance tomb of D. Jorge de Melo, underneath a complicated retable with saints framed in pilasters. There is a good two-storeyed renaissance cloister in the convent, with trees in the garth and another Manueline cloister with capitals in designs of vegetables; the large chapter house with a groined ceiling should be seen.

The 18th-century Seminary in the Praça do Municipio is a very pleasing building and houses a Museum, with various good ivories and a set of twelve 16th-century polychrome terracotta bas-reliefs. There is also some good Portuguese furniture and pictures. The Sé in the same Praça has an enormous 18th-century façade flanked by two towers topped by octagonal pyramids; the interior has a lovely groined and painted ceiling and unusual mahogany choir stalls. The architectural 17th-century high altar retable with panels should be noticed, and also the pictures in all the side altars, which show how well worth while would be an exhaustive study of the 17th- and 18th-century painters of Portugal. The Sacristy is delightfully gaudy, with 18th-century *pau santo* vestment chests, splendid English embroidered 15th-century vestments and fine church plate. There is also a unique cloister with an exquisitely graceful baroque pediment containing an oval window above every arch and urns topped by flambeaux between. The José Regio Folk Art Museum and the hand-woven carpet and tapestry factory are both worth a visit.

The Robinson cork factory at Portalegre is also worth visiting; the enormous pressure under which cork tiling and belting is now made is most impressive, and the visitor is amused to see the complicated processes by which so many familiar objects are produced, from the vast piles of raw bark stacked below.

The Palacio Amarelo in the Largo de Cristovão Falcão has splendid ironwork over the twelve lovely 17th-century windows, and there is an unusual tower on top of the building, and inside a fine black and white marble staircase.

About 12 kilometres north of Portalegre towards Marvão are the ruins of MEDOBRIGA—now called ARAMENHA, where great quantities of Roman remains have been found including a marble portico, but most have been moved to the museum at Belem.

CASTELO DE VIDE, with an estalagem and some good though modest hotels and pensions, is one of the many spas of Portugal, much frequented in the season, and big fairs are held here on 15th January and 10th August. The town is on a hill with a deep valley below and on the top of a mountain opposite is the little chapel of Senhora da Penha in which a light is put at night by a woodcutter who has his cottage in that remote spot, so it looks like a large star shining out from far above. Most beautiful mountains and hills and very fine vegetation surround the town, which is a good centre for seeing some remote Alentejo towns such as Crato, Nisa and Marvão. The city is very curious, as there are certain streets and squares that have been untouched since the 15th and 16th centuries; at the entrance is the splendid granite Fonte do Martinho, built before 1586. Even the more modern lower parts of the place are filled with 17th- and 18th-century houses with lovely iron grilles over the windows.

The Praça D. Pedro V has some exquisite small baroque palaces surrounding it, including the hospital, which is in the house where Mousinho da Silveira the liberal statesman was born in 1780, and at one side stands the great church of Santa Maria. The interior has a certain beauty by reason of the height and width of the barnlike structure, and contains good woodwork. Narrow uneven streets lead up to the castle (where the Aragon Ambassadors came to arrange the marriage of King Diniz with Dona Isabel of Aragon, who afterwards became the Holy Queen, Saint Elizabeth of Portugal), through a perfectly preserved 16th-century village. The mediaeval doors and windows are innumerable, and make a most lovely sight, with the shining white-washed cottages, the dark castle above, and the little white chapel of Senhora da Penha on the mountain opposite. The castle is very large with good ogival doorways and one can wander freely about it. The church inside is dedicated to Senhora da Alegria —Our Lady of Joy—and is completely lined with polychrome 17th-century azulejos. Castelo de Vide is full of notable fountains, that of the Vila has a rectangular pyramid roof on renaissance columns.

The road from Castelo de Vide to the Spanish border winds below the great mountain at the top of which is the lost walled city of MARVÃO, called by the Romans Herminio Minor, which looks completely inaccessible from this side, as the battlements crown a great escarpment of rock; but a hidden road to the left winds round and up the back of the hill, through groves of chestnut and walnut trees through which glimpses of the great plain below can be seen. Almost at the top the road passes the old convent of N. S. da Estrêla, founded originally in 1448 and now used as the Misericordia hospital, with large wards and a delightful little cloister; the Gothic doorway and pulpit have been taken from their original positions and grouped together in the groined chapel to the left of the chancel! This church is the scene of a *romaria* on the 8th September. There is an estalagem, the Ninho de Aguias at Marvão, a perfect place for a rest.

One entrance to Marvão is through a narrow mediaeval archway near which is a most curious little, round, Moorish-looking structure, now much restored, but which is called the Jerusalem chapel and may have been originally the Easter Sepulchre. The city was of immense military importance in the Middle Ages, and is still entirely enclosed by great walls, though now the population is hardly more than a few hundreds. Little has been built in the last century, and the narrow, rough, stone-paved streets wind their way through white-washed, flower-bedecked houses and palaces, up to the castle which seems to rise from the living rock on which it is built. The walls are the home of countless kestrels, with almost sky-blue tails, and the view on all sides covers immense distances, as the mountain

PORTALEGRE: 18TH-CENTURY CLOISTER TO SÉ OR CATHEDRAL

MARVÃO: MISERICORDIA

FARO: A SQUARE

SAGRES: PRINCE HENRY THE NAVIGATOR'S FORT

on which the town is built stands isolated, overlooking the plains.

Marvão used to be one of the most attractive and remote towns in Portugal, but now it has become well-known and the road up the mountain-side widened, it is constantly visited by strangers. So all has been cleaned up and the churches restored out of all recognition.

To the north-west of Castelo de Vide, on the Castelo Branco-Estremoz road, stands the curious town of NISA with a fine renaissance fountain, the Fonte da Pipa, and one of the oldest castles in this part of the country. Between Nisa and Castelo de Vide there are strange little circular houses made of granite blocks with the rounded roof covered with turves, called *chafurdões*. These are used by the shepherds for storing grain, or for shelter at night. Little is known of their origin, but the local people think they were first constructed by the Moors. (They are very like the Iron Age round houses at Citânia de Briteiros near Guimareãs.)

Those who love beautiful and extraordinary scenery should drive north of Nisa and see the gorges of the Tagus at PORTAS DE RODÃO. Even there the river is very wide, far wider for instance than the Tiber in Rome. It flows through the mountains which do not overhang the water but descend to it in rolling foothills. The great new bridge across the river springs from side to side high up in the air, for the floods are so great that even the road has had to be cut out of the hills and does not follow the river. Near here is the great dam, Ribeira de Nisa, which has formed a large artificial lake in a tributary of the Tagus, and generates electricity for all the surrounding country, so that you find electric light installed even in the smallest cottage. It is also hoped ultimately to make fertile much of the land which is now only good for one crop a year.

CRATO, due south of Nisa and west of Portalegre, like many of the Alentejo towns is built on a hill rising from the plain. It was captured from the Moors by Afonso Henriques in 1160, and given to the Order of Malta in the next century. The Prior do Crato was one of the unsuccessful pretenders to the throne after the death of the Cardinal-King in 1580, which led to the Spanish domination. From the Praça da Republica, little roads radiate, with iron lanterns suspended across them from the 17th- and 18th-century houses on either side. The former lodging of the Grand Priors has been much rebuilt but has good details and a pleasing loggia.

I

Three kilometres north of Crato, in the village of FLOR DA ROSA, are the conventual buildings founded by the father of the Holy Constable in 1536. They are a most curious example of a fortified monastery, with great towers and battlements, and there is an interesting cloister.

ALTER DO CHÃO on the road from Crato to Estremoz is grouped round a castle with several good towers on one side of the main square, which has a black and white wavy tesselated pavement. In the same great Praça da Republica stands a beautiful white marble fountain dated 1556, with elegant columns holding up the cupola. Three kilometres distant is the Estação Zootecnica de Alter. This was originally a royal stud, but has now become the main national horse-breeding centre and experimental farm. Stallions are sent all over the country, horses trained and mules are bred. Between Alter do Chão and the village of Seda to the west is the Roman bridge of VILA FORMOSA, which is of great length with six round arches, and has been in use for twenty centuries.

The forgotten town of AVIZ, built on a granite rock above the river of the same name, stands in the great central plain of the Alentejo. The town and castle with its three high towers were built during the 13th century. The conventual church of St. Benedict was rebuilt, as was the convent, at the beginning of the 17th century by Baltasar Alvares. To the left of the entrance to the church is the image of Senhora da Orada, said to have been given by B. Nuno Alvares. The High Altar has a magnificent baroque retable, one of the best of its period in Portugal, but the very large 16th-century sacristy is the oldest part of the actual convent—of the Order of Aviz (an offshoot of the Order of Calatrava), which took its name from this town. Most of the contents of the treasury have been distributed among various other churches and museums and even the huge organ has been almost destroyed. The whole town is most curious and remote, and is difficult to reach except by a road that turns to the left just before Fronteira on the Estremoz–Crato road.

Indeed, the prevailing impression that the traveller carries away from the Alentejo is likely to be one of remoteness—of little towns and villages, church-bejewelled and castle-crowned, set on their hills so far from one another, with such vast sweeps of brown soil and green cork-woods rolling between that their distant whiteness reminds him, almost, of sails on a lonely ocean; of those interminable roads, with their patient archaic traffic so slow-moving that the motorist wonders if they will ever reach their journey's end; most of all, perhaps, of the solitary figures of shepherds, motionless in their hooded cloaks, standing guard over their flocks miles from anywhere, immobile as pillars in the desert.

CHAPTER VIII

THE SOUTH

THE first of the really southern towns of Portugal in feeling and architecture is ALCADER DO SAL, though it is only 50 kilometres along the river Sado from Setubal.

Alcacer is a most singular place, containing architectural remains of almost every period. The houses rise up from the river and the rice fields, which make it very unhealthy at those times of the year when malarial mosquitoes abound, It was settled by the Romans before the Moors came, and was only finally re-taken from the latter in 1217.

The Archaeological Museum in the former church of Espirito Santo contains Moorish, Roman and neolithic remains, and early maps. In the centre of the town the great church of S. Tiago, which was rebuilt in the time of King John V, is lined up to the ceiling with blue and white scriptural azulejos panels. From the castle at the top of the town there is a lovely view of the Sado, with pyramids of glistening salt on the banks which stretch away towards the low-lying rice fields, viridian green in the spring. Inside the castle walls stands Sta. Maria do Castelo, a Romanesque church, unusual in the south of Portugal; there are good statues on the altars and two early paintings hang in the chancel. The Blessed Sacrament chapel has a renaissance doorway added, with an iron grille; on the walls are unusual polychrome azulejos of angels and children with plants and trees. Nearby are the ruins of the convent of Ara Coeli, now a great haunt of gypsies, who camp among the tumble-down walls, on which enormous numbers of storks nest.

The Convent of S. Antonio a little way down from the castle was founded in 1524 by one of the Mascarenhas family; it has a good galilee, and a delightful renaissance doorway. Inside, there are two naves curiously dissimilar from each other. Originally there was only one, but later the splendid marble chapel of the Eleven Thousand Virgins was added by one of the sons of the founder. On the outskirts of Alcacer, at one end of the castle hill, is the church of Senhor dos Martires, formerly belonging to the Knights of S.

Tiago, and founded just after the Christian re-conquest of the city. Inside little remains of the original building, but there is a curious octagonal chapel, now used as the sacristy, which is known to have been built in 1333 by the fourth Master of the Order. Near the church is a very early pre-Roman burying ground, in which many interesting archaeological finds have been made. Alcacer do Sal still has a curiously Moorish feeling about it, with its brilliantly white-washed houses and narrow steep streets leading down to the river bank. Here there is a bridge, the first over the Sado, leading to Santiago do Cacem, and the coast road on to Cape St. Vincent and the Algarve. There is an estalagem outside the town.

ALCAÇOVAS due east of Alcacer is a delightful small town with fine palaces, among them that of the Barahonas, with a columned arcade round the patio, and pyramid-like towers. The palace of the Condes das Alcaçovas has much of the original 15th-century Gothic building remaining. In front is the strange little chapel of N. S. da Conceição, the interior decorated with scallop shells. The parish church, with its heavy granite columns, was reconstructed in the 16th century. There are unusual marble Gothic tombs and fine church fittings.

Three kilometres to the west, isolated in the countryside, is the former Dominican convent of N. S. da Esperança, the major part of which was built in the 16th century. The church has good details and very unusual blue and yellow azulejos representing trees, bulls and lions. There are other strange tiles round the chancel, with the sun, and enormous jars and flowers.

A road leads south-east out of Alcaçovas to VIANA DO ALENTEJO about 15 kilometres away. This small city possesses a fine castle, and built right inside its south-east wall is the extraordinary 16th-century parish church. Made of the local granite, the church has flying buttresses ending in pepper-pot turrets, while more pepper-pots stud the castellated balustrade round the whole exterior. Near the town is the large pilgrimage church of N. S. de Aires, a building not unlike the Estrêla church in Lisbon and the church at Meca, near Alenquer, though built a little earlier than these, in 1743. It has two belfries, an octagonal cupola and fine marble decorations, and there is a splendid view from outside. The romaria on the fourth Sunday of September is one of the most popular in this part of the Alentejo.

In the little town of ALVITO, 12 kilometres south of Viana, there is a huge late 15th-century fortified country-house or castle. The plan is rectangular, with round towers at each corner and the whole place is remarkably well preserved. There are two rooms in the keep with splendid ceilings and armorial bosses; the windows are very interesting, some Manueline, others Moorish.

Rather more than a kilometre to the north of VIDIGUEIRA, where there is a small archaeological museum, is the Quinta do Carmo, built on the site of an old Carmelite convent. The late 16th-century church contains interesting tombs; it was here that the body of Vasco da Gama, which had been sent from Cochin in 1539, lay until it was moved to the Jeronimos Church at Belem, near Lisbon, in 1898. There are some good 16th- and 17th-century Italianate canvases, and a pleasing cloister.

.   .   .   .   .   .

FERREIRA DO ALENTEJO, 25 kilometres west of Beja on the main road from Lisbon to the south, is a cheerful little town with an extraordinary round chapel like a walnut iced cake, indeed the whole place looks as if it was built of the best French confectionery. There is a 16th-century panel in the Parish Church and an early retable in the Misericordia.

The extremely interesting town of BEJA, with two passable hotels, the Rocha and the Bejense, seems to be lost in the great corn and wheat fields that stretch for so many miles over this part of the Alentejo, tilled by the sparkling, handsome country-people, who are known for their rapid speech.

Mr. Sacheverell Sitwell gives a wonderful description, in *Sacred and Profane Love*, of the approach to the town: "For mile after mile there is a straight road across the plain. Sometimes, to either side there are rows of eucalyptus trees, with the nests of storks high in their branches, sign of Barbary or Tartary, or the far Orient. The white pallor of this landscape is extraordinary. It is not the white of snow or dust. The colour seems to come from its immensity. . . . There is no shade at all except the eucalyptus. Presently far away a white pyramid is seen, with other simple cubical shapes at its feet, on a hill in the very middle of the landscape. That is Beja. . . ."

In addition to its remarkable architectural features, this town has a curious romantic interest, being the home of the reputed author of the famous *Love Letters of a Portuguese Nun*. The real authorship of these letters, of which so many translations have been made into almost every language, is a fascinating literary mystery. The first known edition was published in France in 1669 and was then said to be a translation from the Portuguese, but the originals (if Portuguese originals there be) have never been found. The letters are to a French officer, and the nun was at the convent of Conceição, now a museum. She is supposed to have been a Soror Mariana Alcoforado, who traditionally lived in this convent at the relevant period, and who ended her long life as Sister Portress. The convent is very interesting, though it cannot be said to be beautiful, with wide Arabic arches along the façade supporting a rich open-work decorated Gothic balustrade. There is a rather badly-proportioned square tower at one end, with a pointed steeple on top. The chapter house off the ogival cloister has a lovely 15th-century doorway and a fine painted ceiling, with Persian-carpet-like patterned azulejos round. The cloister itself is most peculiar with gothic arches, the walls and even the architraves of the arches being lined with metallic blue and white 17th-century carpet tiles. The church contains some azulejos panels dated 1741, of the life of the Blessed Virgin and St. John the Baptist, and the museum has fine pictures, porcelain, statues and early coins. Near the Conceição, in the Largo Sta. Maria, is the church of Sta. Maria, originally built in the 13th century, but rebuilt in the 15th. The façade of this, like the Hermitage of S. André not far off, is an astonishing sight in Portugal—both are plastered over, and might well be in Mexico, with their curious suggestion of adobe building. The classical interior is good, with splendid baroque altars and a Tree of Jesse in the chapel of Our Lady of the Rosary on the left.

The Archaeological Museum next to the Town Hall has some interesting exhibits, among them the grille through which Soror Mariana is reputed to have talked to her French lover; there is also a series of photographs of buildings in the town which have now been pulled down. The Hospital, known to have been built before 1489, in the Rua Dom Manoel I, was unique of its type, with the original cloistered patios and wards with groined ceilings. It has now been moved to a modern building.

In the 18th century the castle of Beja had forty towers, but now it is a pale shadow of what it was. However, the noble marble keep, built by King Diniz in 1310 and not unlike that at Estremoz, still stands. It has an elegant double row of battlements, and from it can be seen the Porta de Evora, the only Roman arch now remaining in the walls of Beja. There is a small Military Museum in the castle.

The Hermitage of S. André, in the same kind of tubular and adobe-like Gothic as Sta. Maria and also the church of S. Bras at Evora, and several others in the Alentejo and the Algarve, was founded by King Sancho I in commemoration of the taking of Beja from the Moors in 1162 and has lately been restored.

Just outside the town, to the north, there is now an important air-base, used by the German Air Force to train jet pilots and for testing and repairs.

A road leads due east from Beja via SERPA to Moura. The former, a walled town, has the remains of a castle and is entered by a mediaeval gateway. The convent of S. Antonio, built in 1463 and altered later, should be seen. This church, also, is like S. André at Beja but it contains 18th-century azulejos panels of the life of S. Francis and a tiny little cloister at one side. Serpa is the centre of a district celebrated for its choral singing, which bears a distinct resemblance to the polyphonic formerly used in the Choir School at Evora, from which it is presumed to have been copied by the country-people. The Pousada de São-Gens is a good place to stay.

MOURA, one of the towns near the River Guadiana, lies in fine lush country, with oddly-shaped decorated chimneys on the little houses, especially in the Rua de Arouche. In the main square there is a charming Regency marble fountain built in 1815, with an inscription and medallion of King John VI. The Municipal Library possesses an interesting 17th-century panel of S. Francis. In the same square the parish church of S. João Baptista, with its Manueline doorway, has a good marble pulpit and an unusual 17th-century set of polychrome azulejos of the Cardinal Virtues. On the outskirts of the town the Hospital occupies the former Convento do Carmo, the first Carmel to be founded in Portugal, soon after 1251. The church, lately restored, has a good renaissance doorway and three naves, of which the ceilings should be noticed. The tombs include one with an inscription stating that the dead man died of laughing! The sacristy and refectory ceilings are also very fine and the square classical two-storeyed cloister with marble pillars is good.

Fifty kilometres from Moura near the strange remote frontier town of BARRANCOS, stands the ruined castle of NOUDAR with little houses falling to pieces round it. In the 17th century it is known to have had four hundred inhabitants, a Misericordia and a hospital. A century later there were only two hundred people, and now no one lives in this haunted isolated place.

About 53 kilometres south-east of Beja, MERTOLA on the Guadiana is a lovely small walled town, with flat-roofed white-washed houses falling in narrow steep streets to the river at its confluence with the Oeiras. The 13th-century parish church has a renaissance doorway; it is low and large, with heavy columns, and is the only church in Portugal which has five naves.

The small town of CASTRO VERDE on the austere bare road to the south from Ferreira do Alentejo has some curious and delightful things in it. The church of Chagas, rebuilt when Philip II of Spain was also King of Portugal, has a nave lined with strange little Dutch-like blue azulejos, representing birds, flowers and windmills. The parish church, dedicated to N. S. da Conceição, is of more interest for it is completely lined right up to the ceiling with 18th-century azulejos, those below in patterns, and above huge panels of the battle of Ourique, dated 1713.

. . . . . .

The Algarve, the southernmost province of Portugal, is being so rapidly developed as a tourist centre that there are now a great many good hotels and roadhouses or estalagems. Fortunately the development is being carried out with discretion.

The main road to the southern coast of Portugal goes on from Castro Verde through the extremely beautiful Serra do Malhão to S. BRAS DE ALPORTEL, near which is one of the very comfortable *pousadas* or inns founded by the "Secretariado Nacional de Informação". Four main roads meet in this town, one going on south to Faro, one west to Loulé, while the third runs south-east to the Spanish frontier at VILA REAL DE S. ANTONIO, from which there is a ferry over the Guadiana into Spain. Curiously enough nothing existed on this site before the Marquês de Pombal decided to build a town here in 1774, when the whole place was erected in five months, on the same kind of pre-fabricated plan that Pombal adopted when rebuilding the lower part of Lisbon after the earthquake. All the stone window and door frames and other fittings for

Vila Real were brought from the capital ready made. The town as a whole is very attractive, and the Praça do Marquês de Pombal is surrounded by low Pombaline houses with a black and white marble pavement, the design stretching out like the rays of the sun.

Three kilometres up the Guadiana at CASTRO MARIM are big semi-circular walls surrounding a square castle with round towers. Inside the walls are also the ruins of the 14th-century church of S. Tiago. The fort of S. Sebastião, on another hill to the south-west, was built by King John IV, father of Catherine of Bragança; he was a great fortifier, and as we saw, built the many little forts which one sees between Lisbon and Cascais on the banks of the Tagus.

Returning from Vila Real de S. Antonio to Faro and the West, the road more or less follows the coast, passing through Tavira and Olhão; the wild flowers on the first stretch are extraordinary in spring, especially the various *leguminosae*: something like forty different sorts of these can be found, all unfamiliar to English travellers and some quite exquisite. TAVIRA, already rather Moorish-looking, is a beautiful town. The Misericordia church has an exceedingly fine renaissance doorway with figures standing at either corner of the pediment, and in the centre a niche with stone curtains draped round Our Lady of Mercy. Inside are rococo gilt wood altars, dated 1760, and azulejos panels on the Works of Mercy. There are wonderful rococo boiseries in most of the churches, particularly in those of S. Paulo and the Carmo. A 1st-century Greek inscription, the only one to be found in Portugal, was discovered in 1856 in the tiny village of SANTA LUZIA near Tavira.

OLHÃO, which is definitely more like a North African town than a European one, is of singular beauty and strangeness, its cube-shaped brilliantly white houses have flat roofs on which the inhabitants sit. It is a great fishing town and the men here go as far as Setubal and Lisbon on their voyages; a number even go to American waters every year, but always return for the three winter months; so many of the houses in Olhão have American comforts and luxuries put in by these roving seamen.

At MILREU, not far from Olhão, there are very remarkable Roman remains, including baths and mosaics, and a building which is thought to be a 3rd-century Christian church, all set in superbly beautiful country. Nearby is the fine 18th-century palace of ESTOI, owned by the Visconde de Estoi, which is not unlike Queluz, with a formal park with fountains and statued staircases. Unfortunately there are numerous 19th-century additions to the palace.

FARO, 8 kilometres from Olhão, with an international airport, is one of the largest towns in the Algarve. During Lent there are most unusual night processions through the streets, when members of the Confraternities from the various parishes walk slowly along dressed in strange black hoods. The name of the town is thought to be Arabic; and with the recapture of this town from the Moors in 1249 ended their rule in Portugal. In the 15th century the Jews established a printing press, which produced various well-known books, and there is still a very large Jewish colony possessing two Synagogues, though in general the Jews have been absorbed by the Portuguese, who have always freely inter-married with them. The city was almost entirely destroyed by the English commanded by the Earl of Essex in 1596, when Portugal was under the Spanish domination; they took all the books of the Bishop of Silves as loot, and these ultimately became the nucleus of the Bodleian Library at Oxford.

In the 18th century Bishop Francisco Gomes de Avelar built a great deal in Faro, including various bridges, the Seminary, the Misericordia Hospital in the central square, and the Arco da Vila, a delightful piece of Italianate architecture. The renaissance Cathedral has an enchanting red Chinoiserie organ, notable baroque details, and a superb late 17th-century altar in the sacristy. The Maritime Museum, near the Hotel Eva and the sea-front, is of absorbing interest to those concerned with sea-fishing in its various forms. The Largo de S. Francisco is a large space in which stands the church of the same name, lined with exceptionally good rococo woodwork, and azulejos panels of the life of the saint. Round the Carmo church, built in 1713, whose pleasing façade has a balustrade between the two high belfries, a big fair takes place every year on the 16th of July.

All along the coast near Faro are dunes and strange seawater lagoons. This is the most projecting part of the South of Portugal and in consequence is right on the route of migrant birds; extraordinary numbers can be seen passing along near the shore both in spring and autumn, usually at dusk or early morning. The whole coast of the Algarve is singularly beautiful, rising to low cliffs, with great rocks and promontories jutting out to sea and warm sandy beaches between.

LOULÉ, situated in one of the most lovely parts of the Algarve, is the scene of a big fair during the last three days of August. The town is famous for the variety and number of those pierced Moorish chimneys, made of mortar or plaster, which adorn every house or little cottage. The parish church, in the Rua de Martins Farto, was given by King Diniz to the Order of S. Tiago in 1280. The interior is large, with curious capitals to the columns; there are fine renaissance archways, and unusual polychrome azulejos panels of St. Michael at the Last Judgment in one of the side chapels. Near the city the pilgrimage church of N. S. da Piedade was rebuilt in 1553 by a tinsmith. To the south-west of Loulé, ALBUFEIRA is one of the most attractive of the coastal towns, with several hotels and estalagems.

One of the earliest cities in Portugal is SILVES, which is possibly Phoenician in origin. It was called Kelb by its Moorish masters, and had at that time thirty thousand inhabitants, most of whom were Arabs. In the 16th century the population was reduced to a hundred and forty people, and various earthquakes in the 18th century destroyed almost the whole town with the exception of the castle and the cathedral. Silves is in a lovely situation on a low hill in the plain which stretches from the Serra de Monchique to the sea. The Gothic Sé is of interest, though not perhaps of great beauty, being built of the local reddish stone with white pointing. The rather heavy interior has some fine rococo altars. The Moorish castle gives a most strange feeling of Africa; enormous cisterns still exist, which were constructed to hold sufficient water for a year's needs, and there are great cellars for keeping food and grain. Outside the town is the Cruz de Portugal, a 15th-century decorated stone crucifix, with a pietá at the back.

PORTIMÃO, beautifully placed on the lovely estuary of the Arade, is a rambling town smelling strongly of fish, as after Setubal it is one of the chief centres in Portugal of the sardine-canning industry. A couple of kilometres away on the coast is PRAIA DA ROCHA, for long the most popular seaside resort for visitors in the Algarve. There is a very fine beach with splendid sands and rocks and lovely bathing, for the sea is warm almost all the year round. The two hotels, both good, are the Algarve and the Bela Vista and others are being built. Four kilometres to the west of Portimão the luxurious Penina Golf Hotel at Montes de Alvor has a championship course and is one of the best hotels in the country. A road leads north from Portimão to the beautiful SERRA DE MONCHIQUE, the range of hills which shelters all this stretch of coast from the north, and runs out almost to Cape St. Vincent. It is remarkable for the beauty and variety of its wild flowers, including some unique sorts, which can be seen at their best in April and May. All through the Algarve the mimosas flower in February, and the almond-blossom a little earlier; the whole countryside is smothered in a foam of blossom then, a lovely sight.

Right up in the mountains is CALDAS DE MONCHIQUE, a little spa with medicinal waters which are exceptionally good for rheumatism and indigestion. As in most spas the buildings are dreary, with the old-fashioned Vichy atmosphere of polished copper and mahogany, but the surroundings are so lovely with the great forest or *mata*, and splendid walks over the hills, that the spa can be forgotten. Huge rocks stand out of the rough ground as the road rises to MONCHIQUE, which is a picturesque little village. The view over the plain to the sea from the top of Picotam hill near by is one of the most beautiful in Portugal; but all round Monchique there are roads with superb vistas.

About 5 kilometres north-east of Mexilhoeira between Portimão and Lagos are the stone neolithic tombs at ALCALÁ. LAGOS, where big fairs are held on the 16th and 17th of August, and from the 12th to the 14th of October, has a bay of great size which is said to be able to hold one hundred and forty-seven warships, and used to be frequently visited by British naval units. It was here that Prince Henry the Navigator had his shipyards, and re-fitted his exploring fleets between their voyages of discovery. The western entrance to Lagos from the sea is by the Ponta da Piedade, which is like a fantastic cathedral, with spires and arches weathered out of the soft orange rock; there are enclosed pools whose only approach is from the sea, and great caverns and towers and minarets in the cliffs.

In Lagos itself there are fine buildings round the Praça da Republica, including the singular Customs House, under whose arches the only slave market in Portugal was held. At one side is the Misericordia, particularly rich in 18th-century carved woodwork, and the Paço do Governo has a splendid coat of arms on the façade. In the Rua de Silva Lopes, the tiny chapel of S. Antonio, rebuilt in 1769 after an earthquake, is completely lined with extremely rich rococo gold boiseries, which surround good 18th-century paintings; a statue of the saint has the red sash of a British General of the time of the Peninsular War across his breast! In the chapel is the grave of Colonel Hugo Beatty of the Irish Regiment, who died in 1789; his crest and motto *"non vi sed arte"* is engraved on his tomb. In the little museum off the chapel, there are the vestments used at the last Mass attended by that tragic figure King Sebastian before he embarked on the Moroccan campaign in 1578, from which he never returned.

A narrow track leads up to the Rossio da Trinidade, which dominates the bay and where there are good 17th-century houses and stretches of the original city wall. There is an interesting aqueduct, started in 1490 and finished in 1521, which still brings water to the city from the spring of Paul da Abedueira.

The road from Lagos to Sagres and Cape St. Vincent soon enters a strange, arid country with fewer and fewer houses and scarcely a person to be seen. Between Raposeira and Figueira a turning to the right leads to the chapel of N. S. de Guadalupe, an extraordinary little Romanesque building, dating from the 13th century and possibly a Templar foundation. The columns in the chapel are in coloured stone, which gives a strange Byzantine air to the whole place, and some of the capitals have human faces. Soon the road rises a little and the twin capes of Sagres and St. Vincent are seen in the distance.

SAGRES, the southernmost, cannot but move the traveller. Here the half-English Infante Dom Henrique, surrounded by maps, charts, and experts, plotted the routes taken by all the first Portuguese explorers down the western shores of Africa, which later led to the discovery of the Cape route to India. A fortress, with the Prince's arms over the entrance, stands at the neck of the long narrow promontory; in the courtyard, on the ground, lies an enormous stone compass-dial, said to have been used by the Prince himself for his calculations, and within the enclosure are the ruins of a house and small chapel which may well be those in which he lived and worshipped. One can, and should, visit Sagres in spite of the spate of building (Pousada do Infante and Hotel da Baleeira both excellent), and gaze across the bay at Cape St. Vincent, the "Sacred Promontory" of the ancients—sacred to them because there the setting Sun, sinking into the Atlantic, looked one hundred times his normal size, and above the beating of the waves could be heard the hiss of his extinguishing fires.

For the English visitor, CAPE ST. VINCENT, the most south-western point of Europe, has other associations. It was off these cliffs that the battle of Cape St. Vincent was fought in 1797, when Lord Jarvis and Nelson beat the French, and earlier in 1770 Rodney had put the Spanish Navy to flight. (It was also to this promontory that the body of St. Vincent was brought by the ravens in the legend: these birds still appear on the Arms of the City of Lisbon, and tame ravens are to be found in many of the wine shops of the capital, walking about on the floor and making friends with the customers.) Certain of the plants here are unique: *Scilla vicentina*, *Helianthemum origanifolium*, *Astragalum potarium*, and *Centaurea vicentina*. At the extremity of the cape D. Henrique built his Vila do Infante in the 15th century, but nothing now remains of it save perhaps the small semi-ruined chapel dedicated to St. Catherine.

A good main road runs near the coast from Lagos up to Alcacer do Sal through Aljezur, Odemira and Santiago do Cacem, through beautiful, rather desolate country; the few people to be met on the road are exceptional-looking, tall and well-made, with glowing black eyes.

SANTIAGO DO CACEM, which has one of the good government *pousadas* not far off, presents a most curious appearance from a distance; as so often in Portugal, the cemetery lies inside the walls of the castle crowning the hill on whose slopes the town is built, so that the funeral sable shapes of cypresses stand up above the grey masonry of the citadel. On the way up to the castle, the Misericordia church has a renaissance side door and pleasing baroque work within. Just beyond it, the splendid old houses in the Praça do Conde de Bracial surround an agreeable obelisk in the centre. The parish church has been much restored during the centuries, but there is a 14th-century high relief of St. James the Greater fighting the Moors. In the sacristy are two early paintings on panels. Just above is the castle, built by the Templars; a little path goes right round under the great walls and towers, with lovely views over the town and the distant country; the low whining of the large clay whistles on the windmills across the valley comes gently through the air, changing as the wind changes.

A road leads west from Santiago do Cacem to SINES, famous as the birthplace of Vasco da Gama. From here, after the Convention of Evora Monte in 1834, Dom Miguel went into exile on board the English ship "Stag". Sines is a very pretty town, nearly half-way between Cape Espichel and Cape St. Vincent, but is so remote and difficult to get to that it is almost unknown to foreigners. It is one of the few places left in Portugal which has a town crier, who walks through the streets making announcements about all the things that have been lost and found, and what fishing boats are coming in from the sea. The minute harbour is protected by a huge bastion of natural rock, backed by a steep slope crowned with the white houses of the town. The anchorage is very good in summer, but in winter a south-west wind often drives right into the bay. There are great lobster floats near the shore, constructed of planks with a large pole in the centre, from which depend vast nets full of lobsters and crawfish, swimming about in the water till they are hauled up and despatched to the Lisbon market. There is a castle, and the house where Vasco da Gama was born (since rebuilt), as well as the little hermitage chapel of N. S. das Salas, begun by the explorer, but only finished after his death.

A lighthouse stands on the end of Cape Sines, and on either side stretch endless cliffs with occasional beaches, in this almost unpopulated part of the country. On a tiny island off the coast, Pessegueiro, are the ruins of a fortress and of a church. If a motor boat is hired from Sines to this island, a further excursion can also be arranged to take in VILA NOVA DE MILFONTES, down the coast, once a flourishing town but later sacked by Algerian pirates. An extremely rare large-flowered species of gorse, *Ulex spectabilis*, is a remarkable feature of this very lonely stretch of country.

FERREIRA DO ALENTEJO: "ICED CAKE" CHURCH

BEJA: 15TH-CENTURY CHURCH OF S. MARIA. ("ADOBE" BUILDING)

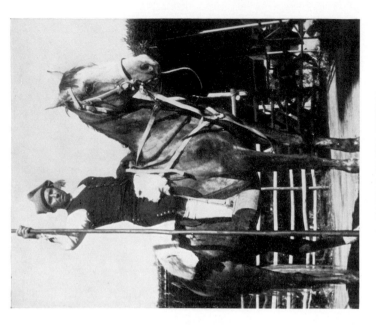

A CAMPINO IN THE RIBATEJO

CASTLE OF ALMOUROL

CHAPTER IX

ESTREMADURA

STUDYING the map of Portugal in connection with Wellington's campaigns, it is not easy at first to realise that Lisbon in fact lies at the tip of a sort of blunt-ended peninsula—indeed at the first glance, the reader may wonder why the lines of Torres Vedras should have been much of an impediment to the march of the French on the capital. But before the marshy land of the Tagus valley was drained and the river confined within its present channels, the most practicable route to Lisbon was precisely down the road, on higher ground and firmer going, from Leiria southwards; and the capital with its riches, its prestige, and its superb harbour was always the goal, a goal protected on three sides from attack. To the west lay the Atlantic, to the south the broad tidal river, to the east the leagues of impassable marsh country; down the strip of high ground ran the only line of approach, with the sand-dunes pressing in to narrow it on the right and the unreclaimed marshes on the left. It is no accident that the greatest of battles for Portuguese freedom, Aljubarrota, should also have taken place along this strip, centuries before Torres Vedras.

Before reaching Caldas da Rainha, on this old road north from Lisbon, stands the lovely little walled town of OBIDOS, with a good *pousada* in the old Castle. It has all been much restored, the walls indeed having been practically rebuilt with regular battlements all the way round, but nothing can destroy its charm. The castle, which has also suffered restoration, was a good specimen of mediaeval fortification, though now it is difficult to trace the original work. There are no new houses in the place, so that on going through the great gatehouse, which is gay with azulejos, one feels as if one had stepped back three hundred years into a singularly and indeed unnaturally clean and polished town of the period; the narrow streets still have their mediaeval paving of large rough stones, and the shining white houses and the small *largos* are all delightful in their effect, with the gay washing put out to dry on the naked rocks inside the walls.

Near the town in the Quinta da Capeleira lived in the 17th century Josefa d'Ayala y Cabrera, better known as Josefa of Obidos, the daughter of a local man and a Sevillian mother. Josefa had extraordinary and varied talents, for she was a painter, a miniaturist, an etcher, a modeller in terracotta, a silver-worker and a calligrapher. The paintings attributed to her vary considerably in quality, and many of them must be by her pupils; it is known that she had a big school of painting at Obidos. Her father was also an artist, and a picture of his of the Crucifixion is now in the passage leading to the choir of the Misericordia church in Peniche.

Obidos can be entered by four gateways and two posterns. The castle encloses the *pousada* in a 16th-century palace with Manueline windows, and the keep has an inscription over the doorway stating that it was built in 1413. The most remarkable church in the town is the Parish one of Sta. Maria which contains a splendid renaissance tomb, on which is a carved stone group of the Pietá, with St. John and St. Mary Magdalene. The roof is painted in polychrome and decorative azulejos reach right up to a frieze of paintings by Josefa. The Misericordia nearby was founded by Queen Leonor, who made Caldas da Rainha popular; it has an early baroque doorway above which in a niche stands a coloured glazed china statue of the Virgin. The altars are gold renaissance work and there are certain good painted panels in the church, including more work by Josefa.

Just outside the town on the Caldas da Rainha road is the extraordinary hexagonal church of Senhor da Pedra, the scene of a *romaria* on the 3rd May. It was built by the same architect as the Mitra Palace, now the Lisbon Museum, between 1740 and 1747 and is a most singular edifice, especially the exterior, with its great lantern. Inside the church is of little interest though there are some fine 18th-century chairs in the sacristy.

ATOUGUIA DA BALEIA, on the Peniche road, remains much as it was in the middle ages, when it was an important place. There is a Gothic fountain, looking, with its arched entrance, rather like a small castle, at one end of the little town and there are also the pillory and the castle ruins. The Parish Church of S. Leonardo at the entrance to the place is a beautifully-proportioned early Gothic building with a fine apse, the interior boasts Romanesque capitals to the columns, with human and animal heads, and the original Gothic windows remain; but by far the most remarkable thing in the church is a stone high relief of the Nativity, which forms the altar-front in a side chapel to the right. It is a 14th-century work representing the Blessed Virgin lying in bed, with the Holy Child rising Blake-like from her body and St. Joseph with a Gothic beard and hair sitting at the foot. In one of the Virgin's hands is a book and in the other a flat zinnia-like daisy; her lovely head rests on a pillow, and the bedclothes fall in large stiff folds, while behind stand the donkey and the ox. It is curiously like the tomb of Don Lope de Fontecha at Burgos in Spain.

The town of PENICHE is a big deep-sea fishing centre. It is most picturesque, with terrific rocks and deep caves in the surrounding cliffs. It was the scene in 1589 of a landing by an English force of twelve thousand men who came to fight for the Prior do Crato, the Pretender to the Portuguese throne. The major part of the fortifications date from the time of D. João IV and the town contains many lovely houses and churches. On the extreme westerly point of the promontory on which Peniche stands is the sanctuary of N. S. dos Remedios, a tiny chapel, hollowed out of the cliffs and completely lined with azulejos panels which glitter in the semi-darkness.

The BERLENGAS ISLANDS lie about 12 kilometres out to sea. Motor boats leave in the summer months from Peniche and take about one and a half hours over the crossing. They are a group of rocky granite islands, of which the largest, called Berlenga Grande, is roughly a square mile in size; on this are the ruins of a monastery and the fort of S. João Baptista, which justs out into the sea and is only linked with the island by a narrow causeway. Visitors can sleep in the *pousada* which has been made in the fort. Moreover, the island is so curious and interesting, with its large number of rabbits and its strange flora, that for those who do not mind the sea crossing it is well worth while making the effort to see it.

Between Obidos and Caldas da Rainha, up a side road to the right, lies the village of GAEIRAS with the Peninsular War Museum founded by one of the Pinto Basto family; it is housed in their quinta right in the village itself, a private museum, but the family are usually most kind in showing it to visitors and students. There is a collection of fire-arms and contemporary maps and prints of the engagements and battles, but some of the most interesting exhibits are the letters from Wellington, Lord Strangford and Beresford, as well as from Ney, Junot and the ex-King of Spain, Joseph Bonaparte.

About 6 kilometres north of Obidos the main road enters CALDAS DA RAINHA, a town which during the Second World War became the "résidence forcé" of a great number of refugees who fled to Portugal from all over Europe and who could not obtain visas to go on to any other country. Caldas is an attractive clean place with good hotels, the Central, the Lisbonense and the Rosa, as there is a famous spa for rheumatism with a large Free Hospital, founded by Queen Leonor in the 15th century and later rebuilt by D. João V. The town is also known for its large pottery factories; some of the ware is made in the form of leaves, fruit and animals, but unfortunately the colours are often crude. Caldas is a good centre for excursions over this part of Portugal, for both Alcobaça and Batalha as well as Leiria and Tomar and the extraordinary Lagoa de Obidos are all within easy reach.

The town does not contain much of architectural interest, except the early Manueline parish church of Nossa Senhora do Populo, which was actually built in 1500 as the chapel of Queen Leonor's Hospital. It is a charming building, now sunk below the level of the street, with a very peculiar tower-like belfry in which the bells hang in open arches. This is not, as Watson states, the only Manueline church tower now remaining in the country; there is at least one other, that of S. João Baptista at Tomar. Inside, the famous Gothic font has been much restored and is now of little interest. The whole of the interior walls are covered with blue and yellow 17th-century azulejos, very gay and charming, especially the ingenious design and arrangement round the High Altar, on which is a polychrome wood statue of the Blessed Virgin. The church has a great feeling of warmth and is much used. The fronts and ends of the two side altars are encrusted with black, lustre, green and brown tiles of the 16th century; a cross in the same colours is inserted in the centre of each; these cut right across the main design and are presumably a later addition.

The great feature of the church however, is the very peculiar chancel arch of five curves, rising to the central one with, above it, a rather lovely early triptych of the Crucifixion, in a carved and gilt frame of architectural design which follows the curves of the arch; the whole effect is of a looped stone curtain with a shaped picture suspended against it.

ESTREMADURA

A road leads from Caldas down to FOZ DO ARELHO, 10 kilometres away, passing the LAGOA DE OBIDOS, a sea-water lagoon which is usually cut off from the sea by a sand-bank; this like that at Albufeira near Sesimbra, is opened at intervals to let in the fresh sea water, and so clean it out; the breach then silts up again. Only those who are fond of the sea should stay at Foz do Arelho where there is Mr. Harbord's excellent hotel, the Facho, for the Atlantic is so near that one feels as if one were in a liner. The lagoon is singularly beautiful, with low hills and moors rolling down to its flat shores; it is full of fish: eels, lampreys, soles and shell-fish, and there is rough shooting.

The Pousada de S. Martinho is at Alfeizerão on the direct road from Caldas to the north.

Alcobaça and Batalha lie farther north. These two great national shrines, bearing for the Portuguese such a weight of patriotic sentiment, the Victory over the Spaniards and the Victory over the Moors, have their differing beauties of style and period, their differences of atmosphere—Alcobaça, as a wise European has said, has the greater faith. But one thing they have in common—the glory of the sun-soaked local stone. It is impossible to describe; all one can say is that Alcobaça is gold washed and tipped with grey, and that Batalha is grey flushed with gold.

The Monastery of Santa Maria at ALCOBAÇA (Hotel Bau) was originally founded by D. Afonso Henriques in 1152 in thanksgiving for the recapture of Santarem from the Mussulmans. It was a Cistercian foundation and the plan is practically identical with that of Clairvaux. The whole church is of the same height and is the largest in the country. The interior is astounding, with two long lines of immensely tall, clustered white columns stretching away into the distance; all the rococo woodwork and plaster over the columns put in in 1770 by William Elsden, the English architect who worked for Pombal, have been taken out in the drastic restorations, so although the original beauty of the edifice has been restored, the church seems to have lost its life. On either side at the top of the great nave stand the splendid gothic tombs of D. Pedro I and of his mistress, Inez de Castro. In the right transept is an extraordinarily lovely renaissance painted terracotta group of the death of St. Bernard, though it was frightfully injured by Napoleon's soldiers. Most of the life-size monks surrounding the dying saint have lost their heads, but their bodies are very beautiful in their drooping grief, and a number of cherubs with musical instruments still have little sad, fat faces.

The Abbey itself demonstrates, as do almost all over-restored churches, the extreme difficulty of how to re-furnish the stripped altars. The high altar at Alcobaça has a most lovely crucifix, but ludicrous modern iron candlesticks on either side, and the little wooden pulpit is both ugly and shabby. Behind the high altar there are a number of chapels which are barely furnished, like those in Lisbon Cathedral, and the Blessed Sacrament Chapel is hidden away near the sacristy, which was built by João de Castilho in 1519, re-done after the earthquake in 1755, and has now yet again been entirely restored. To the left of the nave a door leads into a cloister in which is a shrine with an exquisite 15th-century polychrome stone statue of the Virgin and Child; a steep staircase leads up to the vast dortor, which has quantities of canvases stacked against the walls. Off the cloisters are also the splendid refectory with a reading pulpit and the big kitchen which so impressed Beckford, not unlike that at Sintra, lined with pale washed-blue tiles which give a curious underwater effect, enhanced by the sound of rushing water running through the fish tank at one end. In the centre the great fireplace is surmounted by a huge open chimney, rising to the full height of the building. The lovely chapter-house now has standing round it enormous coloured terracotta statues of saints and angels, which were made by the 17th- and 18th-century monks, and used to stand in the Transept chapels of the Abbey. A pair of lovely, young, curiously sexless kilted angels, with wind-blown hair and very sweet expressions, should be noticed.

The Sala dos Reis to the left of the main entrance to the church is most curious, with its big earthenware statues of Portuguese Kings clothed in 18th-century dress. Round the room, which is now staring with whitewash, there is a good border of Juncal 18th-century azulejos, depicting the foundation of the monastery and a manuscript tile panel with its history. There is also an enormous bronze soup tureen of heroic size, said to have been taken by the Portuguese at the battle of Aljubarrota in 1385, when the soldiers' soup was made in it!

One of the things many people miss at Alcobaça is the little cemetery outside the door of the vestibule which leads from the sacristy to the sanctuary In this deserted garden stands the graceful and peculiarly stylised little 18th-century chapel of N. S. do Destêrro or of the Entombment, rather tiresomely encumbered outside with funerary houses or chapels; the wall of the raised terrace on which it stands is decorated with some very amusing and highly unreligious azulejos of hunting scenes, including one of stags being lassoed, and another of a gentleman who has been treed by a bear! The whole place is very quiet and sweet—roses bloom, a stream rushes in a stone channel below the parapet, and the inhabitants of Alcobaça who live beyond the Monastery, to save going round the great building and along the tree-shaded market-place on the north side, nip through the garden and take a short cut through the vestibule and the nave, emerging down the steps below the great rococo façade, in the centre of which the seven-course Cistercian doorway is set like an archaic jewel in rich paste.

NAZARÉ, 13 kilometres north-west of Alcobaça, is one of the most fascinating places in Europe, not for its architectural features, but because of its inhabitants. They are alleged to be Phoenician in origin, and the name of the nearby promontory of Peniche lends colour to the theory, as does their appearance. A high proportion of the people are grey-eyed and black-browed, with fine straight noses coming down almost in a line with the forehead, like the profiles on Greek vases; and they cling, as no other community in Portugal does, to their own peculiar form of dress, a sort of rough harsh wool tartan in large broken squares of brilliant colours—reds, pinks, blues, greens, clear yellows, buff and orangey shades; the women wear this in the form of full pleated skirts, stitched close over the hips, the men as shirts and trousers—but a man will wear pink tartan trousers below an orange tartan shirt, and both may be liberally patched with yet some other shade. The effect is indescribably brilliant and surprising in the modern world of drab garments. The women usually wear over their heads a black fringed shawl falling to below the waist, with a curious little cloth peak above the forehead, and gold dangling ear-rings in the form of crescent moons —their skirts are bunched out with three or four layers of petticoats. scalloped round the hem.

The whole place is given over to fishing, and the gaily-dressed population haunts the broad sandy beach and the sea-front behind it. The boats are as picturesque as the people, long and rather narrow, the prows terminating in a high sharp point; they are often brightly painted. Tractors are now used, but a few pair of oxen still sleep and ruminate among the nets till such time as they are yoked to the boats to haul them up; the women sit about drying salted fish on rush mats in the sun, nursing babies, mending nets or merely gossiping, while tiny boys and girls, as gaily clad as their elders, run and play, or mind still smaller mites—the whole place has a strange peace and dignity, full of serene self-containedness—"The world forgetting, By the world forgot." Many even of the younger people have never been so far as Caldas da Rainha, only a few miles away. Most of all is the visitor aware of the antique peace and remoteness towards sun-down, when those strangely-shaped boats are coming in round the headland beyond the bay, and the women sit in black circles on the white sand, the shawls hiding their gay skirts, awaiting the return of their men, like Norns, or some beings from another world.

In winter fishing is given up, and since the Atlantic gales drive straight into the bay the boats are pulled right up off the beach into the streets and squares of the little town; it is a strange sensation, in November, to drive down the hill into the main square, and find one's progress blocked by an immense boat, filling the road-way and towering above the car. During those stormy months, nets are made and mended, and boats and tackle repaired, and no doubt those petticoats scalloped, till spring returns and the boats go down to the sea again and the quiet oxen to the beach.

The Sitio, reached by a funicular, on the high cliff top, has a superb view of the town far, far below and the sandy coast stretching away to the south for miles. The renaissance church is beautiful, with delicately painted pillars, azulejos and a general impression of muted richness. There are several hotels down in the town.

Between Alcobaça and Batalha lies the village of ALJUBARROTA, scene of the great battle of August 14th, 1385, when John I finally beat the Castilians and secured Portugal's independence. One wonders whether one of the very primitive cottages housed the valiant baker's wife who on that famous day rushed out and slew twelve Spaniards with the long-handled bread-shovel! Before a church in the village stand two strange Victorian box tombs; on one of them, dated 1869, a stone figure lies under a pleated stone eiderdown, with his head on a small carved pillow.

About 6 kilometres beyond Aljubarrota are the cross-roads of which the right-hand turn leads to PORTO DE MOS, home of the curious Legua pottery, with a castle on an eminence, while the left-hand road goes to JUNCAL, where there was formerly the azulejos factory founded in 1770 by José Rodrigues da Silva e Sousa.

The Estalagem do Cruzeiro on the main road has a good restaurant and rooms for those wishing to stay.

Farther on towards Batalha the restored chapel of S. JORGE DE ALJUBARROTA stands on the right of the road, on the spot where the Holy Constable Nuno Alvares raised his standard before the battle; in a niche on the left of the door there always stands a beaker of water and a mug for thirsty travellers. This act of charity for the wayfarer has been kept up by the same family since the 15th century, and is said to commemorate Alvares' thirst during the heat of the battle.

The monastery of Our Lady of Victory at BATALHA, perhaps Portugal's greatest national shrine, was begun by John I in 1388 in fulfilment of a vow made before the Battle of Aljubarrota. The old road to the north approaches it by a bridge over the river Lena, with delicious Gothic-revival lodges at either end, and then swings round to where the superb West front of the great Gothic building is seen below on the right. It is possible that the 14th-century English craftsman Henry Yevele was engaged on the Abbey, as much of the detail shows English influence. This is one of the few churches in Portugal with stained glass windows.

The interior, like that at Alcobaça, has been so stripped in drastic restorations that it has become a beautiful whited sepulchre, though the double line of tall columns is hardly less lovely than at the former place. To the right of the entrance is the square Founder's Chapel (1426–34) built as the resting-place of John I and his English Queen, Philippa of Lancaster; they lie hand in hand on a high Gothic sarcophagus, with the tombs of their brilliant sons around them. To the left of the nave is the Royal Cloister and beyond it, the in many ways more attractive cloister of D. Afonso. The former is very exuberant Manueline, and off it is the astonishing and lovely Chapter House, over sixty feet square, without any central shaft, where Portugal's unknown soldier lies guarded by a sentinel.

Behind the chancel of the church stand the extraordinary "Capelas Imperfeitas" or Unfinished Chapels, surrounding a large octagonal space; they were begun by D. Duarte in 1435, but he died three years later and they were only resumed by D. Manoel I, who embellished the walls and doors with the form of decoration which bears his name; but he did not finish them either, because he became so entranced with the great church he was building at Belem. So the chapels still stand roofless, unused and desolate, the splendour of their magnificent intricacy of carving exposed to the sun and the rain.

Ten kilometres north of Batalha one reaches LEIRIA, with a good country hotel, the Liz. It is an agreeable town with a Roman bridge over the River Liz, and the castle of Dom Diniz and his holy Queen, St. Elizabeth of Portugal, largely rebuilt, standing up conspicuously on a lofty rock in the midst. The Bishop's Palace has been turned into a library and museum, and the renaissance cathedral is dignified, though without great interest. The Sanctuary of N. S. da Encarnação just outside the town has a long staircase up to it with chapels and statues, rather different to and more countryfied than those at Bom Jesus and Lamego; there is a most entrancing view over the pine forests from the terrace outside this church.

For between Leiria and the sea lies the great State Forest of Leiria, which has the distinction, probably unique in the world, of having been maintained *as a forest* since the 13th century, when D. Diniz (*O Lavrador*) planted it to control the shifting sand-dunes; the only possible rival is the Forest of the Bakony in Hungary. This long history of man's control makes it, to silvi-culturalists, one of the most interesting forests in existence. An elaborate system of watch-towers connected by telephones, and forest roads intersecting it in all directions, protect it from fire; cutting is regularly and scientifically carried out. The tree chiefly grown is *P. pinaster*, but here, as in all State-controlled forests in Portugal the trees are not tapped for resin till two years before they are scheduled for felling. Along the sea-fringe is carried out that complicated process of creating "false dunes" referred to in Chapter II, and sowing the protected areas behind them with seeds of the seven or eight "sand-fixing" plants, under a cover of cut *mata*, till the soil so "fixed" is ready to receive the young pines, which can be seen thriving astonishingly on what, a few years before, was a white waste of shifting sand. The officers of the Serviço Florestal are always most courteously willing to show to visitors who are seriously interested the areas developed so successfully, by this remarkable treatment.

The Glass Factory of MARINHA GRANDE, half-way between Leiria and the sea, was started by an Englishman named John Beare in 1748, but it was when William Stephens bought the then small factory in 1769 that it was developed under the protection of the Marquês of Pombal, who lent Stephens 80,000 cruzados and gave him the right to cut wood in the State forest. On William's death in 1802 his brother John carried on the factory, and in 1826 gave effect to an agreement they had made together that it should be given to the State of Portugal. The factory is still working, employs a great number of people and is still owned by the State. Stephens must have been one of the first manufacturers in the modern world who looked after the education of his work-people; he had them taught music and drawing. Among the village families corruptions of the foreign names of the first workmen can still be found, such as Birne and Gall.

A little way north of Leiria is that baroque marvel in the wilderness, MILAGRES, which few travellers ever see. The best way to reach it is *not*, as books and police alike advise, by taking a long and terribly bad side road from Leiria, but to go on up the main Oporto road to where, just short of the village of Boa Vista, at a small turning on the left, two signposts say respectively "Pinheiros 3 kms." and "Matas Nacionais" (National Forests). In the village of Pinheiros, turn right; the rough road dips down to a beautiful semi-ruined bridge, and climbs in about 3 kilometres to the huge exotic shrine which can be seen from miles away standing out on a bluff, with the river below in a green valley. The road ends in a large sandy square with the great church at one end, cottages in a formal row along both sides, and a beautiful octagonal well-house.

The church is a very fine, very wide, very late baroque building. The façade has five arches leading to an open narthex continued right round both sides, surmounted on the first floor by a similar open gallery. Two tall belfries stand at either side, and a conventional baroque pediment in the centre rises to the same height. The interior of the church is soberly rich, with pink, black and indeed every coloured marble decorating the surrounds of the windows and the pulpit, while formal lozenges of pink and black are placed at intervals on the white walls. One of the most interesting features of the church—which in some indefinable way reminds the visitor of Mafra, without seriously resembling that far richer basilica—is the series of unique manuscript azulejos panels round the chancel, where the legend of the miracle which gives the church its name is inscribed in delicate blue writing on a paler blue ground. These tiles were made at Juncal and are dated 1795. They relate how the church was started in 1732 by the rich benefactor of a poor man, Manoel Francisco Mayo, who lived in front of the church (presumably in one of the small peasant houses flanking the great open space before the façade), and after falling off his little donkey cart, was seriously injured, became a beggar, and was then cured by a miracle. The architect of this most splendid building was José da Silva of Juncal, and the tiles were made by his grandson.

Roads lead from both Leiria and Batalha through Fatima to Tomar. FATIMA has become of late years one of the great pilgrimage centres of Europe, and is often compared to Lourdes. Huge concourses of people, often over a hundred thousand strong, assemble on the 13th of each month from May to October inclusive, and camp on the open spaces all around the sanctuary of Our Lady of Fatima, where the Blessed Virgin appeared in 1917 to three peasant children. The scene on those dates is biblical in its power and simplicity. Whole families, with donkeys bearing food in large panniers, crouch round tiny fires lit on the bare ground, or pray in the huge saucer-shaped arena before an altar outside the modern basilica at one end of the great space. Hostels have been built for the sick and for small bands of pilgrims, but for the majority of people, a visit to Fatima means twenty-four hours of prayer and penance, for little sleep can be snatched on the stony ground. Unlike Lourdes, physical miracles at Fatima are comparatively rare, but many cures of spiritual ills are claimed. There are several guest houses run by religious, an estalagem, pensions and an hotel.

Beyond Fatima the road winds down in a series of curves with lovely views on the right of the old town of OUREM, which clusters round its rebuilt castle, set on the top of a sugar-loaf hill. Unlike so many walled towns it still looks alive and thoroughly prosperous, though practically nothing has been built in the last two centuries except the glaring additions to the castle. No car can get in through the narrow archway set in the walls. Just up a very stony alley on the right is the apse of the fine 18th-century Parish Church, which is entered by a side door. Inside there is a double-tiered organ-loft and over the High Altar a quite lovely 18th-century picture of Our Lady of Mercy, like a blue-cloaked bird sheltering a number of people clad in all colours. In front, a female figure, looking like the young Queen Victoria in a spiked crown, holds a scroll with a drawing on it of the façade of the church. Another scroll states that this church was rebuilt by D. José I in 1756 after an earthquake, though the rest of the town seems to have been little affected. The Gothic tomb in the crypt under the chancel has, like the castle, been very drastically restored.

TOMAR, 20 kilometres farther on, contains that most amazing conglomeration of buildings in Portugal, the great Templars' Monastery, called the Convent of Christ; its round church and the series of seven cloisters range in date from the 12th to the 17th centuries, and crown a hill just outside the town. The buildings, which were sacked by the French in 1810, have now practically undergone a second sacking, for such drastic restorations have been made that much of the old charm has to be imagined. It should be remembered that the guides have to be pressed to show the whole convent, as it is of great size. The Order of Christ was the restored Portuguese branch of the Templars, after the disgrace of the main Order.

The nucleus and heart of this astonishing place is the polygon sixteen-arched Templars' Church, dating from the 12th century; round it the rest of the buildings have gradually been added, so that there is now a church within a church, most odd. The most notable additions are Manueline and early renaissance, and are mainly by João de Castilho, whose work shows the transition between the two —especially remarkable is the magnificent main entrance, recessed in under a crocketed curtain arch, and the open balustrade, repeating endlessly, among other motifs, the square Maltese Cross of the Order of Christ, which runs right round the top of the building, like a trimming of the richest and heaviest lace. The pillars of the early octagonal baldacchino-like two-storeyed edifice over the central altar in the round church are brightly painted, and on the surrounding walls are some interesting Primitives, including one of the Resurrection, with a view of Lisbon at the beginning of the 16th century. The nave, which was added at this same period, contains nothing of interest.

Of the seven cloisters, the latest and perhaps the loveliest is that of the Felipes, built in 1557 by Diogo de Torralva. It is a great two-storey Palladian structure, more like a gallery than a normal cloister; the pillars have lovely carved stone capitals, and there is a later baroque fountain in the centre. The small cloister of Sta. Barbara, next to the Hospital cloister, is entered from the first floor, with the frightening and grotesque Manueline window in the West end of the nave only too clearly to be seen. One side of the Hospital cloister rises up to yet a third storey, set slightly back, and quite lovely in its originality.

The great T-shaped dormitory corridor upstairs should be seen. It has a plain wood coffered ceiling and a chapel at the intersection; this has low relief panels in the roof. The cells are large, and off the corridor is the calefactory where the monks could warm themselves at the fire before going to bed, while at one end is a washing fountain dated 1617. The window of one of the cells looks on to the Micha cloister, constructed over the main water cistern. A good deal of the convent is now used as a Missionary College and the boys eat at long marble tables in the refectory, which has a pair of lovely reading ambones with low reliefs of angels and armorial motifs on them. The windows look out on to the Claustro dos Corvos, the garth of which is bright with flowers.

The Cemetery Cloister, constructed by Henry the Navigator, has been almost entirely rebuilt, but contains charming orange trees. The body of Baltasar de Faria, who introduced the Inquisition into Portugal, used to be shown in a glass-topped coffin like Lenin's, but has now been decently covered with a stone! The next cloister, the Claustro da Lavagem has been largely rebuilt, as has the castle just beyond.

On the way down to Tomar, the tiny basilica of N. S. da Conceição should not be missed, as it is almost the best example of early renaissance work in Portugal, and is possibly also by Diogo de Torralva. The guide to the Convent of Christ has the key and will take the visitor there. Outside, it is quite plain and solid, like an unbattlemented fortress, but the interior is exquisite, with three tiny naves and lovely pure Corinthian columns.

The town itself is delightful, with narrow twisting streets, and every now and then a wide square. It is the scene every few years of the Feast of the Tabuleiros described in Chapter II. There is the excellent Estalagem de Santa Iria on an island in the river as well as a good hotel, the Templários. The Parish Church of S. João Baptista is in a pretty square, with a lovely 18th-century palace, now a hospital, opposite. Inside the church are six Primitives by Gregorio Lopes, which have all been cleaned, and a lovely pair of Primitive grisaille saints hang in the baptistery. The church is an unusually light Gothic building; the famous stone Manueline pulpit has been much restored and there is a Manueline façade and bell tower. The sacristan possesses the keys of all the other churches in Tomar.

Across the narrow river Nabão that runs through the town, stands the convent and church of Santa Iria, with a renaissance doorway; inside there is an extraordinary archway to one of the chapels, with medallions in high relief of heads of Brazilian Red Indians! There are good boiseries on the altars. Farther on is the 13th-century church of Santa Maria do Olival which has undergone extremely drastic restoration. Back in the town, at 73 Rua Nova, there is a 15th-century Jewish Synagogue, the key of which is in the Turismo office.

The great dam at Castelo do Bode is not far from Tomar and is an amazing piece of engineering. There is an Estalagem overlooking the huge artificial lake.

South-west of Tomar lies the charming town of TORRES NOVAS, on a little river, the Almonda, crossed by narrow bridges. At the entrance from Tomar an unnaturally long 18th-century building should be noticed, with rows of over forty windows in the façade.

The best church in Torres Novas is the Misericordia, with a splendid renaissance door, above which is a high-relief of the Visitation. If the church is shut, entrance can be obtained through the house at the side. There is a great feeling of warm richness and beauty about the interior. The nave is lined with very good early patterned azulejos right up to the coffered ceiling, which is painted in gold and brown formal motifs and dated 1678. A queer white stone architectural frame surrounds the three altars facing the nave, set on a kind of stage, as in the Misericordia at Torres Vedras. There are good gilt wood retables, and the High Altar has an interesting renaissance frontal with four heads of saints in polychrome bas-relief.

GOLEGÃ, where the great horse-fair described in Chapter II takes place, is 7½ kilometres from Torres Novas, but except in fair-time there is not much to see. The road leads on to a bridge over the Tagus, whence one can reach Abrantes along the south bank.

A road due east out of Torres Novas leads to Barquinha and on to Abrantes by the north bank of the Tagus. About two miles north of Barquinha lies the little village of ATALAIA with the renaissance church of N. S. da Assunção The walls are covered with beautiful patterned azulejos which surround lovely tile panels in amusing tile frames, so the whole effect with the white columns and elegant arches of the naves, is quite delightful.

Near the small town of Tancos the exquisite castle of AL-MOUROL, a Templars' foundation, stands on a little island in the middle of the Tagus. A boat can be hired to take the visitor across to the castle, which, like Bodiam, and unlike all other Portuguese castles, has no history.

Farther up the Tagus ABRANTES stands on a hill above the river, here linked to the south bank by a bridge. The town played a critical part in the Peninsular War, as it is the key to central Portugal, and was taken in 1807 by Junot, who was therefore created Duke of Abrantes by Napoleon. In the Largo da Misericordia stands the renaissance church of the same name, with a beautiful side doorway with a group of Our Lady of Mercy, signed Gaspar Denis 1548. The church can be seen by applying at the neighbouring hospital, which was founded in 1532. In the interior there is a good 16th-century pulpit, and an early 18th-century restoration fortunately left lovely exuberant gold boiseries and the fine rococo frames to a set of Primitives which undoubtedly belong to the Lisbon school. On the right is a quite exquisite Annunciation, with Our Lady in dark green and Gabriel in white, on the left a very lovely meeting between Our Lady and St. Elizabeth. Through the sacristy a staircase leads to the Casa do Definitorio or the Board-room of the hospital, built at the end of the 18th century, with fine woodwork of the same period.

A little farther up is the church of S. João, founded by St. Elizabeth in 1300, in which King John I heard Mass before he marched for the battle of Aljubarrota. It was much restored in 1589 during the Spanish domination and the interior is a good example of how in Portugal the transition from one architectural mode to another took considerably longer than in the more central parts of Europe. It is now immense; the caissoned ceiling, marbled pale green and grey, is curious and charming and the High Altar is a good example of baroque work. There are lovely polychrome statues in

NAZARÉ: THE BEACH

NAZARÉ: WOMEN HELPING TO HAUL IN FISHING BOATS

CASTELO BRANCO: THE STAIRCASE OF THE KINGS IN THE GARDENS OF THE BISHOP'S PALACE

the church and fine renaissance details in the side chapels, and the altars are very rich, rather resembling those in the chapel of the Three Kings in S. Marcos near Coimbra; in the third chapel on the right is a superb very Spanish-looking polychrome Pietà. There is a peculiar circular stone pulpit on a very delicate carved pillar, rather recalling one at Coimbra. The choir-stalls have painted backs—the paintings on the left are vertical, those on the right shallow and horizontal, to allow room for the 18th-century organ in walnut-wood.

The castle walls enclose a garrison and a huge space scattered with mulberry trees. The church of Sta. Maria do Castelo, now turned into the Regional Museum, has some good tombs and a touching Gothic head of Christ; its custodian has the key of the castle keep, from which there is a very fine view.

There is a first-class hotel, the Turismo de Abrantes, just outside the town at the top of the hill.

Near Abrantes, about half a mile from MOURISCAS, which is on the Mação road, is the extremely interesting little chapel of N. S. dos Matos. It was built in 1664, possibly by some English recusant, as on the altar there is a representation of the Virgin with four angels and the prayer: "Domina, intercede pro Anglia ut convertatur".

The castle of BELVER, built by the Knights of Malta in 1194 and restored by Nuno Alvares Pereira in 1390, stands on the banks of the Tagus. The keep crowns a steep cliff and much of the original work is left. The entrance is through a round archway and there are square towers at intervals along the walls. At the side is a chapel, formerly the scene of a big *romaria* on the 25th April, in which is a chestnut altar-piece with a good figure of St. Blaize.

．　　．　　．　　．　　．　　．

The road south-west between Torres Novas and Santarem goes through pleasant wooded country in which some great landowner has planted a number of cypresses, which give an unusual and Italianate effect to the landscape. SANTAREM, of which there is a lovely view from this road, is one of the earliest and most interesting towns near Lisbon, In the middle of the 7th century the body of Santa Iria (or St. Irene) was brought here and soon afterwards the town was conquered by the Moors and only re-taken by the Crusaders in the 12th century. At one time the city boasted of fifteen hospitals, thirteen parishes and fourteen convents, but a large

L

part of the mediaeval and earlier buildings were destroyed in the last century, and unfortunately the destruction still goes on, now under the name of "urbanização" or town planning.

The city, built on a hill above the Tagus and with a good hotel, the Abidis, in the Rua Guilherme de Azevedo, is large and pleasant with several big squares and open spaces; many streets still retain 16th- and 17th-century features. One of the outstanding buildings is the Seminary, formerly the Jesuit College, in the Praça Sá da Bandeira, with its huge façade bristling with windows, some of which enclose statues. The church inside is disappointing with a poor late painted ceiling, though some of the side altars have Bernini-like marbles. The marble and alabaster High Altar is enclosed by salomonic columns, and a very fine pair of 18th-century carved alabaster Jesuit Saints stand on either side. The 16th-century tympanum over the fourth altar on the right is a polychrome wood low-relief of the four and twenty Elders of the Apocalypse in Adoration before the Book of Truth. A staircase leads from the sacristy to the really splendid central corridor, nearly as large as that at Tomar, which runs the length of the building. The corridor is tall and narrow with white stone barrel-vaulting and very lovely blue pictorial tile panels between the little doors leading into the rooms.

The octagonal church of N. S. da Piedale opposite was built by Jacome Mendes in 1664 to commemorate a victory over the Spaniards at Ameixal and there are Latin inscriptions over the side doors relating to the battle. On the other side, in the Campo de Sá da Bandeira is the former convent of S. Francisco, now a barracks, with an ogival cloister, In the church there is a most unusual choir set in the nave, now used as a dining-room by the soldiers.

The Rua Capelo e Ivens, lined with good shops, leads to the Milagre church where there are four very large and agreeable early Victorian rectangular panels in the nave depicting the story of the miracle which occurred in the 13th century, when lights appeared above a consecrated Host which had been stolen from this church. Three renaissance arches with high-relief medallion heads divide the nave from the chancel. In the sacristy there is a little Victorian crib in a glass case and a Primitive panel of St. Jerome. The sacristan, who lives down the steps on the farther side of the church, also has the key to the little chapel in the Travessa das Esteiras, built in 1654, on the site of the house where the miracle happened. The singular

church of Marvila has an exceptionally fine, extremely lofty interior, the three aisles are covered with diamond-patterned azulejos,
increasing in size till they reach the plain coffered roof. The whole
church gives a most singular impression of height and even of
austerity, very unlike most Portuguese churches.

The former church of S. João de Alporão, now a museum, contains the decorated Gothic tomb of D. Duarte de Meneses, built by
his wife, and only containing one tooth, as the knight's body was
hacked to pieces by the Moors and nothing remained for his widow
to bury but this pathetic relic! A long avenue leads to the Portas do
Sol from which can be seen the whole valley of the Tagus. Palgrave,
who accompanied Tennyson to Portugal in 1859, describes this view
"as one of the great panoramic landscapes of Europe". Over the
river at ALPIARÇA, there is a fascinating museum, the Casa dos
Patudos, well worth visiting for the paintings, porcelain and
furniture.

Nearly 14 kilometres inland from Santarem the little town of
ALMOSTER has a very fine much restored Bernardine convent
founded in 1289. The church contains exceptional late 17th-century
baroque gold woodwork, with writhing seaphim and leaves and
flowers and a wonderful 14th-century carved wooden crucifix on a
lateral altar. There are also the remains of a 14th-century cloister.

MUGE on the other side of the Tagus below Santarem, where so
many palaeolithic remains have been found, can be reached by a
ferry, and the railway line crosses the river just below. All this open
and rather unpopulated country belongs to the Cadaval family and
is famous for its sport, which includes coursing on horseback with
greyhounds over the great pastures. For here we are practically in
the Ribatejo, the country of the river and the flat plains, of bull-
breeding and horse-breeding and superb horsemanship, where the
boys are, as they say, born in the saddle, and the great slow-moving
white or orange sails of the boats on the upper reaches of the Tagus
make such a surprising background to statuesque groups of horses,
and the noble shapes of bulls at pasture. The high-bred tempera-
mental creatures seem to have infected the people hereabout with
something of their own ardours and fervours, for the *campinos* of the
Ribatejo are traditionally wild and passionate, great singers of *fados*,
and consumed often with a vague deep melancholy like that of their
own landscape in a winter's twilight.

CHAPTER X

BEIRA BAIXA AND THE SERRA DA ESTRÊLA

ONE of the most strangely and profoundly indigenous parts of Portugal—perhaps precisely because it is, owing to its remoteness, one of the least visited—is that stretch of country running down inside the Spanish frontier from well north of the Serra da Estrêla to where the Tagus crosses the border south of Castelo Branco. The northern part is hilly; in the centre comes the lovely wide orchard-strewn cup of the Cova da Beira—where flourish the tangerine-coloured lambs—presided over by the graceful mass of the Serra da Guardunha on one side, and the long blue line of the Serra da Estrêla itself on the other; to the south the hills swell again, with a most Spanish and un-Portuguese breadth and sweep of outline, till they sink to the Tagus, to rise once more in the Alentejo near Portalegre and Marvão.

It is an awkward place to visit, but it should be visited all the same. There are good hotels at each end—the Hotel de Turismo at Guarda, and the similarly named hotel at Castelo Branco; at Covilhã, in the middle, one of the ideal centres for excursions, there is as yet no hotel up to foreign standards.

There is one of the excellently planned government *pousadas* on the high stretch of road between Gouveia and Manteigas. This is called the Pousada de São Lourenço and is magnificently placed.

Mr. Harbord, of the Hotel do Facho at Foz do Arelho, really understands about comfort, and for the northern end of the Serra da Estrêla, whether for walking or botanising, visitors are strongly recommended to make their headquarters at his other establishment, the Hotel Urgeiriça at Canas de Senhorim. (Good beds, boiling-hot water, open fires, nice food; individual châlets or cottages for those who want complete privacy.) North of Mangualde, up the headwaters of the Dão, is some splendid country—and here, on the road to Trancoso and Pinhel, is what must on no account be missed, the astonishing complete mediaeval ensemble of the tiny town of AGUIAR DA BEIRA.

The approach is dramatic, along a watershed road, at one point through a stretch of pure granite landscape, a shallow high-lying valley of granite slabs, granite slopes, and rounded granite summits topped with granite boulders—the most impressive piece of desolation imaginable. The town itself lies high, heaped up on the slope below its so-called "Castelo", with lovely wide sweeps of view away to the distant hills of Spain. The small ancient main square, rudely paved, is on a steepish tilt—in the centre rises the most graceful of *pelourinhos*, a long slender shaft above a four-stepped base, on a large roughly-levelled paved platform; at the upper end stands a little square keep with toothed battlements; below this another square squat building, also battlemented with a fine pointed arch in its face, puzzles the visitor till he climbs right up to it, and finds that its top is not a roof but a mediaeval council-chamber, open to the sky, approached by a few steps on the upper side, and with a stone bench running round below the machicolations—for all the world like the famous 12th-century one at Bragança, save for its tinyness, and that it is unroofed. The pointed doorway below gives on to the town spring—again, as at Bragança. Massive walls overhung by trees, and solid stone houses with flattened roofs surround this exquisite, and exquisitely complete little *praça*—for good measure, one of the houses has an outside stone staircase leading up to a little porch supported on stone pillars, and so that nothing may be lacking, the dark spire of a cypress at the lower end cuts sharply into the vast multi-coloured view. It is an untouched, diagrammatically complete example of the heart and centre of a mediaeval Portuguese town.

The churches are simple. The Misericordia—even Aguiar da Beira has its Misericordia—has charming primitive painted ceilings. The Igreja Matriz is remarkable for the curious decoration of the chancel arch, wooden emblems carved in high-relief and painted white with touches of gilding—in Guarda we shall see where the local church decorators got the idea. Right up at the top of the town, at one end of a huge dusty open space is the most interesting of all, N. S. do Castelo, which has an outside pulpit built against the wall, an early Gothic chancel arch, and a very curious—and very northern and Gothic—statue of Our Lady of the Milk; the retable of the High Altar, like the rest of the church, is so tiny and simple as to be extremely touching. The view from outside the door is as vast and magnificent as the little church itself is humble.

The "Castelo" is a puzzle. The *Guide Bleu* says airily that it is a *château fort* of the epoch of Dom Diniz. On the spot this statement is self-evidently rubbish. Dom Diniz built real castles, and with mortar; this curious structure is dry-stone built, the walls are nowhere more than six or seven feet high, and run round the summit of the hill enclosing vast granite blocks far higher than themselves, as do so many Iron-Age forts. It could never conceivably have been roofed. It might be Iron-Age, it might be "country Roman"—i.e., built by the locals in imitation of a Roman *castrum*; if the Visigoths ever built without mortar (they did not at S. Frutuosos near Braga) it might be early Visigothic. Like so much else in Portugal, it awaits thorough excavation and elucidation.

About 6 kilometres beyond Aguiar da Beira the small road on which it lies hits the big north-west south-east road from Lamego to Trancoso and Pinhel; TRANCOSO is another 20-odd kilometres down this. It lies high, at over two thousand six hundred feet, and keeps most of its splendid double walls, over which towers the 12th-century castle, restored again and again in the 13th, 14th and 16th centuries. It is a noble place, with wonderful views, seldom visited, to their great loss, by foreigners.

Four kilometres below Trancoso runs the still larger main road from Mangualde to Pinhel and the Spanish frontier. Almost at the junction a small road branches off north-east towards Vila Nova de Foscoa; those who wish to see one of the most unusual castles in Portugal should take it, and carry on for about 21 kilometres to where a road marked "Meda" branches off to the left, and then wriggle their way along this, over very poor going, to the really splendid little granite-built town of PENEDONO, with its castle perched on the summit of the living rock. It is quite small and almost triangular in design; a solitary keep with a high arched doorway between two projecting towers at one side, and square towers at the angles; the tops of the towers are boldly corbelled out below the machicolations, and the whole thing much more recalls some small French castle, or even Caerlaverock in Dumfriesshire—also triangular—than the castles usually to be met with in Portugal, with their huge *enceintes* and curtain walls.

Back on the main road, another 30 kilometres brings one to PINHEL, a small town with a romantic and troubled history, like so many of these border towns, but little now to show for it save a good deal of the old walls, with some picturesque gateways, a couple of towers of the 14th-century castle, and a Romanesque church. The road on from here to Figueira de Castelo Rodrigo is called the *"excomungada"*, because of its curliness; it rises to nearly three thousand feet at the crest of the Serra da Marofa, a strange wild deserted place, the landscape being of a prevailing ochreous tint.

Only the very plucky tourist, with a pretty plucky car, will make his way on to the peculiar little oval town of ALMEIDA, lying within its truly extraordinary star-shaped fortifications; it is probably shorter in the long run to follow the "excommunicate" road on to Figueira de Castelo Rodrigo, and from there to run south to Almeida, round two sides of a triangle, rather than to bounce and crash along the small and much shorter cross-country road through Vale Verde. Here one is only three or four miles from the frontier, and from the time of D. Sancho down to the Peninsular War, Almeida was a military post of the first importance; in the 18th century, from which the present fortifications mainly date, it was the strongest fortified place in Portugal after Elvas, which in some ways it resembles. But at Almeida the great walls faced with granite, the ditch nearly forty feet deep, the sharp salients and re-entrant angles are so distinct from the town itself, and so unencumbered by outside buildings, that it is far easier to see the whole design than it is at Elvas. Vauban himself is said to have put some finishing touches to it, and during the Restoration period a Dutch Jesuit called Cosmander—who for some mysterious reason held a Colonel's rank in the Portuguese army, and was a sort of von Herbert, apparently—is said to have worked on the fortifications. During the Peninsular War Massena and Wellington took the place in turns.

The Serra da Estrêla interposes itself like a great granite barrier, nearly seventy miles long, between Beira Baixa and the outer world. So far very few roads cross it, that from Gouveia to Guarda and Belmonte is at the northern end, and the one from Castelo Branco to Lousã via Pamphilhosa da Serra is to the south: this latter is first class and the bridge over the Zêzere has been rebuilt. Another road has been constructed from Manteigas through the deep valley which splits the north end of the Serra into two parallel ridges, and joins that which runs up into the hills from Covilhã; now that this is completed it greatly aids the exploring tourist. What would aid him still more would be the production of a large-scale contoured map of the Serra; it seems incredible, but no real map of this great range, such as walkers or ski-runners need, exists—even the Forestry Service can only produce an innacurate little diagram. The Department of Turismo is very anxious to encourage ski-ing and winter-sports in the Serra; but they have not yet realised that ski-ing (as indeed all other forms of turismo) requires good and detailed maps. (The National Information Office issue guides in all languages and sketch maps of the chief cities of Portugal, but not, as yet, of the Serra de Estrêla or other country parts. They do, however, produce, every month, an up-to-date guide to Lisbon, with a reasonably clear map.)

Some parts of the Serra afford rough ski-ing, as high up the snow may lie from November to April. The headquarters of the Portuguese Ski Club are at Covilhã, and above it, at PENHAS DA SAUDE, is the only winter-sports hotel in Portugal—incidentally a very good one, though very expensive. This places lies at four thousand five hundred feet, above the tree-line; if there is no snow at Penhas, there is pretty sure to be some at TORRE, fifteen hundred feet higher up, where the Ski Club has built a hut. Porters can be hired at Penhas to carry food and bedding to the hut, which has no caretaker, and where nothing is provided but bare bunks and—usually—fuel; it is important to take a few cooking utensils too, as there are none. Rather amusing races are sometimes organised at the New Year Carnival by the Ski Club.

The Serra da Estrêla is a splendid place, maps or no. The road from GOUVEIA, on the west side, swings up in great loops over the steep rocky slopes to flatten out on the vast rolling summit ridge; here barley ripens at five thousand feet, but it must be sown before the end of September. South of the road, for miles and miles, either barley grows or sheep graze the short mountain turf, with its especial and lovely flora; a breed of dog peculiar to the region, whose thick coats and ruffs recall Canadian huskies, guard the flocks from the wolves which still infest these lonely hills; the dogs nourish themselves by sucking the ewes' milk. In spite of these depredations, Serra cheeses are justly famous. To the south of this transverse road, too, lies the chain of small lakes, cupped in hollows of the granite along the heights; one or two of them still have trout, and can be fished, for the simple but unexpected reason that they lie too high for vines to grow! The trout-fishing of northern Portugal, magnificent fifty years ago, is now practically non-existent, because the ingenious peasants have discovered that by spraying the river pools with the sulphate of copper doled out to them to protect their vineyards, they can kill the fish—and, as they tell you with naïve satisfaction, "if you skim the fish off *quickly*, they are not poisonous at all; they are very good to eat!" Riding and bull-fighting apart, the Portuguese are on the whole not very keen sportsmen, good as their Association footballers are; and this destruction of their trout-streams does not seem to arouse any particular public dismay or indignation.

There is a strange change of aspect and vegetation on descending by the dull, dusty, steep and extremely frightening road from Poio Negro, the dismal collection of Sanatoria and shacks on the summit crest, to Manteigas—not wholly due to the efforts of the Forestry Service, considerable as their plantations are; it is another climate. MANTEIGAS is a little town squashed and cramped into a hot narrow hollow between mountain ranges, unremarkable for anything save as the starting-point for visiting the only two "stations" where yews in their wild state may still be seen growing in Portugal. The most accessible of these is at the Poço do Inferno, a gorge with waterfalls about 10 kilometres up a Forestry Service road from Manteigas—there are just five or six yew trees grouped in the rocky glen, and botanists will be interested to see them.

The road on to Guarda leaves the upper valley of the Zêzere (which doubles back so strangely on itself, first within the Serra, and then down the flat land to the east of it) and passes over open uplands, great sheep-country, with country factories in the villages where the wool is spun and woven into those gaily-striped blankets used by the peasants all over Portugal. Curiously enough the dyeing is not done in a factory, but out in the fields, near the wells; the water is drawn up to fill great cauldrons, in which the dye and the wool are boiled together over open fires; the long hanks of red or green or blue yarn drying in the sun, draped for a hundred yards or more over the stone walls, are a surprising and vivid sight. Today the dyes are synthetic; they used to come from Germany, but are now imported—so the peasants tell you, and the drums by the wells seem to confirm it—from Russia.

GUARDA lies high above the plain on a northern buttress of the Serra, at a height of over three thousand feet; it is extremely picturesque, with arcaded houses in many of the streets, the arcades all of different shapes and sizes. For a town of its size it has surprisingly few monuments—besides the Sé there is little but the Misericordia church; this has a splendid baroque façade, and the long low building of the adjoining hospital matches it in a modest and comely fashion; the interior was entirely restored about 1910, and though well done contains little of interest—perhaps it never did; but the courtyard of the hospital is pretty.

The Sé or Cathedral, with its great pinnacled buttresses and flying-buttresses and its richly balustraded roof, instantly strikes the visitor familiar with the churches of Normandy as being extraordinarily French-looking—so he is not surprised, on opening his *Guide Bleu*, to learn that it was built in imitation of Batalha, where the Anglo-French influence was so strong. But here the tender golden-grey limestone is replaced by the dour uncompromising local granite, giving a dark harsh splendour to the great fabric. It was begun at the beginning of the 15th century and finished about the middle of the 16th. The design is complicated as well as rich; there are curious hexagonal half-height towers in the angles of the transepts. Like French churches, it is rich in gargoyles; there is supposed to be a very rude one on the side facing Spain—Guarda, with Celeorico and Trancoso, formed part of the eastern defence system—but it has either been removed, or is very hard to spot. The West door is Manueline.

The interior is very noble, immensely long and lofty, with heavy fat sausage-like groining; the West pillars of the transept arch are in rope-twist design. There are some most delicate windows high up in both transepts. The High Altar has a renaissance retable, with gilt figures in high relief on a white ground, obviously the inspiration for the church in Aguiar da Beira already described; but the choir stalls are heavy, poor, and surprisingly few in number. The fourth chapel on the left is used as the sacristy, and has a pretty renaissance doorway.

Outside the town and well below it, in a loop of the road to the railway-station—which incidentally is 7 kilometres away—stands the small Romanesque chapel of Mileu; actually it is almost transition to Gothic, for the chancel arch is pointed, but the splayed windows still have round heads. The grotesques of some of the capitals by the chancel arch are painted in lively colours. An old man at the cottage next door has the key, and, surprisingly, brings it at once. It is a sweet place, so small and humble, standing among the fields and chestnut trees.

Guarda has an excellent hotel, the Turismo, which is a good centre from which to visit both Almeida and the other towns near the frontier, already described, and some of the lesser places round this end of the Serra da Estrêla, which cannot be included in a hurried tour, but are well worth seeing if one has a day in hand. Such are CELORICO DA BEIRA, away to the west, with its very large granite-built castle, said to be of Roman origin, as it well might be—the keep was pulled down in the last century; and there are as usual fine old houses in the town. Or SEIA—sometimes spelt CEIA —on the west slope of the Serra beyond Gouvcia, where at one point Wellington had his headquarters in the Casa das Obras, now the Municipal Offices; and beyond it OLIVEIRO DO HOSPITAL, originally, as its name implies, belonging to the Order of Hospitallers, which has a Gothic chapel in the parish church with some early tombs—14th century; on one of these are kneeling figures of the founder and his wife, a rather unusual thing in Portugal. Farther on still, always just off the big Pinhel-Coimbra main road, is the very old village of LOUROSA, with a remarkable 10th-century church, dated 950; it is basilican in plan, but has been so totally restored in the last thirty years that the great, almost unique interest it formerly held for the historian is largely destroyed.

Then, doubling back again northwards along the Mangualde road, there is FORNOS DE ALGÔDRES, with its splendid Albuquerque family mansion; and 5 kilometres to the north-east Algôdres itself, near which, off the Matança road, is a very fine dolmen. All this country is extremely muddling to visit, as many of these places are not marked on the map; but the persistent traveller with time and a car can find them all by repeated inquiries. There is another of these basilica-type churches at MUXAGATA, 12 kilometres north-east of Fornos de Algôdres—altogether this is an amusing and unusual day's expedition to make, either from Guarda or from Urgeiriça—but lunch must be taken. Wine, as always, can be bought anywhere *en route*.

The first stretch of the big road down the east side of the Serra, from Guarda towards Castelo Branco and the south, is exceptionally beautiful, and one should avoid taking it in the afternoon, when the sun is in one's eyes. The white ribbon winds above a deep valley, on whose sides are set great chestnuts in faultless groups—ahead lie the sun-filled lowlands of Beira Baixa, with the blue outline of the Serra da Guardunha beyond. Some distance after the road has reached the plain, and about 20 kilometres from Guarda, the little town of BELMONTE, with its castle at one end, is conspicuous on a ridge to the left. This would be worth visiting for its own sake, even if it were not the birthplace of Pedro Alvares Cabral, the discoverer of Brazil, it has so much charm. The Castle—really one of Dom Diniz' —has a machicolated keep and a pretty Manueline double window in the curtain wall; but the entrance front has been so heavily restored, largely in cement, of all things, as to have little interest, except for the stark way in which it rises from an open space of slabs of living granite. Opposite the entrance, some distance away, is a small rectangular roofless building with a stone bench running round inside its low walls—presumably, as at Aguiar da Beira, the mediaeval Council-house; but it too appears to have been considerably restored.

But the most charming thing in Belmonte is the little Igreja Velha, the old church of S. Tiago, in which—presumably and according to tradition—Cabral was baptised and made his First Communion, and where now, early in September, they deck out the statue of Our Lady of Good Hope to carry through the streets in the silver-painted boat representing Cabral's exploring vessel. Much of the church is very early; the door is pointed, though the chancel arch is round; to the left of this is a tiny Gothic tomb-chapel with narrow arches, and there is a crocketed tomb-niche in the North wall, and close to it a tiny pentagonal pulpit in carved granite projecting from the wall, with a minute granite canopy over it—almost a doll's pulpit! Most unusual. There is a small round-headed light over the chancel arch, and outside the North wall of the church is the renaissance funerary chapel of the Cabral family, in a very ruinous state; it is entered from the church. A few paces away stands a minute isolated belfry. The whole thing is so small and so complete, up there on the windy slabs below the castle walls, away from the little town, with the great plain spread out below, that it is peculiarly appealing.

(Incidentally, to avoid confusion it should perhaps be mentioned that several guide books refer to this as the parish church, but this is a mistake; the parish church, large and modern, is at the far side of the town.)

BEIRA BAIXA AND THE SERRA DA ESTRÊLA

After COVILHÃ—which has the steepest and narrowest streets imaginable, a most astonishing network of telephone wires spreading out from a church tower, and the usual number of amusing old houses and churches, but contains nothing of outstanding interest— the next town on the Castelo Branco road is FUNDÃO, set in orchard country with a good archaeological museum; it has the curious distinction of being one of the few places in Portugal where snow falls almost every winter, set as it is between the Serras of Guardunha and Estrêla. The walk up the Serra da Guardunha starts from ALCONGOSTA, 3 kilometres away; the Pyramid, the highest point, is over three thousand six hundred feet, and one can descend via the small mediaeval church of N. S. da Orada, which has an interesting little 14th-century alabaster retable.

.   .   .   .   .   .

There are two quite astonishing towns in this region, which the hardy and enterprising traveller will not wish to miss—though, owing to their remoteness, they are in fact hardly ever visited; Penamacor and the unique Monsanto. They lie right off the main road, away to the east, near the Spanish frontier. The really barbarous road to Penamacor leads off from the outskirts of Fundão, and climbs over the northern spur of the Serra da Guardunha; presently the rich red earth, the orchards and chestnut trees of the Cova da Beira are left behind, and the endless arable begins, barley and wheat, extending for miles between extremely isolated villages with huge threshing-floors and acres of ricks; there are a few cork-oaks here and there, and olives in the hollows, but mostly, over these great rolling uplands, the plough and the cistus and wild lavender simply fight it out.

PENAMACOR lies high, covering the slopes and summit of a hill crowned with the vast enclosure of the castle, with its little keep, cracked from top to bottom, rising like the castle of Belmonte from the naked granite; within the great walls, pierced by a deep arched and fortified mediaeval gateway, lies a whole village of low granite houses, massively built of huge blocks, where goats and chickens, rabbits and ducks, peck, nibble and hop in the dust—most of the doorways are white-washed, and stand out sharply from the shadows; the spiky strings of drying red peppers dangle, a brilliant carmine, under the eaves. Of the castle buildings proper, little is left save the keep, the gateway, and a curious belfry with a conical turret. This town within a town has its own tiny church, S. Pedro; the retables of the side altars are in yellow relief on white, as at Guarda—presumably at Penamacor they cannot afford gilding; there is a pretty stoup carved with St. Peter's keys against a pillar, and a nice early statue of Our Lady.

The rest of the town heaps itself up against this summit, from above resembling a sea of flattened brown roofs; the streets are incredibly narrow, and wind up and down, or plunge steeply downhill towards Spain. Many of the houses really do have those Manueline windows so frequently mentioned in guide books, but in fact so seldom seen—often corrugated iron is much more in evidence! Apart from these, and the general picturesqueness, there are not many buildings of major interest; the Misericordia, up by the castle, was recently pulled down, and the Parish Church has nothing much to attract attention but a stone in the wall with a rough inscription, dated 1267, recording a miracle by which a Portuguese escaped from the Moors in a trunk!

The road on to Monsanto keeps fairly close to the frontier, and though attractive is incredibly dusty; and if, as sometimes happens, all the sign-posts have been painted out and left so for weeks on end, it is hard to find one's way. MONSANTO has been much boomed abroad as "the most Portuguese village"—(*a aldeia mais Portuguesa*) —but this is hardly fair to other Portuguese villages, for it is in fact unique, in antiquity as in eccentricity—one imagines that the upper part of it looks to-day much as it looked when Citânia de Briteiros, the Iron-Age town in the Minho, was still inhabited. This upper part is squashed up against the slope of an extremely steep hill below a square-built fortress, between rounded granite boulders anything from thirty to sixty feet in diameter and height; the small, low, but immensely massive houses are built in them and under them and against them and between them, the strangest possible sight. The steep narrow alleys are just steps cut in the granite, or slanting slabs of granite without steps; no wheeled traffic is possible, and a laden donkey blocks them completely. The town is cleaned by rain, if at all; there are neat gutters, paved or hollowed out of the rock, in front of the houses, into which slops are emptied from windows— this is all the "plumbing" that the top half of Monsanto has! It probably gives one a unique idea, in Europe to-day, of mediaeval or pre-mediaeval sanitation. But it is strangely attractive—the inhabitants love flowers, and of course have no gardens, so high up on each little dwelling, beyond the reach of the passing goat or donkey, iron rings or granite blocks project from the walls, on which are lodged large round earthenware bowls, with bright flowers growing in them, or sweet herbs for cooking; as at Penamacor, in early autumn the house-fronts are further brightened by dangling scarlet strings of drying paprika.

The whole of Monsanto must stretch between three and four hundred feet up the hillside, and not so far off the vertical either; the roofs of the lower and more level part of the town are set so close that looking down on them from above is like looking down on the overlapping rugs in a mosque. Into this part a car can, with precaution, creep; there is a church with a clock-tower, and a little square or two, in one of which stands a graceful pillory and surely the tiniest Misericordia church in Portugal; the holder of the key, alas, takes it with him when, like everyone else in Monsanto, he goes to till his fields down in the plain below. This astonishing and primitive place is full of most splendidly handsome and well-built men and women, young and old alike, the women very heavily adorned with gold chains and ear-rings; in an all-Portugal inter-village competition for teams of singers and dancers in their local costumes, Monsanto won hands down, and small wonder.

The by-road which goes to Monsanto, and nowhere else, turns off. from the Pernamacor road at PROENÇA-A-VELHA, and if time allows it is worth going into the 16th-century Misericordia there to look at the great gold retable above the High Altar, with its paintings of the life of the Virgin. From Proença-a-Velha one can either wriggle back to the main Castelo Branco road, or force one's way south on smaller roads to IDANHA-A-NOVA, an archaic town on the way from Castelo Branco to the Spanish frontier, where the inhabitants are also highly picturesque; it has some pretty 18th-century houses and a fair renaissance church. From here the frontier road leads one either back to Castelo Branco, or on, Spainwards, to the watering-place of MONFORTINHO, where there is one of the best hotels in Portugal, the Fonte Santa. It is an admirable place for a restful stay, and the waters, as is the way of waters, are alleged to cure practically everything.

CASTELO BRANCO, with its large squares and general air of

prosperity and bustle, is a complete contrast to Monsanto and its neighbours, and contains one supremely interesting thing, the great formal garden and statued staircase belonging to the former Bishop's Palace, now being adapted as a museum. Unfortunately the gardens are practically impossible to get into, even by applying at the Turismo Office in the excellent Hotel de Turismo, in the Campo da Patria, the splendidly wide main square of the town; it is to be hoped that in time the Municipal authorities will see their way to having the key kept there, available to the eager foreign sight-seer. For really it is the most remarkable thing of its kind in Portugal. The great garden contains, besides the usual patterns of clipped box punctuated by stone urns, a long stone-bordered pool filled with marble arabesques, which in their turn are filled with beds of flowers in bloom, most peculiar; beyond is the usual water-tank with azulejos on its walls—but most unusually beautiful in its shape and in the grouping of the urns and obelisks which surround it; and from one corner rises that astonishing staircase, flanked on either side by seven crowned statues of kings—it rather reminds one of the Court of the Kings outside N. S. dos Remedios at Lamego.

Opposite this palace, at the farther end, is the Misericordia, in the former Graça Convent; the Manueline doorway is thin and poor, and there is nothing else. The Sé is a vast renaissance vault of agreeable proportions, but contains nothing of interest; the retables are late, and cruelly re-gilt.

Another church just worth seeing is N. S. da Piedade, a very small building; the chancel ceiling has a curious raised design in white on white, for all the world like a paper lace d'oyley, very amusing; and the chancel arch, in carved wood also painted white, is rich and pretty.

The former Fonseca palace in the Campo da Patria, now the Camara or Municipal Offices, was built early in the 17th century, and has a beautiful and distinguished façade. Next door to it is the regional museum (de Tavares Proença) which is crowded and ill-arranged, but contains a few good things, notably a 16th-century painting of the Entombment, originally beautiful but cruelly over-restored, and a remarkable one of St. Anthony; there are some fine Flemish tapestries, fortunately in very good condition. A diligent search fails to reveal the three menhirs mentioned in the *Guide Bleu*, but the English visitor may be interested or moved to see a rough

MONSANTO

MONSANTO: FLUTE PLAYER

COIMBRA: SACRISTY OF S. ANTONIO DOS OLIVAIS, SHOWING PANELS OF THE LIFE OF ST. ANTHONY IN ROCOCO SURROUNDS, WITH AZULEJOS BELOW

slate tomb-slab with a Latin inscription recording that Thomas Stewart, Armiger, of the 31st Regiment of the British Army, died at Castelo Branco on the 19th of August 1810, aged 20.

A narrow road leads out of this square, through a fine mediaeval archway, the Arco do Pelame, to a little cobbled square, in which stands the ancient Camara (the present one was only purchased from the Fonseca family in 1935); it is a charming little building with an outside staircase leading up to a gallery over an arcaded loggia. The Castle, high on the hill above the town, has little of interest in itself, but the old village huddled round it, as so often in Portuguese towns, has hardly changed in the last two hundred years, and is highly picturesque. One last thing to be sought out is the Chafariz (or fountain) of São Marcos. A chafariz is not a fountain which plays, it is a flowing spout at which to fill waterpots; they are usually most decorative and this one is, with a wide-spreading wall behind it, and rising in the centre a panel with a crowned coat of arms, the square cross of the Order of Christ, and a rather elongated and barrel-like version of the armillary sphere. This decorative treatment of the daily water-supply, which is so striking all through Portugal, is probably a lingering relic of the Moorish influence; the Mahomedans, forbidden wine, hold water in great esteem and treat it almost with reverence, and the visitor familiar with Turkey will be constantly reminded of the dignified fountains of Broussa and Istanbul by the beautiful chafarizes of Portugal.

CHAPTER XI

COIMBRA AND THE MONDEGO

THE Portuguese have a great affection for the Mondego because it is the only one of their three great rivers which is Portuguese from end to end; the Douro and the Tagus both rise in Spain—indeed flying over the Peninsula far beyond Madrid, one sees the Tagus, already a notable stream. The Mondego rises in the Serra da Estrêla, swings in a great loop round its north-east end, and flows on, joined by its confluent the Dão, past the end of the Serra do Bussaco to Coimbra, and so down through the flat alluvial plain to the sea at Figueira da Foz. (Foz means a river-mouth in Portuguese.)

It is beautiful throughout its length. Close to the sea it runs through tidal marshes where the saltings, between their rushy containing banks, have a dull metallic glitter; above, almost as far as Coimbra, stretches the flat rich valley land, growing rice, and taller greener maize than on the surrounding slopes. Poplars fringe its banks, both here, and where it runs below the pink and white University town heaped up on its hill, from whence sailing boats can be taken at the Portagem, down the Mondego to Montemor-o-Velho, a delightful trip of some four hours. The river is navigable for a surprising distance; right up to its confluence with the Dão above Penacova, the high-prowed narrow river boats may be seen, dark snake-like shapes moored in groups along the white gravel banks beside the channel. The usual remarkable ingenuity of the Portuguese is displayed in the use they make of this river, both as a waterway and for irrigation. Throughout the upper reaches water-wheels are used to pump water to fields along the banks—fragile-looking structures twenty to thirty feet across, with wooden slats which take the force of the current and turn the wheel; to every second or third slat is lashed a wide-mouthed jar of course local earthenware at such an angle that it fills at the bottom of the circle and empties at the top, in a shower of wind-blown silver spray, into a long wooden tray, from which the water descends through a pipe to run along narrow open troughs, hollowed out of slender tree-trunks, often for two hundred yards or more, to the thirsty fields with their irrigation channels—the impetus of the descent is sufficient even to carry it uphill for a certain distance. The number of jars is regulated by the force of the current; they are put on and taken off according to the strength of the flow. But in order to keep a good head of water at the foot of the wheels, low hedges of wattle and brushwood are built across the bed of the stream at frequent intervals, which force the water into narrow channels at either side where the wheels stand; out in the main channel where the boats go up and down are brush-wood gates which are opened and closed as required. The whole thing looks extremely Heath Robinson, but in fact it is an almost perfect example of the simplest means to a given end being in fact the most efficient—everything is made, or cut, or forged locally, and put in by local labour.

COIMBRA, the mediaeval successor to the Roman Conimbriga a few miles to the south, lies up the Mondego, 42 kilometres from its mouth. The University, founded in 1290, is one of the oldest in Europe, and has remained the premier centre of learning in Portugal —consequently the city is extraordinarily rich in buildings and works of art. Those arriving at the main-line station, Coimbra B, which is a mile from the town, can take the little local train into the central station Coimbra A, or a taxi or tram from the station yard. There are some hotels, the best and most expensive being the Astoria, but the other and cheaper ones are clean with good and ample food, and there are several boarding-houses.

The University which crowns the hill on which Coimbra is built was re-organised by Pombal in 1772. He founded or re-founded chairs of modern languages, mathematics, physics and medicine, though this last faculty dates in Coimbra from the 14th century. He also planned an observatory, a laboratory and botanical gardens, some of the loveliest in Europe, these last two being designed by William Elsden, the Englishman, who was often employed by Pombal in his various building schemes. The Laboratorio Quimico is a charming formal building not unlike a super-sized English orangery and plainly revealing in the general proportions, its country of origin. But now many of the University buildings and the mediaeval village surrounding them, have been destroyed by the modern Portuguese passion for what is aptly named "urbanização", so with the exception of the Library there is very little of interest left in the University. The courtyard has a certain air of spaciousness

and grace with the renaissance chapel and library to one side, and
some fine classical doorways lead into the buildings called the
"Estudos Gerais", a name which recalls the primitive classification
of all Universities, "Studium Generale". At one side there is a
terrace with a bird's-eye view of the roofs of the old town below
and the wide river valley beyond. The Sala das Armas in the University Building has delightful polychrome tiled panels and indeed all
the azulejos are good, but most of the rooms are filled with heavy
furniture standing against damask-covered walls with poor portraits
above, though there is one splendid room, the Sala dos Exames
Privados, which has a good ceiling and interesting portraits of former
Rectors. The room is decorated in the particular colour of the
faculty—apparently these colours are traditional in Universities all
over Europe.

However, the University possesses one unique jewel in the great
secular baroque Library, built by D. João V between 1717 and
1728. It consists of three lofty rooms, so elegantly proportioned that
their size is almost unnoticed, with painted ceilings, and galleries
running round the book-lined walls. These galleries, their exquisite
balustrades and slender graceful supporting columns are richly
painted and gilt, each room in a different colour—a matchless green,
a deeper green, and the third in an astonishing shade between
lacquer-red and tango. The whole thing is uniquely original and
indescribably beautiful. Happy the students who, like Dr. Salazar,
have pursued their studies here!

Perhaps the most famous sight in Coimbra after the Library is the
Augustinian Monastery of Santa Cruz in the centre of the town,
founded by D. Afonso I and rebuilt by D. Manoel I at the beginning
of the 16th century. The façade is very curious, with a separate
baroque porch placed in front of the fine Manueline front. The
church is narrow and quite delightful with patterned blue azulejos on
the walls and a splendid red and gold organ with three thousand
pipes. The pulpit is by João de Ruão, a Frenchman, and the Foun-
ders' tombs are Manueline. Unhappily the work of restoration has
been particularly drastic in this church and its dependencies. The
very lovely double cloister with a renaissance fountain in the centre
has exceptionally fine 18th-century polychrome azulejos panels
round the walls. These were actually being pulled out on the orders
of the Commission of Ancient Monuments, to be removed from the

lower to the upper cloister; some visitors, observing that out of forty-two tiles removed, twenty-two were broken into over three pieces, made urgent protests in high quarters, and the tiles were saved—it is feared only temporarily. But this, and the destruction of so many of the University and other buildings, is a typical example of the reckless injury to Portugal's architectural heritage which is going on, and the English visitor, who has seen so much of his own country's inheritance destroyed first by the ignorant restorations of the 19th century, and latterly by town-planning, finds it heart-rending to watch the Portuguese bureaucracy itself inflicting as much damage by modern restoration on its own glorious buildings. The more he loves Portugal, the keener his dismay and distress. There was little enough excuse in Victorian England, but at least it should be remembered that serious photography did not then exist, that illustrations had to be made from sketches, and that the general level of standards of comparison and knowledge was therefore very low; in the 20th century this is no longer the case. But if these violent depredations continue unchecked one really wonders how much will be left in time to come.

A staircase leads from the cloister at Santa Cruz to the upper choir, which should not be missed. At the top of these stairs are some extremely interesting azulejos panels of standing clerical figures on plain grounds, a little more elaborate than those in the Chapter House of Refoios de Lima in the Minho, but obviously from the same factory. The choir-stalls are astounding in the splendour of their workmanship and are almost the only mediaeval ones left in the country. The voyages of Vasco da Gama in gold wood high-relief, dated 1505, form the backs, and figures stand between the seats, indeed they are a most curious blend of Manueline and straight Gothic.

Visitors should certainly ask to be shown the Relic Chapel which is an unusual oval room containing extremely fine reliquaries, a silver bust of St. Teutonio and curious 18th-century tall narrow gold pyramids, each standing on four balls, containing relics of the Saints for each month in the year. The walls of this strange collection are now shining white like a bathroom, but were formerly marbled. There seems no reason why the marbling should not have been renewed, for the present gleaming whitewash takes away considerably from the beauty of the contents of the room, as it does in the Museum at Aveiro and in the Sala dos Reis at Alcobaça.

There is a fine Chapter House, and the Sacristy is very splendid, with brilliant blue and yellow azulejos which make a curiously good background to the important Primitive paintings, which include a Pentecost attributed to Grão Vasco, and four exquisite single panels of saints, some of the most beautiful things in Portugal.

The road from Santa Cruz to the station of Coimbra B passes various churches and convents containing interesting things. The first on the right is the Colegio do Carmo. In the church there are delightful 18th-century paintings of big-hatted clerics in the nave, and a fine architectural gold High Altar retable enclosing good canvases. By the side of the church there is a little double cloister with renaissance arches below and square arches above, and extremely fine azulejos panels in powder-blue, set within unusual red-brown tiled frames. But the sacristy should not be missed, as in it there is a most extraordinary sculpture group of the Entombment of Christ with full-size figures, which although repainted are still deeply interesting. Two men in Jewish clothes and hats hold the Winding Sheet at either end and the Blessed Virgin and the Apostles stand mourning behind. It is reminiscent of the sculptured Entombment in the parish church in Dieppe, though that is much earlier in date.

Next door to the Carmo is the Colegio da Graça, with a somewhat similar interior but of finer quality. Seventeenth-century paintings are set in the High Altar reredos and there is a delightful gilt garniture to the chancel arch. A pair of very fine painted rococo side chapels stand on either side of the High Altar, with angels holding up coats of arms, and the silvered wooden sanctuary lamps should be noticed.

Farther up the same road, higher than the street level, is the interesting church of Santa Justa, now belonging to the Capuchins, which well shows the transition from renaissance through baroque to Joanine architecture. Inside there is an ornate gold retable with salomonic columns and cherubs, with a high-relief of God the Father and a pair of lovely angels on either side. In the sacristy there are four quite beautiful 17th-century painted panels behind the vestment chest, and some delicious carved wooden angels. The two pictures of St. Paul and St. Peter are particularly worth seeing.

. . . . . .

The Machado de Castro Museum in the old Episcopal Palace near the University is justly famous for its superb polychrome Gothic sculpture, a revelation of Portuguese 14th-century work, and later terracotta, as well as church vessels, canvases, furniture and pottery. Just below the Museum is the old Cathedral, or Sé Velha, in which St. Anthony of Padua was ordained priest. It was once one of the most remarkable Romanesque buildings in Portugal, particularly the exterior, but has undergone such drastic restoration that the interior now gives the impression of having been stripped like a taxidermist's skeleton, to the bone, though the splendid Flemish carved reredos remains. At one time the University Press functioned in the cloister, which is now also being restored.

A lane leads from the Sé Velha up the Rua dos Coutinhos to the Colegio Novo and the Misericordia. The entrance is just opposite the entrancing little mediaeval fortified house, the Torre de Anto. The renaissance chapel is exceptionally fine, with two arch-topped ambones facing the congregation on either side of the High Altar. Just beyond is the two-storeyed renaissance cloister dated 1596 which has a good polychrome groined ceiling with head bosses and is very reminiscent of that of the Felipes at Tomar.

Above the Museum stands the Sé Nova at one side of which is a lovely 18th-century building, formerly the Jesuit College, Inside, the church is very large with golden altars and a huge wide barrel ceiling, and all the furnishings are of heroic size, including splendid pairs of baroque angels which stand nonchalantly about.

. . . .

A tram labelled Olivais starts outside the church of Santa Cruz and goes up by the back of the University, out to the suburbs of Coimbra, passing on the way the entrance to the Park of Santa Cruz which contains a multitude of delightful formal staircases with cascading fountains, statues and gazebos. There are lovely views of the Mondego valley below, and the tram ultimately reaches the little village of OLIVAIS, in which is the small church of S. Antonio where the Saint entered the Franciscan Order. Two minutes walk along the village street leads to three open arches at the bottom of a flight of steps giving on to the little church, where there is a *romaria* on Whit Monday. At each side of the steps are six shrines with rough country-made life-size painted figures of the Passion.

Inside the church there are very fine early blue and white tiled compositions of the life of St. Anthony and a delicate stone renaissance chancel arch. The two side altars have good rococo work with draped gold wood curtains and lovely detached glories above, and the High Altar has a pleasing retable. But the chief feature in the church is the sacristy which though tiny, is exquisite and must be seen. There are six most beautiful 18th-century tempera panels of the Life of St. Anthony with painted flowered surrounds in formal architectural-shaped gold boiseries and very fine vestment chests and a good painted ceiling, though this is in poor condition.

The tram returns to Coimbra by a different route and passes in less than half a mile, the little village of CELAS in which is the convent from which came so many of the best exhibits of the Coimbra Museum. There is a lovely unspoilt square in front of the convent's very unusual doorway; the key can be obtained from a little cottage at the side. The buildings have been immensely pulled about and restored, but there is a single-storeyed Gothic cloister with narrow arches and very interesting capitals to the columns, of full-length figures. One side was filled deep with bay leaves drying for the market, making a most delicious smell, and thus giving a small feeling of life to the deserted place. The Nuns' Choir, with a polychrome bas-relief of the Baptism of Christ, has plain wooden stalls, but a lovely gilded grille separates it from the good octagonal church which has a fine groined ceiling with gold bosses, and on the walls are pretty pale blue tile panels surrounded by formal yellow tiled frames. In the right-hand chapel stands an early statue of St. Onofrio with a kneeling child. The sacristy contains a wonderful polychrome high-relief of St. John the Evangelist in his vat of boiling oil, and St. Martin below, and there is a good early panel of the Ecce Homo. In the chapel opposite is a splendid 18th-century polychrome rococo *pietà* in a contemporary case.

On the other side of the Mondego from Coimbra stand by the river the ruins of the former Gothic convent of Santa Clara, and the Quinta das Lagrimas, with an 18th-century house and tall old trees in the garden near the spring where Inez de Castro was murdered. On the hill behind stands the immensely long Convent and Church of Santa Clara-a-Nova, which should on no account be missed as it is one of the most noble churches in Portugal, and has a superb renaissance cloister.

Inside, the church gives an impression of great height and size with its huge stone coffered roof and immense Doric pilasters. On the fourteen side altars are a series of most remarkable 17th-century polychrome wood bas-relief panels of the lives of St. Francis and the Holy Queen, St. Elizabeth of Portugal, who founded the original Poor Clare convent here when she was a widow. They are in perfect condition and set in salomonic-columned retables. At one end of the church are two beautiful polychrome Gothic stone tombs, one of a child. The chancel is superb and has a great gold retable round the silver shrine to which the body of St. Elizabeth was removed in 1696. Round the chancel are six lovely early 18th-century painted canvases with two particularly charming ones of the translation of the relics, with Pepysian figures holding up the canopy.

The sacristy is not beautiful, but in it is a rather sinister exhibit in a glass case, the grave clothes of the Holy Queen which were taken off the body when it was put into the new silver shrine. In the choir at the end of the church stands the splendid original Gothic stone tomb of the Saint which she ordered in 1330 when she was still alive. The great coffer is surrounded by polychrome stone figures of her nuns on one side, and the Apostles on the other, the Queen herself dressed as a Poor Clare is lying on the top; the whole thing stands on the backs of couchant lions. In the same choir is a charming red and gold box-organ dated 1745, a lovely painted ceiling and certain good pictures.

The quite perfect double cloister built by Dom João V is even better than that of the Felipes at Tomar, which it also greatly resembles though built so much later. It is very large and has a most beautifully kept garth. The sacristan should be asked to show the Upper Choir which has very interesting things in it, including a kind of museum of ecclesiastical art. There are seventeen early frescoes on the backs of the choir stalls and a balcony, looking down into the church, has a little altar with two charming angels, and there is a pair to the red and gold box-organ below. This choir is nearly as long as the church and has superb early polychrome statues and very fine painted retables to the four side altars, and there are interesting pictures, among them being one of the nuns carrying the coffin of their foundress, presumably painted when the relics were first translated in 1677.

CONIMBRIGA, the great Roman town referred to in Chapter I

is an easy drive 14 kilometres south from Coimbra; the turning is on the left in Condeixa, and is marked. There are still large numbers of baths, villas and tessellated pavements with hunting scenes and the swastika, then unsullied, as well as a hot-and-cold-water system.

A road to the west out of Pombal leads to LOURIÇAL, a big late 17th-century convent, now again in possession of a community of Poor Clares. The convent has huge grey walls with a few barred windows and a fine baroque doorway. The church has another fine doorway but inside it it is covered from floor to ceiling with late Reckitts-blue tiled panels of the Life of Christ and of St. Francis and St. Clare. Down a lane is another much smaller renaissance church, very simple, with agreeable azulejos in geometric patterns. Opposite the convent entrance is the delightful little Misericordia, with a tiny belfry and a pillared portico up a flight of steps, flanked by a lower building, through the windows of which can be seen a pleasant wooden ceiling and a painted and gilt altar-piece.

SOURE, north-east of Louriçal, is a pretty low-lying town on the river of the same name. The Parish Church has a renaissance Blessed Sacrament chapel with a sculptured stone retable, a box-panelled ceiling with decorative paintings and two good iron grilles. On the left of the High Altar is a noble 14th-century polychrome stone image of Our Lady of Finisterre, and in the sacristy are five Primitive Portuguese panels in good condition, of Pentecost and the four evangelists; St. John looking extremely Greek is perhaps the best, and St. Luke in his doctor's hat is most amusing.

But the most beautiful thing in Soure is the Misericordia in the next *largo*, slightly uphill from the Parish Church. The key can be obtained at the chemist's on the corner. The simple façade dated 1652 frames a renaissance doorway, and inside, the beatiful church is untouched, for the local Misericordia have never had the means to restore it, but are now said to be giving it over to the civic authorities. The painted wooden barrel ceiling is exceptionally fine with a kind of Vanbrugh-like abandonment and imagination about the brushwork. Angels in ribboned buskins with noble-savage head-dresses roughly outlined in smoky grey disport themselves among formal bouquets and architectural details, in the predominant colours of Indian red, grey and black. The remarkable proscenium painting on the front of the chancel arch is much more formal and Pannini in feeling, filled as it is with architectural features. There is a delicate Hepplewhite pulpit and an interesting long rectangular 18th-century picture of Christ sitting at table in the house of Simon.

Between Soure and Condeixa lies the lovely tiny village of EGA, with a plain square palace with Manueline windows, built by the Order of Christ in the 14th century and set on a little hill. The Parish Church standing, as is so usual, on a formal terrace with a parapet in front, has an almost complete set of azulejos Stations of the Cross let into the exterior walls; inside there are two fine renaissance side chapels with painted low-relief panelled cupolas and polychrome statues, and on the High Altar, set in the 16th-century retable, there is a triptych of the same date which was shown in a remarkable Exhibition of Portuguese Primitives in Lisbon, and was then restored. The central panel shows a nobleman, D. Afonso de Lencastre, dressed in a cloak of the Order of Christ kneeling at the feet of Our Lady, and in the side panels are St. Paul and St. Peter. The delicious little renaissance pulpit should be noticed with its architectural details in low-relief, of tiny faded gilt angels' heads.

CONDEIXA, off the main Coimbra–Lisbon road, contains lovely palaces and country houses, indeed it is one of the richest towns in Portugal in "*solares*". A little river runs through the main square and is canalised into a delightful Edwardian washing-tank lined with blue tiles, on which are nosegays of wild flowers. This water has been diverted from Alcabideque (the original Roman water works with a square Roman tower, which provided the water supply for Conimbriga).

·　·　·　·　·　·

A road goes west from Santa Clara-a-Nova in Coimbra on the south side of the Mondego to Montemor-o-Velho which is on the north side, and on to Figueira da Foz. MONTEMOR-O-VELHO is a charming little town, half asleep in the sun. It has a mediaeval castle and two attractive churches in strongly contrasted positions. Nossa Senhora dos Anjos stands on the main road, beside a small muddy tributary of the Mondego, and gets flooded regularly every winter; it has a beautiful 16th-century chapel and doorway with very light, delicate carving, and contains the early 16th-century tomb of Diogo de Azambuja, the founder of the church, and carved stone retables.

A steep stony little street, too narrow for cars, leads up between picturesque primitive houses to the rather over-restored but still beautiful 11th-century castle, which gives a wide wonderful view over the soft level greenness of the broad valley of the Lower Mondego. The second church, S. Maria da Alcaçova, stands within the castle walls, but the key lives down in the town, and should be collected before the hot climb up from whoever now looks after it. The church is Gothic, with a nave and two aisles, very pure and plain—the arches are supported on pairs of cable-twisted white columns, quite lovely and very unusual. The chapel to the south of the chancel is filled in to form a shallow curve, topped by a coffer-vaulted semi-dome, and all round the curve are reliefs carved in wood and painted in grisaille, the main theme being the Last Supper —somehow it is curiously moving, so tiny and so sincere. On the north of the aisle is a stone figure of St. Peter, which strongly recalls the Grão Vasco painting at Viseu. The walls of the castle also enclose the town cemetery and are the haunt of innumerable kestrels. The Misericordia chapel contains good renaissance polychrome sculptures, among them being an Entombment which is certainly from the Coimbra school.

Beyond Montemor, stone-paved causeways lead through the rice fields, flooded in the spring, to the QUINTA DA FOJA with a house rebuilt after a fire on the old plans. It is built along one side of a great courtyard, with square turrets topped by pyramids at either end, stables and outbuildings on the other three sides and an arched gateway in the centre. This is one of the largest rice-growing properties in Portugal and also has a great stud farm with upwards of fifty brood mares.

FIGUEIRA DA FOZ with an excellent luxury hotel, the Grande Hotel da Figueira, and several others, lies at the mouth of the Mondego and is a popular seaside place, with good bathing. There are fine views from the Alto da Vela and the Alto da Bandeira. The Municipal Museum, open between 11 and 5 on weekdays and 4 on Sundays, is at present installed in the splendid Casa do Paço, on the walls of which are the best collection of Dutch tiles in Portugal and indeed in the world; there are some seven thousand of them. Unlike the local product of huge compositions, each consisting of hundreds of tiles, these have an individual painting on each. Some are of 17th-century country scenes, and some biblical, but the most remarkable are the series of nearly two thousand knights on horseback in shades of sepia and terracotta on a white ground; each one different, some are of kings and princes and have initials on the harness, but the greater number are of galloping or fighting horsemen in every variety of dress, riding caparisoned and leaping chargers. There is an Archaeological section in the Museum which also contains good pictures and the great "Pano de Tavira", a tapestry made in Portugal in the 18th century, and some early sculpture.

Nearly all the village churches lying between Figueira and Coimbra have noble renaissance retables in "pedra de Ançã", the local stone, as there was a great school of sculpture in Coimbra in the 16th and 17th centuries.

The main road from Figueira to Coimbra returns by Montemor-o-Velho on the north of the river, through TENTUGAL, an interesting small town with the remains of a big convent and various churches and old houses. In the Misericordia there is a good doorway with figures above and a splendid stone high-relief renaissance reredos. The Parish Church of N. S. da Assunção is Gothic, with another stone reredos.

A turning leads up to the left between the villages of Martinho de Arvore and S. João do Campo, to the beautifully placed 15th-century church of SÃO MARCOS, with the remains of a Jeronymite Convent. It is not easy to find, though only four or five kilometres from the main road, for the lane is a real country one, but in the church are some of the most remarkable tombs in Portugal. (Those interested should consult Watson's "Portuguese Architecture" before visiting this remote and important place.) A broad grass sward leads up to the buildings, with a very noble pillory at one end, and the agreeable baroque façade of the church at the other. A delightful little porticoed house stands on the left and is linked to the church by a singularly lovely renaissance archway with three low-relief figures above. Inside the church, which has been well restored, the famous chapel of the Magi to the left of the chancel is the purest and most perfect renaissance. Built in 1556, the original retable which gave the chapel its name has long since disappeared, but the details of the angels heads and formal low-relief motifs in this chapel are exceptionally fine. In the nave is the extraordinary tomb (1481) of Fernão Teles de Menêses. The armoured figure lies with the head resting on a stone pillow, whose case is laced on with stone tape! Within the Gothic niche looped curtains fall with incredible delicacy from a crown-like top, behind and on either side of the figure. The soft white of the Ançã stone of which this tomb and the rest of the church are built has not been discoloured by time—it is like milk.

In the chancel there are a pair of Manueline tombs, dated 1522, of a father and son, which though queer and extraordinary, are not beautiful. The smaller simpler tomb of the founder of the church is just beyond them. On the other side of the chancel there is the extremely ornamental renaissance tomb of D. João da Silva, with a splendid central high-relief of the Assumption above the figure of the knight. The High Altar reredos is by Nicolas Chanterene, the sculptor of the retable in the Pena chapel at Sintra. The figures were all repainted in shiny colours at some time in the last century, but even so the beauty and complexity of the various groups are astounding. The central panel represents the Descent from the Cross and is surrounded by scenes from the life of St. Jerome, and the whole edifice is topped by a high-relief of God the Father, with formal vases at the corners of the pediment.

A fire destroyed the greater part of the convent in the last century, but this has now been restored as a country house for the Portuguese Pretender and his family. From it the view over the well-wooded, well-cultivated land to the distant blue haze over the Mondego is as calm and beautiful as an 18th-century French landscape.

A road turns left in S. João do Campo to Cantanhede via Ançã. This, though one of the most delightful drives in Portugal, is very little known, and the traveller by car going north or south between Oporto and Coimbra would do well to take it and avoid the dull, dusty and crowded stretch between Coimbra and Anadia, though this latter town contains the baroque palace of the Marquês de Graciosa. This detour leaves the Figueira da Foz road 7 kilometres outside Coimbra and runs north through Ançã; the quarries from which comes the famous Ançã stone, soft to cut but hardening in the air, lie on either side of it, their steep golden-white surfaces gleaming among the silver of the olive trees which cover the slopes of the wide and shallow valley. Later, the road climbs to uplands of open pasture, so rare in this part of Portugal, set with small thorn bushes and broken by flat out-crops of rock—one might be in Ireland.

CANTANHEDE is a spreading, rather blowsy town, in which the Misericordia church is disappointing, though the formal 1890 tomb in the porch shows how good designing went on in Portugal far later than in most European countries; the sacristy contains two small Parmigianino-like pictures.

The three-naved Parish Church contains renaissance chapels of which the best is that of the Blessed Sacrament; it has a reredos with polychrome figures of prophets and evangelists. A 15th-century Gothic stone image of St. Peter to the left of the chancel arch should be noticed, and indeed many of the statues are worth seeing. One of the side altars has a curious high-relief of Our Lady of Mercy, with her stone mantle covering a host of figures. There is another very similar 16th-century stone Misericordia retable in the Chapel of St. Apolonia at VARZIELA nearby.

A road west out of Cantanhede goes to TOCHA, a typical village in this part of the low-lying coastal country, where the houses are all made of mud bricks hardened in the sun. The Parish Church of S. João Baptista was built during the Spanish domination in 1610. Very fine azulejos panels dated 1763 and made in Coimbra, of ships and other emblems in formal tile frames, line the chancel, and over the High Altar there is a most unusual renaissance baldacchino with a dome, not unlike that by Bramante in the cloisters of San Peitro in Montorio in Rome, which served as the model for the tabernacle in St. Peter's.

．　　．　　．　　．　　．　　．　　．

The country to the east of the main road from Pombal north to Coimbra is little known to the tourist, though it contains some lovely small towns.

ANCIÃO lies 20 kilometres east of Pombal, with an early bridge over a stream under which the Holy Queen is said to have bathed. A lane from Ancião leads to LAGARTEIRA near which is TORRE DE VALE DE TODOS in whose church is a most exquisite stone statue by João de Ruão of N. S. da Graça, with the Holy Child in her arms—her face is completely Anatolian.

FIGUIRÓ DOS VINHOS stands on a hill. The Parish Church has a Spanish renaissance doorway, presumably, made during the Spanish occupation, with St. John the Baptist, the patron of the church, above. In the interior are Gothic images, early 18th-century azulejos panels of biblical scenes, and an organ dated 1689.

Eighteen kilometres to the east lies PEDROGÃO GRANDE,

whose 12th-century Parish church was rebuilt between 1537–39 by the sacristan Jorge Braz, who was also a stonemason.

North of Ancião, PENELA with its castle lies high among the lovely western foothills of the Serra da Estrêla. The 16th-century church of S. Eufemia has an unusual renaissance reredos of the Apostles in the Upper Room.

LOUSÃ is a delightful little town with a fine renaissance Misericordia with a staircase at the side leading up to the hospital and a unique castle for it is built on a slight eminence at the *bottom* of a deep and narrow valley. Twenty kilometres beyond, GOIS stands up looking from the distance like a gigantic pyramid. The Casa da Quinta, now the Town Hall, has good ceilings with allegorical paintings. The recently restored Parish Church has one of the best renaissance tombs in Portugal by Diogo de Torralva (1531); there are 16th-century panels on the High Altar.

All these little villages are set in splendid scenery and were the scene of bitter fighting in the Peninsular War.

. . . .

The long narrow SERRA DO BUSSACO, overlooking the lower plain of the Mondego on one side and the Serra do Caramulo on the other, is chiefly remarkable for two things: its saecular cypresses, and Wellington's victory over the French under Massena; very conveniently for those interested in either trees or history, it also possesses a most luxurious hotel, the Palace, which is 3 kilometres from the watering-place of Luso, with another luxury hotel. The hotel occupies what was formerly a royal hunting palace, built in 19th-century Manueline and plastered with truly horrifying azulejos; at its eastern end stands the old convent of the Barefooted Carmelites, where Wellington spent the night of the battle—a pretty place, with one or two attractive coloured images. To the Englishman it does convey a certain emotion; the small simple cells seem to bring the great Commander very close, and so does the aged olive-tree, standing well out in the fairway of the drive, to which was tied the horse of the "valoroso e glorioso Duque de Wellington", in the splendid local phrase.

Owing to recent planting many of the features of the battlefield are rather hard to identify, even for those who take their Napier and study it on the spot; but the curious may follow small white sign-

WATER WHEEL UP THE MONDEGO

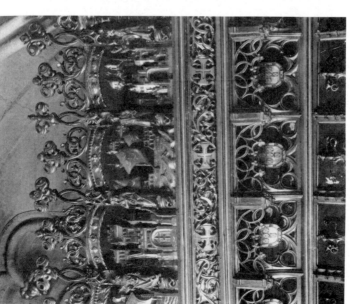

COIMBRA: DETAIL OF CHOIR-STALLS IN "CORO ALTO" IN
SANTA CRUZ

OPORTO: FROM VILA NOVA DE GAIA

(THE OLD PART OF THE TOWN IS SEEN ALONG THE WATER FRONT)

posts and a path through the young pines to the ruined mill which served as Wellington's headquarters on that momentous day—obviously in a comanding position. "Murray's Mill" stands out in the open just below the road to Santa Comba Dão, and here it is easy to trace the line of the French advance up the steep slopes, and the fold of the ground behind the mill in which Murray held his men concealed—to launch them, at the decisive moment, over the crest with such deadly effect. A fine monument outside the northern gate of the forest commemorates the victory, and a modest museum in the village holds a few trophies.

The Cypresses of Bussaco, famous to botanists and tree experts the world over, stand in a walled enclosure several kilometres round, on the southern slope of the mountain, and are almost more romantic in their way than any battle. The generally accepted theory of their origin is that the monks acquired the seeds in the 16th century from a sister community in Mexico, and planted them among the luxuriant growth of the native forest of oaks, cork-oaks, laurestinus, mimosa and tree-heaths, which already clothed the hillside, and still clothe it today. But their size, their rarity, and the extreme beauty of their form and foliage presently made them famous: so famous that in 1643 Pope Urban VIII published a Bull threatening with excommunication anyone who should enter the enclosure and cut or damage "The Trees of Bussaco"—surely a unique episode in the annals of forestry! This edict is carved in stone on a tablet outside the Porta de Coimbra, the great eastern gateway giving on to a broad grassy terrace set with seats and trees, where one may sit the hot summer morning through, fanned by a light breeze, watching the fierce sun draw all the colour out of the great plain of the Mondego, while the cicadas shrill in an absolute orchestra of ecstasy, and the shadows of the pines, their branches lopped almost to the summit, lie across the nearer slopes like groups of black cattle. There is another Papal Bull—much more usual—threatening dire penalties to women who should enter the enclosure and worry the hermits.

The botanical name for these glorious cypresses is *Cupressus lusitanicus*, despite their Mexican origin; the English, with their gift for misnomers, have long called them "Cedars of Goa", though they are not cedars, and did not come from Goa. (But Goa was the easiest name to remember of the foreign-sounding Portuguese colonies, and the trees look like cedars anyhow.) What is fascinating is that the tree in its wild state seems to have disappeared from Mexico—certainly that country imported large quantities of seed from Bussaco during this century. The largest of these splendid trees is over a hundred and twenty feet high, and has a girth of five metres; they tower above the rest of the forest like parasols of green lace. In the last century many more exotic trees were introduced, notably some very fine forms of eucalyptus; paths, some laid out by the monks, others more recent, wind along the shady slopes; the mountain is full of water, and there are fountains and pools and shaded seats—seldom can rare specimens of trees be studied under such idyllic conditions.

One of the many expeditions which can be made from Bussaco is to LORVÃO. The old convent lies at the bottom of a steep glen, densely wooded, with a tiny cramped town crushed up against it. It is L-shaped, and occupies two sides of an enormous courtyard; there must once have been a wall in front of this, but it has gone, leaving a handsome rococo gateway, with traces of painting standing isolated, like the Marble Arch. The façade is austere but very imposing, partly from its immense size, with two fine baroque doorways. The church inside has little architectural merit, but the choir-stalls, covered with carving of an incredible fineness and delicacy, especially the panels in relief above each stall, are exceedingly good, and the grille is lovely. There is an amusing portable organ, like a sedan chair, in painted wood. The famous cupola of tiles has been reconstructed and the whole west end of the church repaired and the roof renewed, owing to subsidence of the foundations and general neglect over the years. A few rich vestments are in the sacristy—but the main charm of the place is the vast façade with its barred windows, and the women sitting in the shadow of the great walls surrounded by a form of white shavings, making toothpicks at incredible speed out of willow wood. In the church are two rather ugly coffins, in *repoussé* silver on red velvet, like a Victorian photograph-frame, of the two daughters of D. Sancho I, transferred to these from old plain coffins in 1713.

SANTA COMBA DÃO lies on the road from Bussaco to Viseu and was the birthplace of Dr. Oliveira Salazar. A marbel plaque on a house in the Largo Alves Mateus shows that Queen Catherine of Bragança stayed there in 1692.

On the Mangualde road OLIVEIRA DO CONDE has a most

beautiful 16th-century country-house with a long low façade on to the street called the Solar dos Albergarias. The parish church of the village contains a stone statue of Our Lady one metre in height which may well date from the 11th century, and there is a good 15th-century Gothic stone tomb of Fernão Gomes de Gois, on which the statue of the knight lies in armour, with figures of a little angel and a child with hands joined. The tomb stands on four lions and has three Gothic inscriptions which are all complete and legible. The maker of the tomb is given as Joham Afonso, 1440, and is not unlike certain of the tombs at São Marcos.

Near CANAS DE SENHORIM is the excellent Hotel Urgeiriça, mentioned in the last chapter, from which the following towns are easily reached by car: Coimbra, Aveiro, Viseu, Lamego and Guarda. The stretch of country between Mangualde and Viseu, and from Canas de Senhorim on to Mangualde is wooded and not very pretty. But MANGUALDE itself has an 18th-century Misericordia with a delightful small baroque façade, and a fine painted ceiling inside, as have most of the churches in this part. The hospital is charming with its little gallery.

However, the most remarkable building in the place is the Palacio Anadia, which has a heavy and imposing pink baroque façade, and is said to contain beautiful things; but the interior is in *no* circumstances shown to the public. Infinitely more beautiful are two other houses in the neighbourhood, the Casa de Corso at TONDELA, built with its two wings meeting in a blunt angle, where the chapel stands, one of the most beautiful baroque doorways in the world; and the Casa da Insua, the superb baroque mansion of the Albuquerque family, in the village of CASTENDO, 12 kilometres up the Aguiar da Beira road from Mangualde. Permission must be sought to see this, and its splendid terrace and courtyard—it is not visible from the road.

Eighteen kilometres north-west of Mangualde lies VISEU, one of the show towns of central Portugal. The market day, which is a very lively one, is on Tuesday. There are lovely little baroque palaces in the town, especially in the Rua Direita. The Carmo, S. Bento, and S. Francisco churches all have exceedingly fine rococo boiseries inside. But the city is justly famous for the Grão Vasco Museum, next to the Cathedral, containing an unrivalled series of Portuguese Primitive paintings of the Viseu School. But the visitor should not let the glory of the paintings deflect him from the sculptures—they also must be seen, and the 12th-century Cathedral itself (the exterior is 16th century), which stands at one side of a great square with the gigantesque 18th-century twin-towered façade of the Misericordia, the interior of which is without interest, on the other.

The nave of the Cathedral has an extraordinary Manueline stone vaulted roof with knotted cable groining supported on 12th-century columns. On the south side of the church there is a very fine renaissance double cloister, even more harmonious and pleasing, though less imposing, than that at Tomar, with which all renaissance cloisters in Portugal must be compared! Adjoining it is the Chapter House, which is very early indeed, with two round-headed windows and most peculiar groining in granite, very heavy, rising to a central circle. A lovely Gothic four-course doorway, with short columns and triangle mouldings, leads to the nave of the Sé itself, its lofty grace a curious contrast to the heavy Primitive solidity of the Chapter House. The chancel has a very rich 17th-century painted ceiling, in tones of Indian red, bronze, green and buff, and extremely elegant choir-stalls with chinoiserie decoration and gilt designs on dark wood, as much like Hepplewhite as those in S. Francisco at Ponte de Lima in the Minho, but far richer. The High Altar has an immensely rich retable, and in the nave the square ambones, carved and palely gilded, are astonishingly beautiful.

The sacristy has practically a ceiling to end all sacristy ceilings, even in Portugal. It is vast, to begin with, and is painted in those same strange, and strangely beautiful, tones of buff and bronze-green and dull Indian red—but the choice of detail for the panels and lozenges inset in the scroll-work and flourishes is most peculiar; boars, apes and satyrs abound. The blue and yellow azulejos on the walls are also very good, and swear at the colours of the ceiling in beautiful indifference.

The best hotel is the Grão Vasco, extremely luxurious, and there is the Estalagem Dom Duarte in the Rua 5 de Outabro.

CHAPTER XII

OPORTO AND BEIRA ALTA

FOR English people it is almost impossible to think of Oporto without also thinking of port, to which the great city on the river originally owed its wealth, fame, and peculiar characteristics—especially the small, rich, highly individual and self-aware English colony, many members of which are the fifth generation to live in Portugal. The history of the wine export trade in the north, developed primarily by the English in response to the need of their navy and mercantile marine for vitamins at sea, and then expanded and adapted to meet the taste of the English squirearchy and aristocracy for a heavy sweet after-dinner wine with which to repel the cold and damp of their native climate, is a fascinating one —the curious should consult the many specialist books on the subject, and the late Rose Macaulay's non-specialist but witty and informative "They Went to Portugal". But history apart, the subject is absorbing. Port is produced by more complicated and elaborate methods than any other wine in the world—by long patience, by delicate blending, by exquisite sensibility in the tasters, by great technical skill; it reminds one more of forestry operations than anything else, in its combining of the slow processes of nature with, on man's part, unsleeping vigilance and expert knowledge.

The small, blue, tightly-bunched grapes which produce port will only thrive on schist, not on granite—so the *País do Vinho* begins above Regua on the Douro, where the schist begins. To Regua, in old days, the shippers came riding in a convoy, thirty or more together, to stay in the Wine House there and do their tasting and buying from the local farmers; now all the great firms have their own quintas, and go up and stay for the vintage period. They grow only a small proportion of the wine they will make on their own land; the rest they usually buy as a growing crop, supplying the casks, the brandy, and a factor to supervise the "making" of the wine in the local farmers' own *adegas*.

For all the scientific skill that is subsequently applied, the grapes are actually crushed by precisely the same method as that which made the brew on which Noah got so very drunk thousands of years before Christ, No substitute has yet been found for the yielding, firm, supple and muscular sole of the naked human foot, though many machines have been tried. Port cannot have the proper colour and flavour unless the skins of the grapes are crushed; on the other hand if the pips are crushed, releasing their tannin content, the wine will be bitter. Man's foot, and man's foot alone, produces this result; so, when their feet have been carefully examined to see that they are healthy, and then thoroughly washed in shallow tubs, into the great *lagares*, built of huge granite slabs, go the teams of treaders, and with linked arms begin to tramp up and down on the cold dark shining masses of grapes. They remove their trousers and wear instead very short and saucy flowered cotton pants in pale blue or pink, but keep on their jackets, and oddly enough usually their hats as well, which creates a very odd effect. The grapes are trodden for four hours and "rested" for six, in a regular rotation; when they have assumed the consistency of rather runny blackcurrent jam the contents of the *lagar* are referred to as the *lagrima*; once fermentation has begun the word *mosta*, or "must", is used.

The *lagrima* is bitterly cold, but fermentation brings warmth, as well as acting as the most complete sterilising agent—all impurities are eliminated by it. Now the temperature of the must is frequently taken, and so is the sugar content, by an ingenious instrument called a saccharinometer, which is plunged into the tank. The ordinary must is run off at 7 to $7\frac{1}{2}$ degrees of sweetness, and mixed as it runs into the great *tonels* or vats with grape brandy, made in the south of Portugal, which arrests the fermentation and "holds" the wine at the required degree of sweetness; if this were not done and fermentation proceeded unchecked, the wine would become like heavy Burgundy, not sweet at all. For blending purposes, small quantities are allowed to ferment on to as low as $4\frac{1}{2}$ or even 4 degrees, while in other *lagares* the must is run off at 12, which is very sweet. But 7 is the average.

Treading is hard work. The *ranchos* vary it, once the *lagrima* is thoroughly fluid, by joining in pairs and prancing about, or even dancing *viras*: to encourage them the *musica*—with a concertina, a banjo or two, and a tambourine—comes up from the village in the evening, and the neighbours either sit on the rim of the *lagar* and beat time, or dance folk-dances on the floor of the *adega*, while the jolly treaders themselves, in those gaily coloured pantettes, dance too, literally "in the drink"—a most picturesque and astonishing sight in the modern world. Talk of "music while you work"—here people make it for themselves! It is in fact much easier to dance knee-deep in must than one might suppose; the granite floor is not in the least slippery, it is firm with a sort of *light* firmness, and the warm skin-and-stem-laden fluid seems to support one while, snapping one's fingers, one puts in the neat precise foot-work that *viras* demand—an unusual and exhilarating experience.

And how it illuminates the Bible!—as all natural processes do, wherever encountered. In a dark chilly *adega*, when treading is beginning, one realises for the first time the full desperate meaning of the words in Isaiah —"I have trodden the wine-press alone". It would be the loneliest thing in the world to step alone into a cold *lagar*, full of the chilly wet fruit, with no one to link arms with—it would seem so impossibly endless. And the phrase—"and of the people there was none to help" is, after a visit to the Douro at vintage-time, quite clearly seen to mean that none of the villagers came up to cheer on the task with music and singing.

Some time during the early spring the wine in the *tonels* is tasted, "refreshed" with yet more brandy, turned and allowed to "run bright"—then about April it is put into casks and sent down, either by rail or in the large-sailed boats which, so astonishingly, negotiate the rapids and savage current of the great river, to Vila Nova de Gaia, across the Douro from Oporto proper, where the wine-lodges are—there to rest, to mature, to be tasted, blended, revived, tasted again and blended again, till after years the noble product of the golden schist and the golden sunshine of the *País do Vinho* comes at last to make peculiarly glad the heart of man, in Britain or America.

Since this account was written, experiments have been made to perfect a wine-press to crush the grapes and now that one has been developed, all the big port wine firms are using this means, though the old methods as here described can still be seen on small farms.

OPORTO, in which the best hotel is the Infante de Sagres, is the second city of Portugal, and has nearly half a million inhabitants;

like Lisbon, it is built on hills above a river, but at Oporto the Douro enters a kind of gorge, spanned by a great double bridge, one level of which joins the lower part of the town to the suburb on the opposite side, while the other spans the top of the high cliffs to Vila Nova de Gaia. The whole thing looks like a singularly dangerous spider's web flung across space.

The town has always been a centre of any revolutionary movement in the country. It was here that the Liberal Revolution of 1820 started and another rising, in 1832, took place against the Absolute King, Dom Miguel. Even in this century the city has been the scene of various abortive insurrections, and in the Peninsular War a good deal of fighting occurred in and around it; it was occupied by Marshal Soult in 1808–9.

Seen from Vila Nova de Gaia, Oporto is dominated by the enormous Bishop's Palace, the Cathedral and the Torre dos Clerigos, the highest tower in Portugal, built from the plans of the Italian, Nicholas Nazzoni, in 1748, It is a curious example of granite rococo, attached to a greyish-pink marble-lined church with a good choir. In the centre of the city stands out the enormously long façade of the Hospital of Santo Antonio, built in 1770–95 by the English architect, John Carr of York, who before he came to Portugal designed Harewood House and the Mausoleum at Wentworth. In the Praça da Universidade opposite the hospital are the two Carmelite churches, side by side. That of the Third Order is later in date (1756–68), one of the exterior walls is covered with an enormous modern azulejos composition.

The Misericordia in the Rua das Flores was also built by Nazzoni in grey granite with an unusual façade, and a lovely white plaster ceiling inside. In the offices next door are some notable 18th-century painted banners, one in particular of the Descent from the Cross in grisaille should be seen, as well as other good pictures. But the painting of major interest is the "Fons Vitae", possibly by Bernard Van Orley (1520) representing Christ on the Cross between the Blessed Virgin and St. John, with the Blood of the Saviour flowing down on the kneeling D. Manoel I, his third wife, Eleanor of Hapsburg, and the children of his two earlier marriages, all clad in brilliant colours. Watson, discussing the authorship of this painting, makes great play with the fact that among the flowers in it are columbines, and that as these are unknown in Portugal, it is clear proof that it is by a foreign hand. But in fact one columbine, *Aquilegia dichroa*, *does* grow in Portugal, and near Oporto, where it was found some years ago.

Near the river, and next door to the Bolsa (Stock Exchange) is the truly extraordinary church of S. Francisco which was built by D. Sancho II in 1233, rebuilt a hundred years later, and finally in the 17th and 18th centuries was filled with the most fantastic collection of rococo gilded wood decoration of almost any church in Portugal. Flowers, birds, fruit, angels, climb up and down the Gothic columns and burgeon out of every altar-piece. In a chapel to the left there is a 15th-century Italian fresco, and in one to the right a Gothic tomb decorated with stone tears; a 16th-century painting of the Baptism of Christ hangs in the chapel of St. John the Baptist.

On the same level is the entrance to the Ordem Terceira Church which is pure Adam in feeling, decorated in black, white and gold. In old days a huge Good Friday Procession would issue forth from here, but the images are so tall that they would now get en-meshed in the overhead tram-cables, so the statues lie forlorn and unseen by the outer world.

Near this church is the Rua do Infante Henrique, where the English Queen gave birth to the future Navigator. This was formerly known as the Rua dos Ingleses and in it stands the British Factory House. This magnificent building was erected in 1785 by the then British Consul in Oporto, William Whitehead. All the furniture is contemporary and is a remarkable tribute to the sober good taste of the British merchants of that day. It is well worth getting an intro-duction to a member of the Factory, in order to see over the interior with its beautifully proportioned rooms, great crystal chandeliers, fine furniture, and lovely painted ceilings. The Factory is *not* a club, as is often supposed, but is a curious survival from the 18th century, for there are only about a dozen members, from the biggest English port wine firms.

At the top of the hill stands the Sé or Cathedral; Romanesque in origin, it is slightly reminiscent of a fortress, like the Sé Velha in Coimbra. At one side is a perfectly proportioned 18th-century loggia attributed to Nazzoni and inside, the church has been restored with care and intelligence, so that many of the 18th-century furnish-ings remain. The Blessed Sacrament chapel to the left of the High Altar should be particularly noted, as the remarkable architectural altar, tabernacle and reredos are all made of solid silver, and come from Valbom near Oporto. The silver glistens dully; it is only taken to pieces and thoroughly cleaned every few years. During the Peninsular War the whole thing was white-washed to hide it from Soult's soldiers. There are extremely ornate choir stalls, and the whole splendid renaissance and early baroque chancel has fortunately been left by the restorers. The sacristy contains charming early 18th-century pictures of the Life of Christ framed in rococo gold behind the vestment chests, which are very fine, with brass-encrusted swags. Behind the sacristy the pointed Gothic cloister and a larger one at the side, lined with good azulejos, have been very much pulled about. The delightful wooden upper storey of the latter was removed some years ago. The guide should be asked to show the chapel of S. Vicente off the cloister, in which is a set of ten polychrome bas-reliefs behind the stalls, and a curious flattened organ with balconies and gold draperies. A glass shrine containing the body of a martyr, dressed entrancingly in a white satin shirt with gold spangles, is on a side altar. The very early Gothic statue of our Lady of Vendome has been moved into the cathedral.

At the side of the Cathedral towers the quite lovely Bishop's palace, built in 1772, with its huge façade, pale yellow-washed with granite windows, now used as Municipal Offices. Not far from the Cathedral in the Largo de Sta. Clara stands the convent of the same name. The exterior is quite plain and gives no indication of the riches and beauty within, for the chapel of this convent is lined with the most superb goldwork in the country. Sacheverell Sitwell rightly calls it "one of the major beauties of baroque art. . . .". The grilles are exceptionally lovely, the ceiling is studded with gold bosses, and the chancel ceiling is all of gold. The polychrome statues are remarkably fine, especially that of St. Clare, in the first chapel to the left; there is a delightful pair of black saints, and a high-relief of the Last Judgment above. On the right stands a beautiful group of the Blessed Virgin, St. Anne, and the Holy Child. The two tiny organs are quite delicious and the pulpit is also good.

On the western side of the city, beyond St. Anthony's Hospital, the Palacio dos Carrancas is now the Museu Nacional de Soares dos Reis, open at 10.0 a.m. every day except Mondays. Built in 1759, the palace is a fine example of domestic architecture of the period, with a granite staircase and well-proportioned rooms. It was the headquarters of the French when they occupied Oporto during the Peninsular War. On their ejection by the English in 1809 it became Wellington's—then Sir Arthur Wellesley's—headquarters and it is said that he here ate the dinner prepared for Marshal Soult, who had fled precipitately.

The Museum is arranged with great care and taste. The Picture Gallery is exceptionally well lighted, and contains two Clouet panels, pastels by Pillement, a Magnasco, and the characteristic Soares dos Reis bust of an English lady. There are also good porcelain and pottery, which show well the development of ceramics in Portugal, for little is known in other countries of the lovely productions of the 18th-century factories of Rato, Mafra, Coimbra, Viana, the Italian factory of Jeronimo Róssi at Massarellos, and the 19th-century porcelain from Vista Alegre. There is also a good collection of coins and medals, including a gold 5th-century Greek bracteate of Arethusa's head, found near Bragança in 1840. The Ethnographical and Historical Museum in the Largo de S. João Novo contains Roman remains, examples of country arts and crafts, weapons, furniture, maps, lace and costumes. It is a fascinating collection.

On a road north of the Museu Nacional stands S. Martinho de Cedofeita, better known than most of the Romanesque churches of which the north of Portugal is full; it takes its unusual name from the belief that it was built with extreme rapidity. An inscription on a slab over the West door ascribes this building to King Theodomir, and puts the date at A.D. 556, but modern experts regard it as being of the 12th century at earliest. What is unusual about the church is its considerable size, and the way in which the three heavy *square* groins of its barrel-vaulted stone roof rest on three pairs of pillars set flat against the walls of the nave. The chancel repeats the plan of the nave, but is lower, with the usual shallow arches recessed into the walls all round, except for the two behind the altar. The capitals of these are plain. The East window is a plain slit without pillars. Exterior details worth noticing are that the West door is square, and has the beginnings of a porch projecting in front of it; the very rich and spirited carving of the capitals of the North and West doors, and the *incised*, not relief, carved figure of the Lamb and Flag in the tympanum of the North door. The cloister which used to adjoin the church was pulled down in the latest restorations.

. . . . . .

On the slopes below N. S. da Serra do Pilar, at VILA NOVA DE GAIA, then open ground, Wellington collected his troops before attacking Oporto. Behind the disappointing church is the astonishing circular cloister, the renaissance arches resting on Ionic columns, so curious and unusual that it must be seen. Near Gaia there is also the church and convent at GRIJO, with a most lovely cloister and an attractive 16th-century church.

About 8½ kilometres to the north-east of Oporto lies the Romanesque church of AGUAS SANTAS, a rather disappointing building. It is much restored and added to and has apparently been altered again since Watson described it, as there are now two wide shallow arches connecting the aisles with the nave. A noteworthy feature is that the little pillars on each side of the small round-headed chancel windows are entirely covered in carving in a strap-net design—not interlaced work, as Watson says, by the way. The remains of an early rose window above the chancel arch are now only visible from the outside.

The Templars' Church at LEÇA DO BALIO lies about 4 kilometres west of Aguas Santas. This early Gothic building is most unusual and splendid, the roof being completely surrounded with a machicolated parapet, as is the top of the corbelled and fortified tower—and a sort of machicolated balcony runs across the West façade above the doorway. The South door is most lovely, the moulding being very richly carved in a design of circles and medallions, and the supporting pillars exquisitely slender—the capital of the right hand one has an astonishing design of clustered stars. Within, the apse, with the central chancel and two smaller side-chapels, strongly recalls the Cistercian church at Odivelas: there is the same bold yet graceful groining, the same arrowy-slender lancet windows. Both the chancel and the North chapel contain fine tombs, and a remarkable bronze of Estêvão Vasques Pimentel who rebuilt the church in 1336. The two aisles, like the nave very lofty, have twin lancet windows both below and in the clerestory, very unusual—the arches are supported on four sets of clustered pillars of the utmost grace, with very fine figure-carving on their capitals, and there is a big—early and simple—rose window in the West end. It is all very austere and fine and blessedly untouched—a complete whole. The remains of the cloister and other buildings are full of fine things, but since Watson's day have been incorporated into a private quinta—it is hard to see them.

VILA DO CONDE, 25 kilometres north-west of Oporto and almost on the sea, is a delightful town dominated by the enormous Convent of Sta. Clara built on a hill above the Ave. The great river façade was erected in the 18th century, and is of extremely satisfying proportions. The church is much earlier, 14th century, with 17th-century decoration and splendid renaissance tombs decorated with bas-reliefs. After the recent restorations, when many of the conventual buildings were demolished, the church stands isolated, as does the small renaissance cloister, left, without apparent reason, in the bare open space between the church and the convent.

All around Oporto, and indeed in the whole of the northern province of Minho, there are 12th- and 13th-century Romanesque churches, each very similar to the next; but what *is* unique is the extraordinary number of rococo and baroque granite churches, especially in the extreme north, which will be referred to in the next two chapters.

.   .   .   .   .   .

Thirty-five kilometres due east of Oporto lies PENAFIEL, a rather gloomy and dirty little town. The best church is that of the Misericordia, which has an extremely fine white plaster ceiling in a restrained design, barrel-vaulted like that—in granite—of the chancel; but the great feature of this church, which alone makes a visit to Penafiel worth while, is the screen surmounting the rather mediocre carving of the Board pew. This is of flat wood, painted, but cut out to follow the design, like those ply-wood cut-out photographs so popular in England in the 1930's. It is unique and quite lovely. In the centre is an exquisite Mercy with two children, very like an early Sir Thomas Lawrence; at the ends are two stately females against architectural backgrounds. In the sacristy are three or four rather good oil paintings and a charming tiny statue of the Assumption to the left of the crucifix.

Another of those water-shed roads, which are such a feature of the north of Portugal, leads from Penafiel to Amarante. On fine days the distant views of the Serra do Marão are magnificent, but the near scenery is dull and bitty—a little of this and a little of that, spindly *Pinus bravus* and eucalyptus; the whole place has a suburban feeling about it, and the buildings, both domestic and church or shrine, are curiously poor compared to those of the countryside round Braga and Viana do Castelo.

AMARANTE, with an excellent hotel, the Silva, is an extremely ancient town, though the present beautiful bridge over the Tamega was only built by Queen Maria I between 1781 and 1790. The original Roman bridge which was reconstructed by S. Gonçalo the local saint in 1200, fell down in 1763. The view from the far side of the river, with the obelisked bridge in the foreground, the amazing richness of the whole convent of S. Gonçalo with a blue and yellow tiled cupola beyond and S. Domingos piled up above, is one of the most beautiful architectural ensembles in Portugal, or indeed in Europe. The south façade of the convent which gives on to a little square above the river is exquisite; the portal, in very Italianate renaissance, is amazingly rich and yet elegant, slender graceful fluted columns with the richest possible carved capitals, pendant bosses, a figure of Our Lady in a shell-topped niche, and five other saints. To the left, quite unconnected with the doorway, the creamy granite of the church, at third-storey level, is suddenly and unexpectedly broken by a graceful arcaded loggia, with 17th-century figures.

Immediately beyond the church is an exquisite two-storey cloister, also renaissance—the remarkable feature of this is the ceiling of the lower storey which, though renaissance, has immensely rich fan-groining, with pendant central bosses—at the four corners, in diamond-wise panels, are painted reliefs of saints. A sort of lobby outside the sacristy (in which are a charming pair of Regency mirrors with Flaxmanlike painted figures) leads from the cloister to the Praça at the East end of the church—this lobby too has a most curious and beautiful ceiling, of shallow box panels of carved wood, painted to look like stone; the carved centre of each panel has then been overpainted in tones of rose and coral. The effect is fantastically lovely.

Beyond the cloister already described is a second, very large and severe, with a single row of round-topped arches below walls and windows above except at the two ends, where a second line of slender pillars supports a flat-topped gallery with a tiled roof. When

visited this cloister had recently been used for dancing at the
romaria, and a wooden dance-floor was still in position, draped
with paper garlands. It was tragic to have missed the *romaria* of
Amarante on the first Saturday and Sunday of June, which is one of
the strangest survivals in Portugal. S. Gonçalo is traditionally the
patron saint of marriages, and during this festival, every bakery in
the town sells special cakes baked in the shape of a phallus, which
as the *Guide Bleu* politely says, "the young men and young women
are not embarrassed both to offer and to ask from one another!"
This is clearly the remains of a fertility cult much older than any
Christian saint, and it would be interesting to know if it is in any
way connected with the prehistoric statues of boars which are so
widely distributed in Tras-os-Montes. Murça, with its famous "pig
of Murça" is not more than about 100 kilometres from Amarante,
and the great boar at Bragança is another 110 kilometres beyond;
the smaller one in the Museum garden at Bragança came from somewhere in the district—a most unusual number in so small an area.
Incidentally it is impossible not to wonder whether the very name
Amarante has not some connection with the cult, which   must
certainly have existed in Roman times.

The interior of S. Gonçalo, which is full of lovely things, gives
the impression of great height. The columns are painted, with
dusky gold and flowered wreaths winding up them, and the magnificent organ case is supported by a pair of huge tritons on either side
of a merman with two black tails! The retable of the chapel just on
the right of the South entrance has some very good paintings indeed.
In the first chapel on the left in the nave are two quite lovely, very
tiny polychrome statues, one at each side of the rather poor retable.
The High Altar itself is magnificent—it is huge and nobly rich, set
like a stage considerably higher than the chancel, with a sweep of
steps up to it and vast gilt salomonic columns flanking a most
splendid boat-like throne; at the top under the roof, a riot of gilt
figures, some with *powdered* hair, repeat the delightful frivolity of the
two be-wigged and buskined angels on either side of the chancel
arch. There is nothing in Portuguese churches more charming than
these angels—they are everywhere; carrying their tapers with a great
air of bustle, their clothes giving an indescribable impression of
fashion, and a rather vacuous look of satisfaction on their nice silly faces.

To the left and under the High Altar is a minute chapel, walls and ceiling alike of carved wood, which contains the polychrome stone tomb of S. Gonçalo, his head lying on two tasselled red stone pillows. The chancel has some beautiful features, especially the windows on either side of the High Altar, with their painted splays and carved and gilt surrounds.

The clock tower is built apart from the Church, and just by it is the lovely, very small round church of S. Domingos. The sacristan of S. Gonçalo has the key. Yet again there are a pair of splendid life-size noble-savage angels staggering under great cornucopias ending in copper sconces in leaf form. The church is tiny and still contains all the original very rich and unspoilt rococo woodwork, and a number of good statues. The gold and white organ-loft is set in an angle of the church, upheld by two baby tritons, and the ambones have angels standing on their canopies.

Farther up the hill the church of São Pedro has a very strange tall and narrow granite and white-washed façade dated 1727; the high bell tower in the centre is surmounted by a large stone mitre and triple cross, and two figures stand on the balconied corners of the façade. The interior has an unusual blue, white and green plaster ceiling. Here are yet another pair of angels holding candles, and on the chancel walls two lovely polychrome high-relief panels in early gold baroque frames; one of them, like the Paólo Uccello in the National Gallery, is dominated by the presence of a large white horse. The rather late High Altar reredos has two huge statues of St. Peter and St. Paul on either side, and a splendid tabernacle with four fat grub-like angels crawling over it. Six agreeable late 18th-century panels of the twelve Apostles, two heads to each picture, with the names painted on formal ribbons below, should be noticed in the sacristy. The crucifix at the back of the Vestment Chest is in a lovely shrine, with a small Persian pattern of tulips and other flowers on a gold ground.

The drive from Amarante to Vale de Cambra via Entre os Rios is as attractive as that from Penafiel to Amarante is dull. (There is a good road up the Douro from Entre os Rios.) It is *not* necessary to return to Penafiel—a perfectly good second-class road cuts through wildish country, and then drops in great loops through pinewoods to the two rivers. The crossing itself, of the Douro and its confluent the Tamega, is splendid. It is perhaps at its best on a September evening, after rain, when the swollen Douro is *really* golden, the hills

AN UPPER REACH OF THE DOURO, SHOWING TERRACED VINEYARDS

AMARANTE: REGENCY BRIDGE OVER THE TAMEGA

FISHING BOAT NEAR AVEIRO

LEÇA DO BALIO: TEMPLARS' CHURCH

dramatic with purple-blue shadows, like the bloom on purple grapes, and the coppery soil on the nearer slopes repeats the pinkish flush from a stormy west. The road winds down to the great golden river, crosses it and winds up on the farther side, so that for a long while the traveller keeps on being confronted with that majestic presence.

Leaving the river, the road climbs to CASTELO DE PAIVA, a village whose scattered houses are embowered in chestnuts and vines; from here on to Arouca it is rough and narrow, but perfectly viable, and the drive is glorious. Great hills, reminiscent of Scotland, rise about one, deep valleys sink away below—there is little planting, and one escapes from the perpetual tyranny of *Pinus bravus* and sees the noble outlines of the hills themselves. For this reason the geological structure of the country is especially clear on this stretch —on the schist, the hills are smooth and sweeping, with great unbroken curves; a bend of the road, and one is on the granite, and the outlines become lumpy and nubbly, with great agglomerations of boulders on the summits. Some distance above the valley we enter the trees again; reaching the level, one turns left, and in a few minutes comes to AROUCA.

This convent of Cistercian nuns owes its riches and its prestige chiefly to the Queen-Saint Mafalda, daughter of D. Sancho I, and divorced wife of Henry I of Castile; she retired to the convent some years before her death in 1256 and finding discipline lax, proceeded to enforce a stricter rule both of dress and conduct. She had some connection with another house of the same Order in Oporto, and each claimed her body. A delightful legend says that her corpse was placed on her favourite mule, who unhesitatingly proceeded to walk, at a reverent pace, to Arouca. Here, accordingly, she now lies embalmed; one can catch a glimpse of her mummified body, richly dressed, in a glass and silver coffin, in which it was placed in 1734.

The treasury is surprisingly rich. In particular there is a very early silver-gilt reliquary, which tradition says belonged to Saint Mafalda herself, and some curious pictures. Local veneration for the saint preserved the treasure—at the time of the Dissolution in 1834 the country people came in and carried off the valuables, which they hid from the authorities; when the force of the persecution had spent itself, they were returned, in some cases by the children of the original preservers.

Except for the church, the whole of the great block of the

conventual buildings, dating from the late 17th and early 18th century, was for long deserted. Now it is filled with boyish voices, for the Salesians have established a large Trade School in the huge place and the unfinished cloisters are being completed.

The church, which now serves the parish, has a very fine 18th-century organ, and in the Coro Baixo are magnificent choir stalls. and some very good pictures. But the great splendour of Arouca was the series of tremendous 18th-century statues of nuns in their habit in black and white and more than life-size, which look down on this choir—stylised, conventional, they yet had a unique beauty and dignity in the still formal folds of their robes and the contrast between the rigidity of their granite forms and the faultless painting of their faces, under the black lines of their granite veils. It will hardly be credited, but they have now been white-washed, and so their unique interest has largely been destroyed.

In the museum in part of the convent there are Portuguese primitives, early sculpture, books, vestments, a 13th-century silver diptych and a remarkable early Roman bangle of fine gold. This was found under a tree in the vicinity. But Arouca has another treasure, which alone should make it almost a place of pilgrimage—a wooden panel on which is carved in low-relief a portrait alleged to be that of St. Teresa. One is forced to believe it true, the force and power of the whole figure is so intense, the intellectual vigour and spiritual illumination of the face so astonishing. Nothing can be learned on the spot as to its history, or its authorship—it is just St. Teresa. Looking at it, one feels that this is almost enough.

During the Peninsular War an Englishwoman named Clara Warre was a nun at Arouca, and was visited there by Field-Marshal Beresford and her brother, afterwards Lt.-Gen. Sir William Warre, whose "Letters from the Peninsula" were published later.

It is a thousand pities that there is as yet no *pousada* or hotel in VALE DE CAMBRA, for it is a charming place—a high-lying valley, green, terraced and fertile, under the pine-clad slopes and bare grey tops of the Serra da Gralheira, watered by the still-flowing Caima. The upper reaches of the river are spanned by a fine Roman bridge; apart from this, the only architectural feature is the very exquisite renaissance church at ROGE, 2 or 3 kilometres beyond the village of Vale de Cambra itself. The façade is very rich and most peculiar, with barley-sugar columns, and barley-sugar curly obelisks

on the roof, also two very finely dressed figures, a charming conceit
—the escutcheon above the door has mermaids on it and the carved
cross out in front is extremely elaborate, on a pedestal of cherubs,
with the cross at the top surmounting the globe. The church tower
is also surmounted by the armillary sphere, and has curly obelisks
and rich gargoyles.

The church is dedicated to Saint Elizabeth, the Holy Queen, and
contains one very amusing sculpture group, alleged to be of her and
her cousin, behind a glass in the retable of the altar on the North
side of the chancel arch—a gentleman, richly attired in an 18th-
century coat, kneels and clasps an equally rich-dressed lady. It
does not look at all saintly, one must confess.

An interesting road leads over the Serra to S. Pedro do Sul past
the village of JUNQUEIRA DA SERRA, whose primitive thatched
granite-built houses recall the dwellings of prehistoric Citânia.
Dropping down to the Vouga valley one passes a splendid house,
formerly a convent, at S. CRUZ DA TRAPA—very elegant and pure
baroque. A great feature of all this country are the curved terraces
of cultivation, strung out, like vivid green horse-shoes, up the bed
of every ravine, between the cindery dusty darkness of the *mata* and
the pines.

S. PEDRO DO SUL, with good hotels at the Termas or Spa 3 kilometres away (particularly the Lisboa), has some beautiful things
in it, but it is almost the most maddening town in which to do any
sight-seeing in all Portugal, that land of difficulty for the tourist.
The magnificent and rather austere baroque convent of the Frades
is now used as the Camara, or Municipal offices; besides its splendid
façades, fronting a vast gravelled open space, and a not very interesting little two-storeyed cloister, its main feature is a very rich church.
The key to this is not, as one might suppose, kept in the Camara
building, but half a kilometre away—the visitor is at first told that
it is impossible to have the key fetched, and more than the usual
immense pertinacity is required to get in, involving a delay of half
an hour or more. The senior Camara officials themselves deplore
this tiresome concealment of one of their country's masterpieces.
The church has splendid gilt retables to the High Altar and the two
side ones, a magnificent Tabernacle, a charming statue of Our Lady
above the High Altar, and two superb angels in the chancel; there
are a pair of very fine silver sanctuary lamps, and the organ,

three-sided and springing out from a fluted base, is lovely—its date is 1729. The sacristy has, as usual, an exquisite ceiling and there is a ravishing polychrome saint to the right of the crucifix.

The Igreja Matriz, standing in the funny little raised square in the centre of the town is fairly easy to get into, being the parish church; but the Misericordia opposite—called locally S. Antonio—defeats the traveller utterly. We tried twice, at an interval of some weeks. On the second visit the key situation was as follows (facts elicited in one-and-a-half hours of diligent inquiry):

One gentleman had had the key of the belfry, but he took it with him when he went to hospital some weeks before, and lost it there. A member of the Misericordia Board had the other key, but he had gone to the seaside for a holiday, and taken it with him. So all one can say is that the quite lovely façade is covered by watery blue and white tiles. There are granite baroque surrounds to the windows and a beautiful tiny, narrow balcony above the copper-green door, which stands opposite the fine early apse of the parish church, and below the imposing balconied front of the Reriz Palace, with its big cornice.

Four roads meet at S. Pedro do Sul; the river road up the Vouga valley from Aveiro, the mountain road over from Vale de Cambra, the magnificent road over the high Serra country to Lamego and the Douro, and the road to Viseu *en route* for Mangualde and Guarda, or Tondela and Bussaco.

North of S. Pedro do Sul, on the Lamego road, the town of CASTRO DAIRE is set on a high cliff, and the road winds up and through it. Some lovely palaces surround the main square, which has a park in the centre. The road between Castro Daire and Lamego goes right over wild uplands, with mountains on either side, passing singular elemental villages apparently sinking into the earth; near the road there are many neolithic remains. Groups of men walk along the road at vintage and harvest time, with flowers in their hats, singing and dancing.

· · · · · ·

The road west from S. Pedro do Sul by the Vouga valley to Aveiro goes through VOUZELA. The Misericordia church has a delightful bright blue tiled and granite façade. Inside there is a noble renaissance retable in polychrome wood high-relief, with panels of the

Holy Women. The bench for the *Mesa* or Board has four red-clad angels standing on the back. Such detail, but particularly the retable, make it worth the visitor's while to send for the key, which here takes only a few moments. Incidentally, the Police Station at Vouzela has one of the most faultless small baroque façades in the world!

The road from Vouzela to the coast winds through woods along the mountainside, with the river Vouga below, to ALBERGARIA-A-VELHA (about 5 kilometres down the Oporto–Lisbon road there is a Government *pousada* at SEREM, Vale do Vouga) and then straight on to SOBREIRO, where the façade of the church is entirely covered with Edwardian tiled pictures of moustachioed benefactors and saints.

AVEIRO, that lovely watery city, is surrounded in the late summer by glistening white mounds of salt among the salt-pans, which stretch to the nearby sea; they stand out against the dull blue mainland horizon like miniature Alps. A canal with formal parapets and obelisks on either side goes from the centre of the town to the coast; motor boats can be taken to explore all the strange, remote and beautiful network of canals and brackish lagoons, which are separated from the sea by endless dunes and saltings, forming the delta of the Vouga. The visitor to Aveiro, where there is an hotel, the Arcada, and the Pousada da Ria not far away, should not be dashed by the approach to the town through a dreary avenue. Only at the other end start the canals and the town proper. Most foreigners visit Aveiro for only one reason, to see the golden rococo interior of the Convent of Jesus, which Mr. Sitwell refers to with such delight in various of his works. But now that the buildings have been turned into a Museum (open at 10.0 a.m. in the summer and 11.0 a.m. in the winter), some of their charm has gone, together with the dust and the marbled walls. Though even now there is still much to take pleasure in, to say nothing of the other lovely buildings in Aveiro The extraordinary chapel of the Convent is completely covered, walls, ceiling and altars, with gilded wood, though it is not so large or so fine as that of Santa Clara in Oporto. A charming series of 17th-century paintings in the chancel depict the Holy Princess, afterwards Santa Joanna, leaving her father, D. Afonso V's house in a coach—not unlike that of Philip II in the Coach Museum at Belem —her entry into the Convent, her life there and holy death. The lower choir contains her tomb in marble marquetrie which is an exceptionally ugly example of renaissance virtuosity.

In the 15th-century cloister are Gothic and renaissance doorways, some with traces remaining of their original colour. The *Coro Alto*, restored in 1731, has singular chinoiserie gold and black decoration to the choir-stalls and ceiling. In the Museum itself there are superb polychrome statues and groups of baroque images and crib figures, as well as vestments and some fine Portuguese Primitives, with the never-to-be-forgotten kitcat portrait of Santa Joanna by Nuno Gonçalves. Here she is dressed as a Princess, with a jewelled cap and low V-shaped open bodice and jewels, but the curious and memorable thing about the picture is the fact that the future saint looks straight out of the panel, exactly full face; and that face is so plain, so strange, so deeply melancholy, with its long, long nose and tiny black eyes and fat square jowl that no royal flattery can have gone into the painting of it. Her exquisitely beautiful right hand lies across her breast, clasping her cloak.

The Saint-Princess died in a little square room, another carved and gilded box, with ravishing "moonlit" pictures all round, including an exquisite death scene on the right. An octagonal chapel off the square landing, with a rich painted octagonal ceiling, has superb polychrome sculptures in niches on the walls—and on the High Altar there is a series of tiny painted panels of New Testament scenes, only five inches high but so vivid, in which the figures, though perfectly recognisable, are only half-length—a thing possibly unique.

At right angles to the strange galleried façade of the Museum is the Cathedral of S. Domingos, in which an unusual impression of light is given by big oval 18th-century windows set high in the walls of the nave. There is a very fine painted ceiling to the side vestibule, not unlike the Misericordia ceiling at Soure, but rather earlier in date. The altars are malachite and pale green and blue in colour and there is a beautiful gold organ. The choir stalls have ten delightful 17th-century panels of the life of St. Dominic behind them and there are other good paintings in the side chapels. The church was built in the 15th century and the early parts still remain agreeably visible through the later additions.

The Carmelite Church is in the same square as the Post Office; a Police Station is in part of the original convent, though when the nuns were turned out in 1910 much was destroyed, and their choir at the West end was pulled down to make the road, so the present façade only dates from that time. However, the 17th-century interior is worth seeing (the key can be got at the cottage attached snailwise to the back of the church), for like the chapel in the Convent of Jesus, the interior is entirely covered with gold woodwork of good quality, and there are some lovely panels in the chancel. One, of the birth of the Virgin, has enchanting details: the baby is being bathed in a wooden tub and the maids are airing the towels in the background. The three statues on the altar are all splendid, St. Teresa, St. John the Evangelist, and St. John of the Cross.

The Misericordia is a 16th-century classical church, high and plain, the façade plastered with blue azulejos, with a good two-storeyed renaissance doorway. Inside there is a very fine 17th-century gold renaissance High Altar retable reaching to the ceiling, with seven good contemporary painted panels inset, the centre one of Our Lady of Mercy, with among those sheltering like chickens under her cloak, a Pope kneeling on a red cushion! A trumpeting angel stands triumphant on top of the small black, white and gold organ. The high gilded stall of the *Mesa* and the gilt overdoors and windows are exceptionally lovely early baroque; one of the gold side altars is picked out with china red.

Near the station, on a piece of open ground, stands the very interesting chapel of Senhor das Barrocas, octagonal in form and recently restored. There is an extremely fine baroque doorway with a window above, surrounded by high-relief classical motifs and heroic size angels, one of which has quite disintegrated. Built between 1722 and 1732, the chapel is a perfect example of classical architecture with baroque decoration. The space in front is delightfully treated with a formal balustrade on which stand two great urns filled with stone foliage. Most of the decoration of the interior is rather later in date and has fine gilt carvings and two tempera panels by Pedro Alexandrino. The open-work ambones are agreeable, and the sacristy has a good painted panelled ceiling.

South of Aveiro, in the town of ILHAVO, an interesting museum exhibits different types of model ships, varieties of ropes and fishing gear, country clothes of various types, and sea pictures, as well as conchological collections. The whole place is charming and holds a pleasant mixture, like many such small country museums. The Parish Church contains two interesting polychrome bas-reliefs, not unlike those in Sta. Clara-a-Nova at Coimbra. There are also two remarkable locally-made statues in polychrome terracotta.

One and a half kilometres south of Ilhavo are the great porcelain works of VISTA ALEGRE, which still produce lovely things. The porcelain is of the same hard type as that produced by Berlin and many of the Belgian factories. The works were begun by José Ferreira Pinto Basto in 1824. When the factory was first founded the craft of packing very fragile china was not understood, so a team of camels was acquired which carried the china to Oporto and even as far as Lisbon; the cost of this strange method of transport must have been more than offset by its advertising value. The new museum, which is fascinating to all lovers of porcelain, contains examples of every different type the factory produced, also some exquisite Biscuit and glass. The entrance to the galleries is next the factory by the chapel of the original Pinto Basto quinta, built at the end of the 17th century. Inside there is the splendid tomb of the Bishop of Miranda, half lying down in his canonicals and mitre. The whole thing, in stone high-relief, is an extraordinary example of very late highly-decorated renaissance work.

. . . . . .

Above Aveiro an enormous lagoon and salt marshes, with curious little villages on the banks, stretch right up to Ovar; there is good shooting in these marshes. OVAR is a singular town, where the women still wear their black pork-pie hats and go bare-foot, and all the men are engaged in fishing. Even now the fishwives in Lisbon are called Varinhas, short for Ovarinhas. The large Parish Church, built on a slight eminence with a beautiful view, has good 18th-century boiseries and two Dom João V tables. In the town are two delightful fountains, of the Hospital and of Casal. There are various little chapels in the place, of which the most interesting are Graça with a painted ceiling, and that of S. Pedro do Calvario in the centre of the town at the top of a high staircase, which contains strange life-size 18th-century sculptures. All this marsh and coastal country is very beautiful, in a monotonous way—grey-green of reeds and water, grey-blue of horizon, seaward and shoreward alike; musical with water's varying sounds, and with the voices of water-birds, Lonely, largely inaccessible save by boat, it still keeps its profound and melancholy charm.

CHAPTER XIII

TRAS-OS-MONTES

THE province of TRAS-OS-MONTES, "beyond the mountains", is as romantic as its name. It projects in a blunt angle into Spain, so that the frontier bounds it on two sides; and in certain towns, like Montalegre and the utterly remote and lost Bragança and Miranda do Douro, a strongly Spanish feeling colours the architecture and the inhabitants. There is a sort of splendid savagery about the climate and the landscape—icy winds sweep in winter over the great rolling uplands; in summer the sun blazes down in intolerable heat and splendour on the endless leagues of barley, on the dessicated villages; the white dust of the roads puffs up through the windows and floor of the car, asphyxiating the motorist. All the same, the tourist who misses out Tras-os-Montes on his visit to Portugal misses one of the noblest bits of country in Europe.

Curiously enough, under the new alignment of the provinces of Portugal this superb district is made to extend south of the Douro, so that it includes the exquisite baroque town of LAMEGO. We use the words "baroque town" advisedly, for whole towns of faultless baroque houses or palaces are extremely rare—but Lamego is such a town.

The central square is laid out as a public garden surrounded by splendid buildings, their dark granite pediments, doorways and window-settings standing out against the prevailing white-washed surfaces. Conspicuous among these is the Bishop's palace, now the Museum, which has some lovely exhibits, in particular several very rich chapels which were removed bodily from the Chagas convent when it was pulled down some years ago. There are some exceedingly fine early polychrome sculptures, and two 14th-century statues of Our Lady of O, representing the Virgin big with child. (This is a favourite Portuguese "devotion"; the odd name comes, in part, from the seven antiphons in the Office of the days before Christmas, all of which begin with O.) The Museum contains a number of pictures, some good, more medium, and a lot of tapestries; of these some are exceptionally fine, though in poor condition. It is a curious fact that Portuguese museums and private houses are often rich in tapestries of all periods. Replicas of the famous Pastrana set depicting Portuguese triumphs in Africa in the 15th century can be seen in the Ministry of Finance in Lisbon.

The Cathedral, off the same square, was originally Romanesque—the lower part of the tower is all that is now left of this period. It has a fine Gothic façade, but otherwise was immensely altered in the 18th century by Nazzoni, who did so much work in Oporto; there is not now much of interest in it except the choir-stalls. The sacristy has two good Chippendale mirrors over the vestment chest and a long-case clock, which looks very English but was actually made in Lamego. Adjoining the Cathedral is a delightful renaissance cloister which contains some curious chapels, of which the most noteworthy is that of St. Anthony; on the side walls of this are two of the largest baroque frames that can ever have been made, surmounted by crowns, but they surround poor canvases.

N. S. de Almocave is a Romanesque church with a good exterior and interesting doors; inside it contains four panels of saints in the chancel, including one lovely picture of a martyr in red. In a chapel on the right of the nave is a fine retable.

On the way up to Chagas church, N. S. da Graça has some good statues in the first chapel on the right. The baroque reredos of the High Altar is most unusual, being pure white, like a wedding cake. The public garden outside this church, at the top of which stands Chagas, is surrounded by good palaces, with views of N. S. dos Remedios, the pilgrimage church just outside the town, at the top of its monumental staircase.

The convent of Chagas was pulled down several years ago, when the Lyceum School was built on the site. However, the church remains, with a fine sober side façade giving on the street, and four huge stone crosses outside. In the interior the great painted ceiling is reminiscent of that at the Misericordia at Soare, but is architectural, and much heavier, with many figures and a formal red cupola. There are lovely gilded retables in this church, particularly those on either side of the chancel. On each side of the High Altar are a delightful pair of Directoire tables, and by one a good Chippendale stool.

The 18th-century pilgrimage of N. S. dos Remedios stands in a park on a high wooded hill outside Lamego (*romaria* from

September 1st to 15th); an enormous granite and white-washed double staircase, with nine landings, leads up to the exquisitely beautiful circular courtyard outside it, which is surrounded by formal high granite pillars, obelisks and arches, some crowned with immense stone figures in Eastern hats and cloaks, or in classical draperies. Balustrades, set with spheres and vases, surrounded the stairways and terraces, and water trickles out of numberless fountains at each level. On the one immediately below this so-called Court of the Kings, outside the church, there is a lovely Palladian arch and a perfect formal fountain, with a merman on a dolphin's back, dated 1869, but which might well have been made a hundred years earlier; opposite is an octagonal pavilion with a chapel inside inscribed 1783, quite lovely in its marriage of granite facings and white walls. The church itself is disappointing; the façade is muddled and without form, and the interior without merit. The great beauty of the place lies in the architectural treatment of the huge staircase and the splendid woods that cover the hill.

A few miles south-east of Lamego, off the Moimenta da Beira road, lies the Cistercian Monastery of S. JOÃO DE TAROUCA, the first of this order to be built in Portugal, founded in 1124. It is chiefly remarkable because it contains a picture of S. Peter very like the famous one at Viseu, and discussion as to which is the more authentic is unceasing.

Close to Tarouca, down the valley of the river Varosa, stands the little town of UCANHA, which has a most unusual feature in its fortified bridge, almost the only one still existing in Portugal, over the river. The road across the bridge actually passes through an arch in the base of the massive square 14th-century tower protecting it.

.   .   .   .   .   .

Going north from Lamego the road drops down to the Douro, crosses it by the big modern bridge at REGUA, where the *País do Vinho* begins, and goes on northwards through Vila Real to Chaves, near the Spanish frontier. The great obstacle to visiting all this country is the paucity of hotels, and it is perhaps worth mentioning at once where the traveller can stay in even the most modest degree of comfort.

The Parque Hotel by the church of N. S. dos Remedios is good and the Estalagem de Lamego at Raposeira nearby is very comfortable. At Chaves the hotel is quite fair; and there are one or two good hotels at the spa of Vidago, south of Chaves, especially the Palace, first class, and the Golf; and at Pedras Salgadas farther south, there are the Avelames and the Pedras Salgadas.

There is the Estalagem do Caçador at Macedo de Cavaleiros, between Mirandela and Bragança and the superb *pousadas* of S. Bartolomeu at Bragança and Santa Caterina at Miranda do Douro. In addition to the hotels at Pedras Salgadas and Vidago, there are also comfortable quarters at the remote Pousada de S. Gonçalo, 15 kilometres west of Vila Real, in a superb situation on the southern slopes of the SERRA DO MARÃO—which like all these Government *pousadas* has good beds, boiling hot water, and perfectly adequate food. The one criticism to be made of it—and this applies to all of them, more or less—is the lack of accommodation for cars and chauffeurs. The Marão *pousada* is 15 kilometres from the nearest town, and lies at three thousand feet; it can accommodate twenty guests, but only has garage space for a few cars, and one room with beds in it as chauffeurs' accommodation. Foreigners *can* hardly tour Portugal otherwise than by car, at present, and a large number take a chauffeur along—to reach an inn nine miles from anywhere at the end of a long hard day, and be told that your car must stand out all night in the pouring rain, and that there is no room at all for your chauffeur, is discouraging, to say the least of it. It is greatly to be hoped that the Turismo Department, which has taken so much trouble, and with such success, to make these *pousadas* comfortable and pretty, will soon remedy this very practical defect. South of Murca, at Alijó in the port wine district, there is the excellent Pousada do Barão de Forrester, which is by far the most comfortable centre for exploring Bragança and the other remote towns of Tras-os-Montes.

VILA REAL, given a Royal Charter by D. Diniz, is a delightful town, with lovely 16th- and 17th-century houses and palaces. In February 1823 the Count of Amarante, who was in command of the troops stationed here, raised the cry of "Death to the Constitution; long live the Absolute King" which was the real start of the Miguelist War. The churches are exceptionally interesting, for this town is also a centre of Portuguese baroque.

The Cathedral of São Domingos in the main square is a lovely Gothic building with many later additions. The gold reredos of the

High Altar is really late renaissance, so architectural is it in feeling.
The Capela Nova or the Clerigos forms the angle between two streets and so is slightly fan-shaped; it has one of the most interesting and strangest baroque façades in the country, the doorway flanked by double pairs of immense granite columns; two Roman Emperor-like figures stand on the pediment, with a statue of St. Peter in the centre. The interior does not come up to the promise of the outside; the ceiling is groined, with painted bosses, and the walls are lined with blue azulejos. But the church of São Pedro, which has a poor, fussy façade and a pair of strange belfries with squat obelisks on top, possesses an exceptionally fine interior, with a painted box-panelled ceiling where the formal flowered pattern is repeated in each section; the chancel ceiling is also exceedingly rich in colouring. The gold woodwork is superb, especially that covering the front of the chancel arch, which is as fine as that in the Carmo church in Viseu.

The road on the left of São Pedro leads to the great terrace-like open space of the Terreiro do Calvario, from which there is a splendid view of the beautiful countryside round Vila Real; below, a strange, deserted, almost fortified-looking building stands in a forgotten, overgrown garden—this is all that remains of the Carmo church, with a porch on six tall slender octagonal granite columns. The church with no discoverable name which stands in the centre of the Terreiro has a blue-tiled façade, and across the sunken road which runs below the terrace stands the little chapel of St. Anthony, built in 1535, with 17th-century azulejos, and a delightful porch standing on twelve granite columns.

The Rua da Misericordia is a lovely long narrow road with 16th- and 17th-century houses above high granite walls on either side, leading to the hospital and church of the Misericordia, which are among the very few uninteresting ones in the country.

From the Bragança road there is a lovely backward view of Vila Real. A turning to the right after 3 kilometres leads to what must be one of the most extraordinary private houses in Europe, the Palace of MATEUS, built in the 18th century and belonging to the Conde de Vila Real. The visitor is usually allowed to see the outside of the house, which is near the road, and sometimes the interior. The main façade consists of a centre block ornamented with statuary and a great coat of arms, and two classical figures of heroic size standing on the balustraded pediment. A double staircase leads down from the main doorway on the first floor to a courtyard, on either side of which are side wings, decorated with high bulbous chimney-like finials at each corner. This courtyard is enclosed by a balustrade on which are poised yet more figures and vases. To the left of the Palace, set back, is the delightful rococo façade of the chapel. The interior of the house has some fine chestnut- and walnut-wood ceilings, carved doorways and swags, as well as some agreeable 17th-century still-life pictures. The inside of the chapel is disappointing, except for a lovely small statue of St. Anne, sitting in a high-backed Queen Anne chair! The garden façade is much plainer, and apparently earlier than the main front; it looks on to a knott garden.

The road past Mateus goes on to Sabrosa and CELEIROS where there is an exquisite early baroque chapel dedicated to St. Anthony, all of granite, with a most strange façade with high-relief floral carvings and a granite frill standing up from the pediment, with birds on vases at the corners and a group of the Crucifixion in the centre.

The main Bragança road runs on through rolling, bare, high arable land to MURÇA, a clean, rather suburban little town, which seems very unnatural in Tras-os-Montes; but it contains some extremely interesting things. The prehistoric Iron Age granite statue of the "Pig of Murça" stands on a plinth in the middle of a public garden; the trees are planted so close all round as to make it difficult to appreciate the extreme oddity of the sculpture.

The façade of the Parish Church is poor, but inside it has some good grey-blue azulejos in the chancel and two fine Primitive paintings of saints which are said to have been taken from the Misericordia. The very tiny baroque façade of this latter church, dated 1692, is quite lovely; it is on the main road, almost at the entrance of the town coming from Vila Real. The embossed carved green doorway is bordered by two pairs of salomonic granite columns, with grapes and vine leaves climbing up them in the manner of the boiseries of the period; above are three octagonal windows, and a delicious curlicue pediment with the Blessed Virgin in a niche, flanked by two smaller similar columns; a cross stands at the top, and at either corner is a vase with a great granite bird perching on it, not unlike those on St. Anthony's chapel at Celeiros. Inside, the little church is almost a ruin, but it still has some beautiful things in it. Above the pulpit is a carved dove representing the Holy Spirit, and there are wood and gesso stalls with roughly painted Franciscan saints in panels on the backs; a white-painted granite retable, so finely carved that it seems incredible that it is made of stone, surrounds the altar, deeply recessed beneath an arch, with steps up to it.

After Murça the really splendid country begins. The road climbs on to the shoulder of a great rolling serra, and for a long way runs at at least fifteen hundred feet; here the barley grows, and in autumn the pale stubble stretches for miles and miles; in each of the two or three solidly-built villages strung out along 30 kilometres of road, the rick-yards must cover a couple of acres. Chestnut trees grow in the hollows—being carefully replanted—and immense cherry trees, as much as thirty feet high, border the road itself here and there. And what vast sweeps of country!—and what colours! Everyone knows the exquisite tone of turf growing over chalk, but how few know the effect of stubble on the peculiar dusty gold of schist soil, with the dark shapes of chestnuts and cork oaks detaching themselves, as the French say, against it. The road by the way is first class, well engineered, and tarmaced all the way to Bragança.

MIRANDELA is exactly half-way between Vila Real and Bragança; it has a splendid mediaeval bridge of seventeen arches over the river Tua, and the town is so attractive, with the wide river valley, the open streets and lovely houses and churches, that it would be a very pleasant place in which to stay, and from which to explore those unknown and unvisited little towns of Tras-os-Montes which lie off the main roads. These include VILA FLOR, 25 kilometres south of Mirandela, which has a good 18th-century palace and a square renaissance fountain on Ionic columns.

In Mirandela, the superb 18th-century Palace of the Tavoras dominates the town, and is strangely Dutch in feeling, like the Queen's House at Kew translated into the granite and whitewash of northern Portugal. In the centre the great triple façade rises a storey higher than at the two sides; the elaborate pediments are decorated with coats of arms and flambeaux, and the window frames are particularly elegant. There is nothing of interest inside the palace, which has long been let out as a school and in private apartments.

The road on to Bragança continues over the high rolling arable of the Serra da Nogueira, with great mountains hull-down on the horizon, and the nearer slopes of the same dull dusty gold with great shapely dark trees. Curiously enough, though most of the road lies at about twelve hundred feet, there are a lot of willows on this stretch, and poplars too—beyond the village of Podence the astonished traveller comes on a huge avenue of lofty straggling poplars, stretching across the sunbaked uplands, which is pure Hobbema—Hobbema in Tras-os-Montes! And all along this route are little granite monuments enclosing shrines.

BRAGANÇA, where during the Peninsular War the 1808 Revolution against Junot started, is a smiling, gay town standing at over two thousand feet above sea level in richly cultivated country—very unlike the usual foreign conception of the place, as being surrounded by gloomy mountains and desolate scenery.

There are nine churches in Bragança, and the tourist should see them all; but here we only have space to describe the most important ones. The Sé or S. João Baptista, formerly a Jesuit church, has a good side door facing on to the main square of the town, Inside there is a beautiful Gothic fan-traceried roof, with red bosses to the groining. The double cloister at the side is typical and the sacristy should not be missed, as in it are two most splendid life-size polychrome statues of St. Ignatius and St. Francis Xavier, and the ceiling consists of 17th-century painted panels of the life of the former; though the painting is poor, the whole decorative effect is quite lovely.

The Misericordia nearby is one of the earliest in Portugal, having been founded in 1418. The hospital has now been moved but the old buildings are used as offices. In the church at the side there is an exceptionally fine faded gold renaissance four-storey retable, all in high-relief, with a polychrome group of Our Lady of Mercy and statues of the four Evangelists, the Crucifixion above, yet higher the Holy Women at the Tomb, and over all, God the Father in splendour.

The Largo de Sepulveda is surrounded by lovely buildings, one of which is the town prison where you can talk to the men through the bars and give them cigarettes or alms as they work in their carpenters' shop. At right angles is an arcaded yellow palace, now the military prison, and opposite there is the fine plain renaissance façade of the church of S. Vicente, where tradition says that D. Pedro the Cruel clandestinely married Inez de Castro. Inside there is an astonishing ceiling, dated 1886, with country-carved figures of the four Evangelists in high-relief at each corner, and the risen

VILA REAL: FAÇADE OF THE CAPELA NOVA OR THE CLERIGOS

SERRA DO MARÃO; GOVERNMENT "POUSADA" OR INN

BRAGANÇA: THE CASTLE

BRAGANÇA: DANCE OF THE PAULITEIROS

Christ with two soldiers in the centre. All these figures are very vivid, and show how the vitality of art in the country districts of Portugal went on far longer than in the more central parts of Europe. There are good gold boiseries on red ground-work in the chancel, and four tall narrow painted panels of the life of Christ.

The Rua Serpa Pinto, with lovely houses on either side, leads up in a series of broad shallow steps from S. Vicente to the Castle, but on the way one should visit the Museum, which is small but well arranged. Out in the garden there is another granite boar, rather smaller than that at Murça, and upstairs there is a very fine 14th-century polychrome statue of the Blessed Virgin, from the church of S. Vicente.

The church of S. Bento, not far from the Museum, was built in 1590, and has a very pure and perfect renaissance granite doorway with the saint in a niche above and a coat of arms at the side. Inside, the barrel ceiling, dated 1763, is quite exceptionally beautiful, being painted all over in a very wild and Italianate manner, with classical and architectural features in sombrely brilliant colours. The High Altar has a delightful gold rococo retable, with black-cloaked cherubs climbing around. The chancel arch is painted in the same style as the ceiling, and the church contains some very fine poly-chrome statues and good 17th-century panels.

The splendid mediaeval citadel of Bragança, with encircling walls and a keep over a hundred feet high, has not been over-restored; its outer buildings are used as barracks, and the great "campo" as a parade-ground. The whole group dominates the town. In a small public garden stands yet a third of those granite effigies of boars—the shaft of the mediaeval pillory has been driven right through its body, and in the upper part of the snout a deep round hole has been hollowed out. This is peculiarly interesting, since in Scotland and Ireland, in early times, the boar was a symbol of Kingship, and was associated with the annointing ceremonies of Kings—at Dunadd in Argyll, close to the famous boar carved in the living rock, is a bowl hollowed out for the anointing oil; it seems possible that in the Bragança boar this bowl was inserted into the figure of the pig itself. On the farther side of the castle church stands the famous 12th-century Town Hall, one of the very few Romanesque civic buildings still in existence; it is massively built over a huge water cistern, is roofed, and lit by small unglazed round arches all round, below which runs a stone bench; a city father is supposed to have sat under each window.

The church of S. Maria do Castelo, beside this extraordinary town hall, has a good baroque façade, but inside is by far the best painted ceiling of any of the churches in Bragança, which may be said to specialize in fine painted ceilings; it consists of a formal treatment of the Assumption of the Blessed Virgin, in all colours, on a partly diapered ground. In a side chapel to the left there is a reredos signed and dated 1657, with three agreeable painted panels enclosed within gilt columns, and at the top, a panel of a red-cloaked saint. Below the keep there is a regular village enclosed within the original outer walls, as at Lisbon and Penamacor.

In this part of Tras-os-Montes there are very distinctive local folk-dances, particularly the Dança dos Pauliteiros which is a stick dance performed by men dressed as women.

During the Inquisition many Jews moved into the wild country round Bragança, and their descendants still remain in remote villages, and continue to practise their Jewish rites. The whole country hereabout is full of strange aspects, which have been fully treated in the great archaeological and historical work, in eleven volumes, written by the late parish priest of the village of BAÇAL, about 5 kilometres from Bragança, who made it his life's work to assemble information about the district—he is justly and gratefully renowned among historians as the Abade de Baçal.

A road leads south-east from Bragança to the extraordinary town of Miranda do Douro, which has a special dialect. On the way the fortified town of OUTEIRO is passed; here the church of Santo Cristo, dated 1698, has an unusual façade with two towers, and gold wood retables inside. About 25 kilometres on, the road reaches VIMIOSO, containing many early houses with coats of arms on their façades, and about 12 kilometres to the south-west stands the great castle of CAMPO DE VIBORAS, from which there is a marvellous view.

It was near Miranda do Douro, which is on the Spanish frontier, that the Marquis of Sarria with Spanish soldiers entered Tras-os-Montes on May 5th, 1762. He declared that he had come to deliver Portugal from the English yoke, and first laid siege to Miranda: later, with little opposition, he captured Bragança and Moncorvo, while the Spanish General O'Reilly marched into Chaves and actually threatened Oporto. But the Portuguese peasants, who always hated the Spaniards, defended themselves rather as the Home Guard might have done in a later war, and repelled the Spanish forces attempting to cross the Douro near Torre de Moncorvo, and held a mountain pass against them at Montalegre. During this extraordinary war the Count Schaumburg-Lippe (whose superb portrait by Reynolds was in the exhibition of the Royal pictures at Burlington House in 1946–47) was nominated Commander-in-Chief of the Anglo-Portuguese forces, as he had been born in England and had served as a young man in the Guards. His soldiers marched north from Lisbon to Abrantes, and in September they routed a Spanish force, which was advancing on Castelo Branco, near Almeida. At the end of the year a treaty was signed, under which all Portuguese territory was evacuated by the Spaniards; it must have been one of the shortest and least sanguinary wars in history. Lippe remained for two more years in Portugal, planning frontier fortifications and re-organising the army.

MIRANDA DO DOURO, set on a high upland, with its splendid renaissance cathedral built by Diogo de Torralva, the Tomar architect, standing up from the town in the distance, is actually perched on the extreme edge of a ravine, overlooking the great gorge across which Wellington is said to have been slung in a basket during the Peninsular War. The town is filled with palaces and houses in a state of disintegration, and has a ruined castle. In the Castanilla (a purely Spanish name) almost all the houses are 16th-century.

South-west of Miranda there is a part of Portugal which may be said to be completely unknown to the tourist. There are no railway lines, the distances are great, and only in the last few years have the minor roads been made fit for cars. A road from Miranda through MOGADOURO goes to ALFÂNDEGA DA FE, and then south-west to TORRE DE MONCORVO, a little town on a hill surrounded by orchards, with two good renaissance churches: the Misericordia has a 16th-century choir, and in the parish church there is a carved wood Gothic triptych of the life of St. Anne. The town with its narrow streets has a number of early escutcheoned houses.

A poor road goes to FREIXO DE ESPADA A CINTA, very near the Spanish frontier, where there is a renaissance Misericordia and the parish church contains a number of 16th-century painted panels. A museum has recently been opened in this remote town. About 35 kilometres south there is another interesting frontier town, FIGUEIRA DE CASTELO RODRIGO. Here one of the churches has a most peculiar arch built entirely of S-shaped stones fitting into one another, with no key-stone. A mile outside to the south-west are the remains of the Cistercian convent of Santa Maria de Aguiar, with a large cruciform three-naved Gothic church containing early 18th-century carved wood stalls, and a chapter-house with a very fine vaulted roof. Actually for visiting this southern part of Tras-os-Montes, Guarda, only about 60 kilometres from Figueira de Castelo Rodrigo, is the best centre.

* * * * * *

Almost the climax of a visit to Tras-os-Montes is the drive from Bragança to Chaves, about 90 kilometres. The road, though extremely curly, is quite good, but it is rough in places, and the summer dust is terrific. For the first part it runs through the sweetest country, for all it lies so high—green pastures with cattle and horses grazing, groves of huge chestnuts, slopes clothed with oaks and hornbeams, and now and again one of those severe villages, built of vast granite blocks; the oxen wear fox-skins, rather like hats, across their foreheads to keep off the flies, and men on horseback, flourishing long staves, gallop along the white dusty tracks.

About 30 kilometres from Bragança is that shattering place VINHAIS, to which little attention is paid in the guide-books, but which is one of the splendours of Portugal. Below the road, at the bottom of a flight of monumental steps, is a huge baroque façade with not one but *two* churches embedded in it—this is the enormous convent of S. Francisco, now the Seminary of the diocese of Bragança. In the upper church, of the Third Order, is probably the finest painted ceiling in Portugal, faultlessly executed with architectural features, flowers and urns, in delicate colours on a creamy ground—very unusual. There are also lovely gilded altars, and such a wealth of first-class polychrome statues as can hardly be credited. The lower, or convent church, also has a beautiful ceiling, and splendid boiseries marbled in blue, cream and gold, extraordinary altars with relics behind glass, and if possible even more and finer polychrome statues—a group of St. Anne and Our Lady to the left of the chancel is particularly lovely. On the right is a most unusual blue and gold relic cupboard like a dove-cote, with a myriad of little glass-fronted pigeon holes, and above the High Altar there is an enormous group of statues depicting the Annunciation. The Blessed Virgin looks up at the Archangel Gabriel who is suspended on wires from the ceiling, and the Holy Spirit is an immense glory is above them both. The choir-stalls are good, but the sacristy is really wonderful, with huge vestment chests with carved red and gold backs which curve upwards and inwards meeting the lines of the barrel ceiling. What is so astonishing, and so satisfying, about Vinhais is that all this unparalleled wealth and splendour of beautiful things, being church property and still in use, is quite untouched and unaltered.

The village has three pensions and would be worth exploring with care. Lovely little houses line the street, and it is set in most beautiful country. About 4 kilometres away at CASTRO DE AVELAR there are the interesting remains of a Romanesque church, with brick arcades outside, unique in Portugal, though there are various examples of this particular Mozarabic style in Spain.

The drive beyond Vinhais is incredible. The road climbs to the watershed, and runs along it—to the right one looks across to the mountains of Spain, to the left over the mountains of Portugal; straight ahead, where the road runs south, the Serra da Estrêla looms up end on, 100 kilometres away, a great blunt blue mass. The road is at over two thousand feet on this stretch, and the country is open and very bare; generally there is a great wind blowing, and for a mile or more behind him the motorist can see his dust streaming away over the brown slopes in the sunset light. One of the great drives of the world.

CHAVES lies within seven miles of the Spanish frontier. The Romans fortified it, as well as building the splendid sixteen-arched bridge which still carries 20th-century traffic over the river; then, and all down the centuries, through Muslim wars and Spanish wars, right to the Peninsular War, it was regarded as the key to Portugal in the north—hence its name. Being so near the frontier it was a great meeting-place for embassages between the two countries, and many royal weddings took place there; now, less exciting, it thrives on a spa with hot springs. There is an estalagem and an hotel.

The castle, which stands at the top of the town, is not over-restored; there are also the remains of Vauban-esque fortifications. The Praça de Camões, below the castle, has at one end the parish church, originally Romanesque, but with renaissance and later additions; the exterior has been so over-restored that little of interest is left, but inside there are three fine naves with rounded arches. The best thing in the church, however, is the rococo organ, marbled in green and gold, with angels standing on the top above a lovely balustrade of painted wood, the whole thing supported by two great malformed gold dwarfs with huge heads, and an immense mask between them.

At right angles is the Misericordia, with a very peculiar façade of two storeys over the narthex, divided by salomonic colums with masked capitals and a pediment, and verandahs under the eaves. Inside are some of the most extraordinary azulejos in Portugal—a set of huge panels of blue and white tiles depicting scenes from the New Testament reach right up to the high painted ceiling, which is dated 1743, and decorated with formal motifs and armillary spheres round a very fine central panel of the Virgin and St. Elizabeth.

At the other end of the square beyond some charming houses with delightful doorways, and the unusual architectural detail of the balcony and verandah being on the *top* floor, is the tiny chapel of Santa Cabeça, with a very chaste and restrained granite façade: the key can be obtained at the house next door, but it will not turn the lock without the application of oil! Inside the panelled ceiling is of gold surrounded by black and pink motifs. The very rich golden retable has lovely small standing angels on either side, and at the back of the altar there are three most unusual Chinese panels, on black grounds; one is of a tiny, vividly-painted, madly-galloping gold horse and rider.

Across the Roman bridge the octagonal church of St. John of God, up a turning to the left, has two huge granite angels draped along the pediment, with an architectural monstrance in the centre; but the road in front of the church is so narrow that it is difficult to see this strange 18th-century conceit. As in so many octagonal churches, the architect does not seem to have known what to do with the interior after completing the good dome; but there are a pair of pleasing ambones.

Just over the Tamega, on the castle side of the river, a straight road through the valley leads to Outeiro Seco and in about 5 kilometres passes on the right the very perfect little Romanesque church of SENHORA DA AZINHEIRA, which has been modestly and well restored. The key can be obtained from a cottage some distance up the road. The exterior has curious corbels with carved heads and there are some early tombs outside the church; on the interior walls are the best series of 16th-century frescoes remaining in Portugal— some of them are dated 1533. A huge figure of St. Christopher can be made out on one wall; the Blessed Virgin with saints, some of whose faces are superbly painted, the Last Supper and a Doom, as well as the Crucifixion and the Entombment are still faintly to be seen.

About 3 kilometres to the north-west of Chaves, near ABOBE-LEIRA, there is a great rock at OUTEIRO MACHADO covered with extraordinary prehistoric carvings.

From Chaves a picturesque road to the south-west leads back in about 66 kilometres to Vila Real. It goes through VIDAGO, the well-known spa whose good hotels have already been referred to; PEDRAS SALGADAS, a somewhat similar spa, and VILA POUCA DE AGUIAR. Beyond RIBEIRA DE PENA, 19 kilometres west of Vila Pouca, there are groups of famous dolmens and neolithic tombs. Off the road from Vila Pouca to Valpaços there is a forestry track to the village of TRES MINAS, which possesses the remains of Roman gold workings, said to be the largest left in Europe, as well as a more modern gold mine which is still worked. Near SERVA there is a Roman castle on top of a hill, surrounded by stepped fortifications. The castle of Aguiar, outside the town, is also most curiously poised —flower-like—on a vast rock.

From Chaves westward to Braga and Oporto is also a splendid drive. The road again climbs up on to high ground, and runs along close to the Spanish frontier, first through groves of immense chestnuts, with again the unusual spectacle of green pastures and grazing oxen; later the land becomes more bare and appears to grow mainly potatoes. A by-road to the right leads out to Montalegre, practically on the frontier, over great bare tracts of heath with huge mountains ahead. Oddly enough this piece of country is much walled, and very peculiar the walls are, dry-built of upright granite slabs twenty inches across, with smaller slabs of schist piled on a slant between them, so that the effect is of shallow looped curtains; also the contrast between the silvery granite and the rusty gold of the schist makes them very decorative. All this is what the late Rodney Gallop calls "the Portuguese Andorra", the TERRAS DE BARROSO, in his "Portugal, a Book of Folk Ways". But even since he wrote, the daily costumes of the people have deteriorated—one now sees none of the knotted kerchiefs on the men's heads, etc., which he describes.

MONTALEGRE is a tiny hill-town, standing high, and dominated by a very splendid late mediaeval castle, with an almost circular outer wall—it has, alas, been heavily restored, and its wild splendour and ruinous grace, with antirrhinums crowning the machicolated battlements and shrubs pushing out between the masonry are all gone. The hot little streets of primitive houses are full of eager and friendly people, who hover round the traveller—about once in six weeks, they tell you, strangers come to Montalegre. Behind the castle with its four great towers stands the granite parish church, looking like a house, since the windows are rectangular with square panes of glass, and the belfry is hidden. The Misericordia, right in the village, has an extraordinary country-made gilt triple reredos surrounded with a perfect riot of plain grey salomonic columns bound with acanthus leaves.

One has to return from Montalegre to the main road by the way one came; still going westward is a superb stretch—actually one of the few really frightening roads in Portugal—as it winds along very precipitous slopes above the upper waters of the Cavado; across the deep-cut valley for miles and miles, one is as it were accompanied by the terrific presence of the SERRA DO GEREZ, a tossing wilderness of grey granite peaks. In the glens hereabouts are silver birches, but with larger and darker leaves than those of Britain—and near a drinking-trough the exquisite fragile pale blue *Wahlenbergia* grows in the ditch. Then, quite without warning, only dropping a few hundred feet, suddenly one finds oneself in another world—all green and *riant*, with vines climbing up the trees and covering great trellises, and the maize tall and full in the ear—the Minho.

CHAPTER XIV

NORTH OF OPORTO: THE MINHO

ETWEEN Oporto and the Spanish frontier, the country is full of interesting and beautiful towns and is remarkably rich in remote, usually deserted conventual buildings, often containing superb baroque and rococo work, with large numbers of Romanesque churches, and many splendid country-houses set in formal gardens. Braga, which has excellent hotels, particularly the Parque, the Elevador and the Sul-Americano, at the summit of the pilgrimage hill of Bom Jesus, about 5 kilometres from the town, is the best centre for exploring this stretch of Portugal by car, though there are clean pensions in most of the little towns, which are linked by country buses.

The great Benedictine monastery, now an agricultural college, in the centre of SANTO TIRSO has one of the most superb baroque façades in Portugal. The single row of nine windows in sets of three occupies three-quarters of the total height of the frontage. Underneath is a wide bed of huge hydrangea bushes, a lovely composition of blue with the granite and white above; there is a raised pediment in the centre and a floridly elegant doorway with a high exotic superstructure at one end. The cloister of the adjoining church is lovely; pointed arches on slender twin columns, with most interesting carved capitals and in the centre a vase-like renaissance fountain adorned with pelicans. The church and cloister are difficult to get into, but the key can be obtained by the porter from the priest's servant upstairs if sufficient persistence is shown. The church is exceptionally large, lofty and splendid; though, like so much else, it has undergone restoration. There are superb black and gold sanctuary lamps and the rococo gold garnitures to the chancel arch and all the windows are quite lovely; the ambones should be noticed, in blue and gold with exquisite fluid gold figures standing on the sounding-boards.

The road over the river Ave, where little boats can be hired for parties of pleasure, leads to VILA NOVA DE FAMALICÃO which is not an attractive town; but the curious abbey church of S. Tiago

223

de Antas, which stands on a hill outside it, up a turning off the Santo Tirso road, is of the early transition period from Romanesque to Gothic, and is unusually large for a Romanesque church in the Peninsula. The apse retains the original structure, but with square renaissance windows inserted. The North and West doors are both pointed; an unusual feature of the former is that it has pilasters, not pillars, and the inner faces of the capitals are carved. The West door of four courses has no carving except on the capitals—there is a primitive and amusing version of a rose-window over it, six cusps round a pierced central stone, surrounded by three bands of plain moulding. Within, though the chancel arch is pointed, the nave windows are round-headed with deep splays. The rose-pink azulejos in the chancel, so frequently reported in guide-books, do not exist, and apparently never have, the chancel being lined with quite ordinary yellow, blue and white patterned tiles. But there are four very fine late painted panels in rococo frames in the chancel where the window embrasures are decorated with formal gold patterns, as is the caissoned roof.

To reach the tiny Romanesque church of SANTA EULALIA near the hamlet of Arnoso, take a turning to the left off the Famalicão–Braga road marked "Arnoso 1 km." — "Villa d'Este 4 kms.", a little past Cruz and before the village of Tebosa. The road beyond Arnoso is very rough, little more than a track, but a plucky car can take it slowly as far as a hamlet below the church of Santo Amaro; from here children will lead the visitor down by a footpath through vineyards and scrub in about seven minutes to the church, which is at the bottom of a valley, and will also bring the key.

It is a typical small 12th-century Romanesque building in very fair preservation, and almost as lost and entangled in briars and bushes as the Sleeping Beauty's castle. Outside are two large granite coffins, shaped to the human body, with granite lids beside them. The East end has a minute lancet window under a small round-headed two-pillared arch. There are typical doors in the North and South sides. The West door has very rich and characteristic carvings of animals and the outer moulding has typical Celtic interlaced ornament; there is a pierced circular window in the tympanum over the door, and also over the South door—the latter restored. All along the South side, under the eaves, runs a band of triply-grooved dog-tooth moulding, and there are carved grotesques and billets under the corbels all round the church, and unusual figures on two of the capitals of the South door.

The interior of the chancel is charming, with four shallow recessed arches supported on small pillars; the East window has, within as without, two tiny pillars supporting the arch. There is a great sense of simplicity and purity about the whole building—the architect's conception was, one feels, as pure as water. In the nave are four larger arches recessed into the North and South walls; there are traces of frescoes on each side of the chancel arch and the consecration crosses can still be seen. The little church has been restored; the retables of three altars have—quite rightly in this case —been removed; the roof of the apse is new, and much of the outer walls also. There are two stones with inscriptions inside the church, and one outside—a man from the village, who seemed to be more or less in charge, said that there had been a second inscription in the outer wall, but search failed to find it—the children said the restoring workmen had built it into the wall again back to front!

.   .   .   .

Between Santo Tirso and Guimarães, a road turns off to the right to Caldas de Vizela, from which a secondary road goes to Felgueiras through most beautiful country above the Vizela valley. Just before Felgueiras is reached, a turning to the left leads to the great Benedictine convent of POMBEIRO at the bottom of a valley. The three-naved Romanesque church has been greatly added to during the centuries, but the façade has a fine transition doorway and a rose window set between two 18th-century towers with square spires. The oldest part of the church is the East end where the two apses on either side of the square chancel are unaltered. The interior contains splendid rococo woodwork and there is a renaissance cloister. The azulejos panels are unusual in representing the story of Noah and the Flood.

Near Negrelos, the monastery of RORIZ has a much-restored romanesque church with a separate bell tower.

.   .   .   .   .   .

The original 12th-century capital of Portugal, GUIMARÃES, is a neat, pretty town, now the centre of the linen trade of the country. The city slopes up to a grassy hill crowned with the 12th-century nine-towered crenellated castle; at the foot of this hill stands the piteously rebuilt palace of the Dukes of Bragança, built round a large square courtyard. It is now a museum with lovely furniture, porcelain and 15th- and 16th-century Portuguese primitives and a set of fine modern copies of the famous Pastrana tapestries in Madrid. A suite is kept for the use of the Portuguese President, and the palace is used for official government entertainments.

Half-way up the grassy mound on which the castle stands is the touching little Romanesque church of S. Miguel do Castelo, in which D. Afonso Henriques, the first king of Portugal, was baptised. This was always a chapel royal, what in England is called a "peculiar"; that is to say, exempt from the ordinary diocesan administration and directly subject to Rome. And even today this parish remains in fact and in law, on a different basis from others.

Guimarães has two museums. The Museu Martins Sarmento, housed in the old Dominican convent in the Rua de Paio Galvão, contains the prehistoric and early finds of the district, in particular those from the Citânias of Briteiros and Sabroso, including the famous Pedra Formosa from Briteiros, and the carved granite doorway from Sabrosos. It is overcrowded, but as well arranged as space permits, and carefully catalogued. It takes its name from the local archaeologist who in the late 19th and early 20th century devoted his whole life and fortune to excavating the Citânia de Briteiros. The other museum is in the small cloister and annexes of the Colegio church of N. S. da Oliveira; it contains some magnificent examples of polychrome sculpture and early paintings and is exquisitely housed in the pretty cloister and adjoining rooms.

This church, on the way up to the castle, is in a lovely extremely early square with Gothic and Manueline palaces, the upper side closed by the arcaded building of the old Town Hall; one can drive right through the arches to emerge into the space on the far side. With the façade of the Colegio these buildings make this square a highly picturesque Gothic ensemble. N. S. da Oliveira was originally an abbey founded in the 10th century; the church was rebuilt by D. João I in commemoration of the victory of Aljubarrota, under the direction of the Toledan architect, Juan Garcia. There is a charming open-sided small Gothic shrine outside the church, which was built in 1342 to commemorate the legend of Wanda, King of the Goths, who consented to his election only if the olive branch which he was carrying put forth leaves when stuck in the ground; it did so on this site.

In the interior of the church there is a wonderful late renaissance silver tabernacle with salomonic columns. The altar front is of repoussé silver on red velvet, in the same photograph-frame style as the two tombs at Lorvão, and the chancel has a lovely baroque vaulted roof, box-panelled, painted in grisaille, with the windows surrounded by similar decoration. The backs to the choir stalls are pure Regency with red damask between pilasters of gilt wood; above are two balconies with swags of musical instruments and there are a pair of huge painted panels of Saints. Indeed, the whole decoration is exuberantly Regency, even to the amusing ambones with white and gilt banisters to their curly stairs, and round gilt canopies above on which eagles stand; and the astonishing number of crystal chandeliers hanging in every part, no less than eighteen *good* ones. At the Feast of the Assumption a ravishing statue of Our Lady, which stands in the church, is carried in procession; she wears the richest possible cloth-of-gold robe and mantle with lace ruffles at the neck and wrists, and a superb silver crown.

The church of S. Francisco, with its original Gothic doorway, stands at right angles to a delightful palace covered with deep powder-blue tiles with rococo granite windows and doors. Entrance to S. Francisco can be obtained through this building. The church has been very thoroughly restored, after some years of semi-abandonment, so now at last the sky no longer shows through the lovely, exceedingly wide, painted grisaille barrel roof. There is a marvellous gold retable to the High Altar with three salomonic columns on either side, and the chapel to the right of the chancel has a polychrome set piece of the Blessed Virgin, St. Anne and the Holy Child. In a chapel in the right transept there is a holy Dolls House at the back of the altar, which is quite entrancing; it was obviously made with great care and love by some kindly parishioner about a hundred years ago. The miniature glass-fronted room contains a black cassocked figure seated at a table in what must be the study; there are books scattered about, a Cardinal's Hat hanging up, tiny chairs are placed on either side of the fireplace, coffee cups and a jug are on a little tripod table, two cats are sitting on the floor, and there is a wealth of amusing detail, including a variety of household utensils! In this church are also two beautiful black and gold ambones, and a lovely light lantern in the transept roof, surrounded by splendid rococo swags topping the chancel and transept arches; in fact this interior is perhaps the most lovely mixture of the rococo and the classical to be found in the north of Portugal.

In the ante-room to the sacristy stands an altar with a very fine high-relief of St. Francis, black and gold on a polychrome ground; below are the Moroccan Martyrs, tiny figures of Moors killing tiny Franciscans, also in black and gold robes. The sacristy has a magnificent ceiling of formal painted panels between richly gilt ribs; there are pleasant pictures and four Sheraton mirrors above the vestment chests; and the Easter Sepulchre, with the Franciscan arms on it and gold gesso curtains held up by angels should be noticed, though the fine furniture which was said to be in this sacristy is no longer there.

Not far from S. Francisco the church of Senhor dos Passos stands on a terrace at the end of a public garden. Its semi-circular, tall, narrow, rococo façade with high belfries must be one of the most curious in the country, with granite figures, blue and white tiles, and a balcony above the doorway. The interior is poor, as if the invention of the architect had been exhausted by the extraordinary exterior.

At S. TORCATO, 6 kilometres to the north-east of Guimarães, up the road to the right of the castle, there is a big modern church to which a pilgrimage is made on the first Sunday in July, and above it is S. Agostinho, a Romanesque 12th-century church with a cloister. The road finally crosses the river Ave and rises to the village of TAIDE, where the astonishing shrine of N. S. DO PORTO DE AVE is more remarkable for its setting than for the church itself. Both above and below the road there extends a vast series of granite stairways, broken by terraces, with balustrades of that splendid combination of white-washed plaster and granite, the parapets set with huge granite flambeaux—with fountains, with trees, with statues, with gardens, with running water, all enhancing and enhanced by the architectural formality. At the bottom of this sequence of terraces is the church, with an octagonal chancel. The ceiling of the nave is charming, with very large shallow box-panels—the ribs white and gold, the panels in a design of white and gold on a soft dull green. There are twin organs in red and gold supported by mermen and centaurs, and twin pulpits. In the octagon itself the doors, the chapels and the windows are as it were trimmed most richly with red marble, and blue, gold and green paint—the pilasters of granite are painted in a curious Chinesey design in green and buff. The sacristy has a good painted ceiling, a pair of delightful mirrors and exceptionally lovely vestment chests. This place is the scene of an enormous *romaria* from the 5th to the 8th of September.

Not far away is FONT' ARCADA, a deeply interesting Romanesque church. There is a fine bas-relief with a tympanum showing the Pascal lamb surmounted by a Maltese cross, as at Ceido Feita. In the interior are traces of 16th-century decoration.

.　　.　　.　　.　　.　　.

Some miles out of Braga on the Braga – Amares – Caldas do Gerez road is the extraordinary Cistercian Convent and church of BOURO, part granite, part plaster, and all falling to pieces. In niches on the faded pink and white 17th-century façade stand five life-size statues of the Kings of Portugal in fancy dress, between a row of balconied windows on the top floor; over the door are a group of the Holy Family in Shakespearian costume, all holding hands. The entrance is through a vast *porte cochère* at the bottom of the ruined granite staircase which leads up to the great church set at right angles to the King-adorned façade. Out at the back is a great range of former store-rooms, over a hundred yards long, ending in a roofless kitchen with the usual huge marble table, granite sinks and ovens, and a large open chimney like the one at Alcobaça, but smaller. The refectory next door is also roofless, and the weather is ruining the frescoes. Close by is a very large one-storey cloister, with round arches and slender granite pillars, and four square granite seats with curved sides surrounding four raised flower-beds with lemon trees; there is also one set of lovely carved doors. A gushing stream runs through to a mill behind. Leading off the cloister is a charming chapter house, with two pointed arches springing from single pillars and a painted glory on the wall above the Abbot's vacant place; the plaster all round the lower part of the walls shows where the azulejos have been torn off.

This splendid place was bought some years ago by a man from Oporto for £130. It was he who unroofed the kitchen and refectory to sell the lead and also removed two tons of ironwork.

The large church itself, used as the parish church, has a shallow vaulted dome and a grey-blue roof with large pink and gold bosses and very rich gilt, red and green decorations with armorial details round the chancel and the transept arches; the latter are very wide and shallow, giving a great effect of lightness. The backs of the choir-stalls consist of twelve gilt and white panels in high relief, gesso on wood, of the life of St. Bernard, with most elegant double pilasters between them. On one side is an exquisite gallery and a number of 18th-century canvases in gold frames hang almost as high as the roof.

The SERRA DO GEREZ on whose southern slopes lies Bouro is an extraordinary mountain range, with magnificent scenery. There are three routes from Braga to Caldas do Gerez, the loveliest being by PINHEIRO. One road goes by Bouro from where a road leads up into the mountains to the sanctuary of N. S. DA ABADIA, where there is a *romaria* from the 10th to the 15th August.

GEREZ is one of the many spas of Portugal. There are several good hotels and the waters are said to be four times stronger than those of Karlsbad. The mountains around can be visited with a guide and there are many foresters' houses which have telephones to help those who get lost. All round here there are great waterfalls, which sometimes, but not always, dry up in the summer.

.   .   .   .   .   .

BRAGA, with a good hotel, the Francfort, is an unexpectedly large town, with buses, whose streets are lined with flowering standard hibiscus in all shades of white, red and purple, which make the late summer scene particularly enchanting. The Goths are known to have been in Braga in 585 and the Moors destroyed the town in 716. In 1040 it was taken by Ferdinand I of Castile, eighteen years before Coimbra fell, when the Bishopric was restored. Braga is one of the few dioceses remaining in the Roman church which has its own liturgy, the Council of Trent having ordered that only those Rites should be retained which were then over two hundred years old. Thus, the Milanese, the Lyons, and the Dominican Rites all remain, and are different, some in greater, some in lesser degree from the Roman. In Braga the difference is only slight; during Mass the priest makes double genuflections and stands aside to show the Sacred Species to the congregation, but it chiefly differs in the arrangement of the Breviary or Liturgical Office. During Holy Week Braga is the scene of great religious processions through the streets, on the lines

BREJOEIRA, NEAR MONÇÃO: THE LAST OF THE GREAT COUNTRY HOUSES TO BE BUILT IN PORTUGAL

GUIMARÃES: TOWN HOUSE

BRAGA: TYPICAL STREET

of the more famous ones at Seville, and on St. John's day, June 24th, there is the unique procession when King David dances in the streets surrounded by his courtiers. The part of the King is always taken by a member of the same family, as it is a hereditary privilege.

The ecclesiastical splendour of the town is largely due to Archbishop Diogo de Sousa, who during his episcopate from 1508 to 1532 built numbers of renaissance and early baroque edifices, and this rebuilding continued under successive prelates, so that the town is one of the great centres of ecclesiastical architecture in Portugal. The façade to every church is granite: Romanesque, renaissance or such florid baroque that the stone is worked to look like gesso; and the whole city, like S. Gimignano, gives the impression of a mass of towers—for almost every church, and they are legion, has two high belfries.

The Sé or Cathedral is the most famous, though it has undergone countless restorations. The original edifice belongs to the 11th and 12th centuries. The exterior is really the more interesting, since the main bulk of the large building is pure Romanesque, with Gothic additions at both East and West ends—there is, however, a most beautiful Romanesque South door. The narthex at the West end is very rich, with graceful delicate clustered pillars, bold groining and a carved balustrade on the façade with six saints in Gothic niches, still bearing traces of colour. The doorway under the groined roof is *just* pointed, but the two courses of carving round it are purely Romanesque in feeling, with the usual strap-work design on the outer course. The space round this early doorway has been filled in with a very late screen, really Perpendicular. The East end is even more curious since it is practically flamboyant—almost the only example of this style in Portugal; the flame-shaped tracery of the balustrade might almost be on the Cathedral at Vendome or the Butter Tower in Rouen. Most unusual also are the slender pinnacles tied to the walls by frail curved buttresses barely three feet long.

The North side of the Sé has been much restored and several encroaching buildings removed, giving a clear view of the edifice. There is a small ecclesiastical museum in an upper gallery reached from the cloister, which is worth seeing. At the east end of the building is a curious tiny semi-circular chapel, a round arch supported on two pillars with carved capitals, admitting to a tiny domed structure with old frescoes. At the west end of this part, an archway leads into a renaissance cloister near the belfry, with several curious chapels including a very odd polychrome relief of Heaven and Hell, and a beautiful Pietá on the east side. On the same side, behind a grille which it is very hard to get opened, is the early Gothic chapel of S. Lourenço, with a most lovely doorway, a pure graceful groined and vaulted roof, and some early tombs.

Inside the Sé almost the only pure Romanesque features left are the pillars supporting the transept arches—the chancel arch itself is of course Gothic, like the chancel. All the chapels in the transepts have been converted to rather insipid renaissance, with flat pilasters, etc. Above the North altar is a quite lovely 14th-century Our Lady; the stone altar front is also very fine, carved in the late 15th century by Basque artists. The West end of the interior is one vast mass of rococo covering everything, almost Spanish in its dark richness; there are a pair of huge organs with a conglomeration of figures, tritons, mermen and dolphins, patches of painted ceiling, a very rich carved and gilt *Coro Alto*, with choir-stalls supported by *very* female caryatides; and the lantern above the *Coro Alto to* is also a surge of gilding.

On August 6th, the feast of the Transfiguration, a singular cere-mony takes place in this Cathedral, when the new grapes are blessed. The rubric for this exists in the 1494 missal, which is the earliest known printed record of the Braga rite, and it is thought that the custom originated in Burgundy and is possibly of Celtic or Roman origin, though it has now vanished in France. It was possibly intro-duced into Braga by Archbishop Geraldus (d. 1108) who was a Frenchman and a Cluniac Monk.

A road behind the Cathedral leads to a Largo with a lovely 18th-century house and the church of S. João do Souto, attached to which is the remarkable Capela dos Coimbras built in 1525, curiously like a little square tower, with a late Gothic window and good carved granite figures on the exterior, some with slight colouring left. A little farther on in yet another square, for Braga is full of open spaces, is the church of S. Cruz with its splendid rococo granite façade and the hospital of S. Marcos with twelve huge figures stand-ing on the top of the lovely baroque granite and white-washed façade.

The Largo de S. Paulo to the west of the Cathedral should be sought out, for it is an exquisite tiny cobbled square, with on one side an archway and a great tower, in front of which is a little square two-storeyed renaissance building, N. S. da Torre, consisting of a tiny chapel above a big porch. The key can be obtained from the house at the side, but the interior is not worth seeing, as it has been entirely redecorated. The same house has the key to the Seminary church, at right angles, with a splendid granite interior. On either side are four rich chapels, and the four Evangelists, of heroic size, in painted wood, stand by. The third side-chapel on the right has a most peculiar high-relief polychrome wood-carving of the Tree of Jesse, Jesse lying at the base clad in a Bishop's mitre and vestments and extremely good small figures clambering about in the tree above. On the same side are fine polychrome statues of S. Ignatius, and of the Assumption, the latter enclosed in a charming wreath of cherubs. There is a very unusual carved wooden screen with panels and pilasters, designed with fruit and flowers, standing inside the main doors.

A road leads from this Largo to the little octagonal chapel of S. Sebastião, very pretty with a blue-tiled façade and a granite and white rectangular chancel with a belfry.

North of the Cathedral in a huge square, the Praça do Conde d'Agrolongo, bordered with trees and surrounded by a lovely group of palaces, is the church of N. S. do Populo, one of the first to be planned after the model of the Gesu in Rome at the beginning of the 17th century, though the formal granite façade is later in date. Inside blue azulejos figures divided by huge flat granite pilasters reach right up to the plain coffered green and white ceiling. There is a grand though rather cold marble-columned reredos to the High Altar. The whole church is splendid in a restrained way, with a lovely choir above the West end on which is a central shrine supported by two tritons on either side of a mask. In the corridor on the way to the sacristy are some fine gilt bas-reliefs and four very unusual late 17th-century pictures of saints, two of them in a kind of court dress, and all in contemporary frames.

Off this largo, at the same end as the church, is the palace of the Biscainhas, with a most lovely façade. In the entrance—really a covered courtyard—six 18th-century granite figures stand on the capitals of the pilasters between the arches leading to the main stairway; little Boswellian men, rather recalling the kings at Bouro. From this entrance court a huge passage leads right through the house to the stables, which give on to the garden at the back. (The whole place is now the property of the city.) The inner staircase has exquisite 18th-century azulejos in the true indigo blue, with landscapes and figures; the front door is at the top of this, and leads into a glazed corridor which runs round an inner patio, green with creepers, surrounding a fountain in the centre. The rooms have some fine pieces of furniture and good ceilings—one room has the walls covered in painted linen landscapes, celadon-grisaille. This part of the house is not normally shown, but the garden is; the garden front is beautiful, with lovely grillages, and there is a charming pavilion.

The church of S. Vicente on the north side of Braga has a wild baroque granite façade with saints and angels, and a Grinling Gibbons wealth of fruit and flowers and winged cherubs' heads, most beautifully carved and composed. There are two dates on the façade, 1598 and 1691, and a legend carved in exquisite lettering saying that the church possesses all the Lateran privileges in return for 2 lbs. of bees-wax, payable in Rome each year. In the interior there is a delightful High Altar frontal of rococo leaves twined round the raven of St. Vincent. The retable is white and gold, very unusual and beautiful. There are good 18th-century painted panels on either side of the nave in rococo frames and a huge white and gold organ-loft upheld by four tritons.

Between S. Vicente and the main road out to Bom Jesus lies the Largo de Guadalupe, a strange diamond-shaped little square surrounded by lovely palaces. The road goes on into a very wide avenue, the Campo de Santa Ana, and on the left stands a long, low white-washed 17th-century building, the Recolimento de S. Gonçalo, which is an almshouse for old ladies. There is a little chapel with an amusing rough painted ceiling of cherubs clasping flowers and cornucopias, and an angel holding an armillary sphere stands on top of the pulpit.

Continuing along the tram lines towards Bom Jesus, the church of S. Vitor on the left should next be visited. The interior is lined with immense blue and white 18th-century azulejos panels with huge figures reaching right up to the plain ceiling. The space above the chancel arch is filled with a gigantic gilt swag, there is a fine gold reredos to the High Altar, and a grisaille organ.

The great pilgrimage church of BOM JESUS stands on top of a densely wooded hill outside Braga, and is surrounded by the good hotels already mentioned, with a funicular as well as a winding road-way leading up to them. The extraordinary 18th-century architectural staircase up to the church is not so beautifully and lightly treated as the very similar though smaller one at N. S. dos Remedios outside Lamego, and there is nothing at Bom Jesus to compare with the Court of the Kings at the former place. The church at the top is very disappointing, having been so often redecorated by various benefactors, whose extremely funny portraits hang in the entrance to the sacristy. Some of the 18th-century octagonal chapels dotted about the woods are delightful, though the groups of statuary in them are extremely late. In the little museum are nice portraits and a good 18th-century picture of the building of the great church. The report that there are canvases by Sequeira in this museum is without foundation. SAMEIRO on a spur of the same hill is another place of pilgrimage with a big modern church.

Four kilometres south of Braga, in the SERRA DA FALPERRA, the chapel of S. Maria Madalena is a lovely example of rococo granite work and the dazzling whitewash showing between the decoration gives a most brilliant effect.

No one in Braga seems to know which road leads to the great convent of Tibães and the very early church of S. Frutuoso, but they are both quite near the town on the Ponte de Lima road. In S. Jeronimo Real, 2 kilometres outside Braga, a sign to the right says S. FRUTUOSO. A narrow lane leads between walls to a cottage where one can obtain the key of the church and convent, which are rather farther on, in a lovely remote country setting. S. Frutuoso is one of the few really early Byzantine churches in the Peninsula, built between 650 and 665 by S. Frutuoso, Bishop of Braga. It is in the form of a Greek Cross, with a central dome lit by four small windows; four arches below the central dome, supported on marble pillars, lead on the East, West and South into tiny semi-circular chapels each surmounted by a semi-dome; these chapels are lit by three round-headed windows. The arch on the North leads into a brick-vaulted vestibule connecting it with the much later church. The capitals of the pillars have very rich carving, some with acanthus design. A band of fine carving runs all round the angles between the arches, under the dome, one foot deep.

The exterior consists of three stone cubes meeting at the dome, and along each wall of each cube are three shallow recessed arches, only two and a half inches deep, alternately pointed and round-topped; the end of each cube is a shallow pediment. This arrangement, though extremely simple, is of great beauty, and this is enhanced by two bands of marble carving of the utmost fineness and delicacy; the upper, of formalised fleurs-de-lis within semi-circles, resting on a cable band, is some four and a half inches deep and runs round the whole building below the cornice and pediment; the lower, cutting the windows mid-way, is of the cable only.

Argument has raged about this rare little building, but it seems certain that it was built before the advent of the Moors, and possibly restored in the 11th century. A confusing feature is a heap of eight marble pillars, just like those within, lying piled up outside, overgrown with weeds!

Formal terraces surround the adjoining conventual church, which has a detached double belfry at the side and a lovely walled space with a fountain in front. Inside, the baroque building has a fine high narrow High Altar retable, bounded by two big salomonic columns. The side altars are very finely gilded and the green, gold and white ambones and the gilt window surrounds are all very rich, as is the chancel arch garniture. There are wonderful green, black and gold choir stalls in the organ-loft with painted panels behind, on which stand cherubs holding wreathed chains, but all this is impossible to see closely as the door into the choir is locked against thieves, and the key seems unobtainable. The sacristy is exceptionally good with a superb vestment chest and above it is a most unusual and beautiful renaissance reliquary, all in the original faded colours; the centre is filled with a panel of the heads of child angels, later in date, and there are a number of lesser reliquaries placed in the centres of gold flowers. There is also a very strange, tall gilded wood monstrance, at least four feet in height, which may have been originally a reliquary.

Returning to the main road at S. Jeronimo Real, a turning on the opposite side signposted Graça leads to the enormous monastery of TIBÃES, at one time the Mother House of the Benedictines in Portugal, set high and commanding wonderful views; on an open space in front an exquisitely fragile cross, set on a very tall slender carved shaft, emphasises the distant country. The church is in use, and the priest lives in part of the building enclosing the cloister; the rest of the huge place has belonged for at least three generations to a private family. There are miles of corridors with cells on either side, rather like the big one at Tomar, but the really splendid feature is the chapter house. This is an enormously long room with a very fine panelled ceiling in a geometric design; immediately below it, all round the room, are a series of extremely interesting portraits, in a sort of frieze, with isolated ones below these again. The lower part of the walls are covered with highly decorative blue and white tiled scenes of Joseph and his Brethren; the blue of the formal architectural surrounds framing each picture stands out beautifully against the whitewash. Few azulejos give such pure visual pleasure as these. There is also an empty library.

There is a cloister beside the church, simple and attractive, with flagstone graves under the arcades—at All Souls the peasants come and outline with herbs and flowers the stones where their relations are buried, for until quite recently it was used as the local cemetery.

The church itself is desolate but has good rococo details, including very intricate carving in dark wood to some of the side altars. The *Coro Alto* contains most remarkable stalls backed by pairs of strange archaic figures in low-relief set in decorated renaissance architectural surrounds upheld by pairs of caryatides. The gardens behind the buildings are lovely; deserted and neglected, with running water, an aqueduct and a huge pond surrounded by trees and shrubs, where the water trickles in from a stone cascade above. There are miniature flights of steps and fountains like those at Bom Jesus; the latter are said to have been copied from Tibães.

PONTE DE LIMA, 30 kilometres north of Braga, is one of the most beautiful little towns in Portugal, partly owing to its situation, partly owing to the wonderful use made of space in it, and, by contrast, to the cramped picturesqueness of some of its few back streets. In front the grey bridge with its lovely line of low arches spans the white stony bed of the river Lima, nearly a quarter of a mile wide, where women wash in the blue pools; the vista of arches ends with the peculiarly beautiful silver-snowy shape of the church of S. Antonio de Torre Velha on the farther bank, with its graceful onion-topped spire. A broad front gives on the bridge, dominated by the square machicolated tower, once part of the fortifications, now the prison, where the charitable may drop cigarettes or money into tiny tapestry buckets, lowered for the purpose by the prisoners, whose cheerful faces appear at the barred windows up above. It is worth walking through an arch to the right of this tower to see the actual entrance to the prison, a flight of stone steps leading up from a miniature square, overlooked by a tiny colonnaded gallery, to a stone walk between the houses at first-floor level—presumably the top of the old city wall. At one end of this, a mediaeval doorway gives access to the gaol itself.

Downstream from the bridge is a magnificent double avenue of huge planes, where one may idle in coolness on seats, and look out from the deep shade to the blinding whiteness of the river-bed and the beauty of the bridge, or walking farther, may admire the curiously austere façade of the renaissance conventual church of S. Antonio dos Frades, and poke into a second church, set at right angles to it, S. Francisco. This latter has a good simple ceiling with red and gilt groining, and very elegant choir-stalls in dark wood with gilt motifs, which are pure Heppelwhite in style, as is the very white organ-loft and even the prie-dieux in the chancel. The retable of the High Altar is immense and very complicated, and has some attractive statues, nice, but not first class, including one of St. Louis of France. The sacristy ceiling is most peculiar, ribs running out to a lozenge in relief in the centre, all richly painted; there are also lovely painted surrounds to the cupboards, blue, white and gold, and two superb Heppelwhite mirrors.

The Igreja Matriz of S. Maria dos Anjos, a very wide three-aisled church, is just off the street leading down to the bridge, and except for the sacristy has only two features of interest, a tiny groined vaulted chapel to the right of the entrance with a very unusual carved retable in dark un-gilded wood, and a retable in the chapel in the North transept with gilt pillars and an arch above, the carving rich but most airy-light. In the sacristy, where so often the best things are tucked away, is a quite exquisite statue of the Virgin and Child, carved in stone and painted, of the late 15th or early 16th century. The niche for the crucifix above the rococo vestment chests has a most unusual and pretty background, red, green and gold designs on wood within the gilded frame, not unlike that in the sacristy of S. Pedro at Amarant.

Opposite the parish church, the Misericordia chapel has been restored. There is a lovely double arcade to the courtyard, and at the West end, a very strange, springing baroque doorway, like that of N. S. da Agonia at Viana do Castelo, which Mr. Sacheverell

Sitwell so aptly describes as "bat-like". Inside the chapel there is a good wooden painted ceiling of cherubs and flowers on a duck-egg blue ground with gold groining. The lovely choir and chapels have a plethora of good boiseries though unfortunately several have been repainted.

Those who wish to see the architecturally interesting but ugly palace of the Marquês de Ponte de Lima (which is said by the *Guide Bleu* to dominate the town, whereas to find it is like looking for a mouse in a sack of potatoes), will save a lot of time by asking for the Hospital, this being its present function. Its peculiarity lies in the combination of crenellations to its façade and two dull towers, and rather pesudo-Manueline windows; they are really more like English perpendicular than straight Manueline. It is about the only ugly thing in the whole delicious place.

At the far end of the bridge one comes to S. Antonio de Torre Velha, whose silver onion spire with its black granite ribs has beckoned so long across the river. Here too is space, beautifully employed. The narrow bridge debouches on to an immense open paved stretch, shaded on one side by the long line of the church, with its white-washed roof; two little rococo shrines, very elegant, mark the approach to the bridge, and a ridiculous but wildly pretty little square shrine with three arches sits out in the sun near the river bank, sheltering a rather foolish-faced coloured saint. Inside, S. Antonio is small and very light, rather like a Regency drawing-room, with fine chandeliers and a Regency pulpit and windows. From here too, Ponte de Lima is seen at its best—the great lines of the distant hills, broken by the dark masses of nearer trees, draw in towards the town, whose square pink and white and buff houses, at once gay and antique-looking, are punctuated by the sharp machico-lations of the palace and the prison, and thrown into relief by the deep green line of the avenue of planes where one sat and smoked an hour before.

Some 6 kilometres upstream from S. Antonio de Torre Velha lies the convent and church of REFOIOS DE LIMA. The façade of the church is one of those pieces of north Portuguese baroque which are at once so simple, so daring and so lovely as to be a guaranteed cure for those who think they don't like this style of architecture. The surface is white; the extravagant outline, the door and the shield-shaped windows above it are in dark granite—and dark granite ribs outline the slender onion-topped spire. And, again, it stands at one end of a huge dusty green open space, with a pillory set on a stepped pedestal fronting it a hundred yards away. Within there is a very elegant austere late renaissance retable to the High Altar, rather classical in feeling, with beautiful life-size polychrome statues set on either side of the Trinity. There are two side-altars set corner-wise to the chancel arch, very rich and unusual; gilt niches with canopies above and fringed pelmets topping all—also gilt; twin pulpits, red and gilt, very rich—and the four side-chapels, two on each side, though more normal in shape are immensely elaborate, with the same fringed gilt pelmets spanning both, all in painted wood, ornamented with gilt vases at each end and in the centre.

Altogether, for all its extravagant austerity outside, this church of Refoios is within incredibly rich. The *Coro Alto* has most elegant classical choir-stalls of dark wood with gilt ornamentation and portrait panels behind them.

The convent adjoining the church on the right and separated from it by a very elegant cloister dated 1621, with classical pillars round a charming obelisked fountain, is a huge massive building with a most picturesque sunk courtyard; beautiful tile-roofed and pillared galleries run across each end, from which flights of granite steps lead down to the ground level, with its wide-arched cart-sheds and barns, where pigs and chickens root and pick among the litter. This, unlike Bouro, is an encouraging place, full of farm hands, and bursting with life and energy. The farm hands eat off the huge marble table in the vast kitchen, with its tile panels of fish, game and hams on the walls, like those at Correio Mor near Lisbon; the refectory, with great tables on marble trestles, serves as a laundry. There are things going on, healthy agricultural things, all over the whole place—the cloister in autumn is piled with sheaves of barley, gold between the faded plaster of the walls and the deep green of the lemon trees by the fountain. The adjoining chapter house contains very good polychrome azulejos of standing clerical figures in 18th-century costume within formal flowered medallions on a plain water-blue ground, very similar to those outside the *Coro Alto* at Santa Cruz in Coimbra.

The valley of the Lima, and indeed the whole of this part of the Minho, is famous for the great number of country-houses of all periods which lie in it, from the 14th-century Quinta dos Nobregas near Ponte da Barca to the Brejoeira Palace built in the early 19th century on the plan of Ajuda in Lisbon. The road from Ponte de Lima up the valley to PONTE DA BARCA is quite lovely. The latter town is delightful, with a 15th-century parish church, a beautiful long 16th-century bridge over the river, and a square with a singular pillory in the centre and a most beautiful arcaded building to one side.

.   .   .   .   .   .

VIANA DO CASTELO, at the mouth of the Lima, contains lovely buildings and is most attractive as a place. The cliff-like hill of S. Luzia towers above it, with an excellent luxury hotel on the top reached by a funicular. The Misericordia, so praised by Watson, in the main square of the town is unlike any other building in Portugal, though the architect of the Misericordia at Chaves may have seen it. It is quite fantastic, with a heavy three-tiered façade supported on granite caryatides; boxes of brightly-coloured geraniums flower through the triple railings and lighten somewhat the very dour and heavy impression. The church, which can be entered through the hospital at the side, has a rough, but boldly-beautiful painted ceiling of formal patterns round four cartouches on a cream ground. There is a lovely gold oval pediment to the High Altar retable, which curves right into the cupola with a cherub playing a trumpet on the very top; interesting twin groups stand on each side, Our Lady and St. Joseph on the right, the Visitation on the left; and a pair of small, delicate, restrained organs are poised on either side of the choir.

Also on this square, which is triangular in shape with a quite exquisite renaissance fountain in the centre, is the very early Town Hall, built on arches. In the Rua da Carreira at the side of the Misericordia stands the lovely long, rococo granite façade of the palace of the Viscondes da Carreira. At the end of this street, a home for old people which occupies the convent of St. Ana has been so much restored that the visitor may think that the church cannot be worth seeing, but this is not so. How often in Portuguese churches the most interesting and beautiful thing about them is their ceilings! This is very much the case with the convent of St. Ana. The chancel has a lovely box-panelled ceiling, a formal design in white and gold between gilt ribs, which makes up for the dull heavy retable—there are moreover two extremely dashing costume angels at the chancel steps. The ceiling of the nave consists of forty-five painted panels of the life of St. Anne set between bright Cambridge-blue ribs. The nuns' choir-stalls are of black and gold lacquer, a curious contrast to the coarse heavy red and gold carving of the backs—they have paintings inset and at the West end is a delightful picture of the Marriage of Cana, the bride and groom wearing wreaths of roses. In the nave are a delicious set of 18th-century painted panels of the corporal and spiritual works of mercy, not unlike Mr. Day's somewhat later conceptions in Sandford and Merton. The pair of benches on either side of the High Altar have three lovely panels at the back with formal Claude-like landscapes.

The ceiling of the sacristy is most unusual; it is panelled, and each panel has a raised design of circles with a round carved boss in the centre; these, like the ribs, are vividly painted in red, blue and gold. On the vestment chest is a seated statue of Our Lady, very rigid and almost Byzantine-looking—though much repainted it is a splendid thing.

Near the church of S. Domingos, the Municipal Museum contains the most complete collection of Portuguese faience in the country. There are also some fine pieces of furniture, both local and from Portuguese India and a few canvases.

At the end of the Rua S. Sebastião to the west of the town there is a vast space on which takes place from August 18th to 20th the three-days "festa" of N. S. da Agonia. Groups of dancers and singers come from all the surrounding villages and form processions, all the participants dressed in country costumes which are still worn in the remoter districts, and many of the women wearing ear-rings made out of Victorian half-sovereigns. Round dances take place every evening in the public garden on the river bank, sometimes accompanied by music but more often by rhythmic hand-clapping by the dancers themselves as well as by the onlookers.

The very singular rococo church of N. S. da Agonia has another bat-inspired façade, with springing granite wings above the doorway. Inside there are pleasing pale gold side altars, and a delightful little gold pulpit, with a very late rococo organ-loft. On the second altar to the right lies a glass coffin containing the waxed-over body of S. Severino, dressed in extraordinary cheapjack clothes, with a gaudy helmet on his head.

North of Viana do Castelo, the pretty little border town of CAMINHA stands on a jutting peninsula between the rivers Minho and Coura, with a castle on an island. In the main square there are 15th-century battlemented buildings and an interesting collegiate church finished in 1556.

Up the Minho, which here forms the border between Spain and Portugal, there are numbers of little villages and towns, almost all with interesting architectural features. At LANHELAS there is a 15th-century fortified country-house; VILA NOVA DE CERVEIRA is a walled town with the ruins of a 13th-century castle, and at LAPELA still stands one of the 14th-century frontier defence towers. MONÇÃO, also a fortified town, is famous for its delicious lampreys and good wine, which can both be sampled at the Pensão Chave d'Ouro, where many gourmets stay in early spring.

At VALENÇA DO MINHO, the frontier town with an international bridge over the river, the excellent Pousada de S. Teotonio is built within the great castle walls.

.　　.　　.　　.　　.　　.

BARCELOS is another of those beautiful small Portuguese towns which, if it were in Italy, would have been the subject of English raptures for a century and a half. Perhaps its main glory is the Campo da Feira, one of the largest and most beautiful open squares in Portugal. It must be a quarter of a mile each way, and has an exquisite fountain on an elaborate raised platform with steps in the centre; this very much recalls the one in front of the Town Hall at Viana do Castelo by João Lopes o Velho, but is even better; it would seem probable that it is by the same hand. A raised balustrade, with a curved paved sweep leading up to it, overlooks the square on the north side; on the south an even more elaborate parapet, adorned with pointless but beautiful arches and obelisks, overlooks the lower part of the town. The whole of the east side is filled by the long low façade of the old Capuchin convent, the front of the church rising in the centre with a typical winged baroque flourish—surely one of the most beautiful buildings in existence; to the west a long stretch of trees and gardens half-masks the line of graceful palaces beside the main road. Finally, the gay dome of Senhor da Cruz, its ornate balustrade and flambeaux looking like a rich octagonal crown, fills the sky in the south-west corner.

Senhor da Cruz is as rich within as without. There are very fine blue azulejos panels right up to the granite dome, which is supported inside on great buttress-like columns. An enormous crystal chandelier hangs from the centre, there is a black and white marble floor and two huge noble-savage angels in their original colouring pose on either side of the High Altar. The most beautiful features are the two side-altars—these are deeply recessed and lined with gilt boiseries; they look like golden caves, but caves canopied with fringed and tasselled gilt pelmets; the frontals are admirable, gilt gesso on wood. The organ and organ-loft too are exquisite, all pale gilding and restrained elegance.

Above the raised parapet on the north side of the Campo da Feira stands the Oblates church of St. Benedict, chiefly remarkable for its ceiling of fifty-five panels of the life of St. Benedict, and there are four good 18th-century pictures hanging on the walls in rococo frames; the ceiling of this church must be one of the finest of its period in Portugal, though some of the canvases are badly in need of restoration.

Barcelos is the centre of a big pottery industry and the ware is sold at the great Thursday fair which takes place in this Campo every week. It is made in little huts at the road-side, the baking being done with charcoal fires in a beehive-shaped mound.

Towards the river Cavado the town changes and becomes more granite and dark in feeling, and very ancient houses line the streets. At one side of the church is the Bragança Palace, now an archaeological museum. Behind the church is a small pottery museum, showing the evolution of the famous Barcelos cockerel. On the other side is a quite fantastic palace used as Municipal offices; on the first floor a row of eighteen enormous formal rococo granite windows stand out from the bright mustard yellow-washed walls and in the centre are a pair of battlemented clock towers.

The Igreja Matriz is very early Gothic, with a West front that retains some Romanesque features, notably the carvings on the four courses of the pointed doorway; the squat tower, too, has round arches, and the square chancel recalls Romanesque buildings—a pretty renaissance doorway has been inserted in the North wall.

The interior is very curious and in a strange way beautiful. The chancel and two adjoining chapels are gracefully vaulted, and the groining is carried down between the narrow lancet windows, giving a great impression of slenderness and grace. The two aisles are separated from the nave by arches carried on graceful clustered pillars; but instead of the white stone or plaster on the walls and above the arches, to which the Anglo-Saxon eye is accustomed, every inch is covered with bright azulejos, so that the whole building is prickly with colour. The chapel of the Blessed Sacrament has a beautiful gilt retable, and the chapel to the right of it, a lovely and unusual black and gold one. There are a number of good polychrome statues, especially in the chapel to the North of the chancel; and on the High Altar, on the left, a dream of one of the Virgin and Child, pure Gothic. The High Altar itself is early, on stone pillars with no frontal. But the cold purity of the original structure of this delightful church, with these exotic enrichments, has immense charm.

From across the River Cavado there is a most beautiful view of Barcelos rising up darkly on the other side. At the end of the 15th-century bridge is a very strange little chapel consisting of a two-storeyed tower with a columned porch all round, and under this bridge floats a water nursery whcrc lampreys are kept until they are sent to market; they are indigenous in most of the Minho rivers.

At BARCA DO LAGO on the Cavado there still exists the ferry which was instituted in the early middle ages to take the multitudes of pilgrims from Portugal over this river to the great shrine of Santiago de Compostella.

Between Barcelos and Braga the lovely Benedictine monastery of Vilar de Frades at AREIAS DE VILAR has a church showing some similarity with the Cathedral at Braga, and on the opposite side of the river at MANHENTE there is a 12th-century church with a battlemented tower.

The Portuguese have a special love for the Minho—partly perhaps as the cradle of their national independence, but also for its green smiling richness, its wealth of splendid towns, and the vitality, up here, of tradition, of dance and song and festival. It is at once a home of and a theme for writers. The scenes of all Camilo Castelo Branco's country novels are laid there—he is the Hardy of the Minho; and Eça de Queiroz' great "Illustre Casa de Ramiro" has a Minho setting as well. "As Pupilas do Senhor Reitor" by Julio Diniz, also brings the northern province with its vine-wreathed trees, its shaded trellised farm-yards with their pendant bunches of grapes, its quiet rivers, its singers and dancers—who are also its plain country-folk—before our eyes again.

CHAPTER XV

MADEIRA AND THE AZORES

THE island of Madeira has certain aspects which make it unique. In the first place, previous to its discovery in 1419 it was totally uninhabited; therefore it has no prehistory; no Stone Age sites, dolmens or stone circles or cairns, no Greek or Roman remains, no early Christian churches, Saxon or Romanesque, no mediaeval castles—in its Atlantic isolation it remained a clean slate, historically speaking, till the early 15th century when, only seventy-two years before the discovery of America, Prince Henry the Navigator's two explorers, Zargo and Teixeira, having first investigated it from the neighbouring island of Porto Santo in the previous year, formally took possession of it for the Portuguese crown. Secondly, it is a place where, for reasons which will be explained later, even the most ardent botanist is liable to be more excited by the introduced or exotic plants than by the native flora, curious and interesting as that is. And finally its system of water-supply in open channels, so vast, so peculiar, and on the spot even so dramatic, has, save to some extent for the Canaries, no parallel elsewhere in the world.

The backbone of the island is a mountain chain stretching roughly east and west for some thirty miles, rising in the centre to six thousand feet; from this central massif long ridges, called *lombos*—or "backs"—run down on all sides to the sea, with deeply-scored valleys or *ribeiros* between them; indeed the whole island is so corrugated with these ridges and valleys, as well as being wholly on a tilt, that a journey of twelve or fifteen miles as the crow flies may easily take two hours or more by car. An exception to this ridged structure is the very remarkable plateau of the PAÜL DA SERRA, down towards the Western end, a great flattened upland space several miles across, where a scanty growth of grass and bracken pushes up between the rocks to nourish countless spindly-legged sheep. It lies at nearly five thousand feet, and on the rare days when it is free from cloud not only commands wonderful views, but is a strange and beautiful place in itself.

AZORES: VILLAGE SHOWING SMALL FIELDS DIVIDED BY DYKES

MADEIRA: PICO FORT, FUNCHAL

MADEIRA: MACHICO

The rocks and soil of Madeira are almost all volcanic—there are a few patches of limestone, coralline in origin, formed in early geological times, lifted up and then eroded to form sedimentary beds at lower levels; but the volcanic rocks prevail, and give to the whole island its predominant and characteristic reddish brown colour, of a tone between copper and chestnut, of rocks and soil alike—a curiously beautiful background to all vegetation, but especially to the vivid shifting green of the vines and the silvery-blue of the tall reeds, or *canas*, which cling to the bronzed ledges of the endless ravines, or fringe their stony beds. In a few places there are cliffs of true columnar basalt, as on Staffa, notably up the valley from Porto da Cruz and in a ravine near Faial, both on the north side of the island, and near the Mount above Funchal; but for the most part the rocks and cliffs are of rough squarish basaltic blocks, or the softer tuff, formed of volcanic ash or mud, with, embedded in it, spheroidal lumps of a much harder greyish rock, which is picked out, like pips out of an orange, and chiselled into setts for paving the roads. The geology of Madeira is worth attention, if only because it imposes its character so deeply on the whole insular civilisation— the compact basalt, which weathers to a grey so dark as to be almost black, furnishes frames to the doors and windows of all the principal buildings—they call it Pedra Viva; the lava pebbles of the beaches and stream-beds pave the garden paths in charming patterns of little grey-brown spheres not much bigger than walnuts.

But above all it is the presence, all over the island, of the soft tuff which gives to Madeira some of its most characteristic features. It can be cut almost as smoothly and precisely as cheese; hence the smooth vertical brown walls of roads which have been driven through a spur of hill or chased out along a slope, and the neat flights of steps cut in these walls, leading up to a path above, or to some flower-smothered *palheiro*, or straw-thatched cottage. Shelters for the road-mender or the wayfarer, with neat rectangular doorways, are scooped out of it along the roadsides; goat-sheds and cow-stalls, equally trim, are hollowed out of it in the high valleys; in places, even human dwellings are so carved out in the solid face of the cliff. And it is the presence of the tuff, easy to cut and yet firm and resistant, which has chiefly made possible the astonishing system of *levadas* or conduits on which the whole water-supply of the island, and its extraordinarily dense cultivation, depends.

For in Madeira water is seldom piped to the towns, as elsewhere in the world it must be. High up, deep in the green wooded hearts of the mountains the moist Atlantic air, condensing on the cloud-shrouded peaks, fills deep springs, or sends waterfalls dashing in filmy spray over the fern-hung cliffs, and turbulent streams roaring down the beds of the ravines. And with simple but brilliant skill these high sources of water are trapped and caught, and carried for miles in open channels cut in the tuff, winding in and out along the contours of the hills till, above the towns or villages which need them, they are released to flow down steep shoots, still in the open air, to bring wealth and fertility to the land below. These channels vary in size from small affairs a few inches each way to the great main *levadas*, thirty inches wide by three feet or more deep, which may have a flow of eighteen gallons per second; some of them have a course of as much as thirty miles. In two or three places where gravitation alone would not suffice, since it was necessary to carry the water to the dry southern half of the island from the moister north, tunnels have been driven slap through the central ridge, an astonishing feat. Two of the most remarkable of these are near the head of the Ribeira da Janela—the higher is some fourteen hundred feet long, and lies at over three thousand four hundred feet above sea-level; the lower lies at just over three thousand one hundred feet, and is two thousand six hundred feet long; even with lamps or torches it takes a good twelve minutes to walk through it, on the damp uneven surface of the path, under the dripping roof, with the loud voice of the water, dashing and roaring along in the channel at one's side, keeping the traveller company all the way.

The water is most rigidly distributed, on so many days or hours per week, to the various villages and estates, and planting operations are arranged for the days when a district "gets water". Even in town gardens, there are scenes of infectious excitement when the water comes down—the rushing, the shouting, the diverting of the bright precious stuff to this plot or that to irrigate the bananas, the vines, the sugar-cane, the maize and the sweet potatoes affects even the foreign onlooker.

·   ·   ·   ·   ·   ·

The climate of Madeira is extraordinarily and steadily mild with a mean annual temperature of 65–67 degrees Fahrenheit; what is more important than the mean, the thermometer practically never falls below 50 degrees. This, with its rich volcanic soil, makes it possible to grow practically anything there, and as a result the gardens of the island almost overwhelm the stranger with the brilliance, variety and luxuriance of their growth—the flowers grow so high (dahlias will run up to eight or nine feet) and the trees are so flowery that it is hard to tell where flowers leave off and trees begin. In June some superb specimens of the *bombax*, their new foliage the colour of flame or of daffodils, tower over the walls and gardens of Funchal—and to see the bombax next to the delicate mauve of the jacaranda in flower is to see something; the crimson of the coral-tree, the vivid yellow of *Grevillea robusta* stand out against the dark green of camphor trees, while the air is heavy with the scent of magnolias thirty feet high. Below come the shrubs: hibiscus of every shade, abutilons, oleanders, the savage fuzzy red of the bottle-brush; and over walls and trees alike ramp the climbers —the small delicate pale blue stars of *Plumbago capensis*, the bigger stars, pinky-mauve or blue, of the passion-flowers, the red or coral or orange trumpets of the bignonias, the more fragile trumpets of ipomaea or convulvulus, white or blue. But above all the visitor to Funchal will remember the bougainvilleas—they smother the whole place. Not the sickly mauve thing which twines sadly in English conservatories, but robust maroons and dark purples and rich plummy reds; one is even of a soft brick-red.

Most of our hot-house plants riot in the open: cinerarias, petunias, begonias—in particular a pale pink one with sprays three feet long— all mixed up with roses, geraniums and pelargoniums, sweet peas and carnations and heliotrope—an unbelievable sight. And it is not only in the gardens of Funchal that there is this profusion and varied glory of colour; round every cottage stand tall arums and Madonna lilies and stocks, while a mesembryanthemum the colour of apple-blossom tumbles in thick pink cascades over their terraced walls. When the arum lilies stray afield, as they invariably do in damp spots, they are cut and used as bedding for the cows!

To give the serious botanist some idea of the variety of foreign trees and shrubs that can be successfully cultivated, in one garden alone (that of the Quinta do Deão) are to be found, well-grown and thriving, a hundred and twenty-two different species of trees and shrubs—from Australia (26), New Zealand (4), the Pacific Islands

(10), China and Japan (12), Malaya and the Indian region (32), Madagascar (8), Africa (12), North America (5), Mexico and Central America (8), South America (24), West Indies (7). (Only one variety in each species has been counted in this list.) And this is only one among nearly forty *quintas*—the local name for a house with fairly extensive grounds—with famous gardens. Curiously, the best gardens were nearly all laid out by Englishmen, between 1760 and 1860, and the trees then planted are of course now in their prime. Mr. Veitch, when H.B.M. Consul in Madeira, built and laid out not less than five quintas—and altogether thirty-five of the most famous are of English origin. Travellers brought trees—Captain Cook himself planted the tulip tree in the Quinta do Val. But one quinta, perhaps the most beautiful of all, Palheiro, lying high above the town, was originally laid out by a French landscape gardener for a Portuguese, the Count de Carvalhal; from his nephew it passed into the hands of the Blandy family, who still add to its beauties and its treasures.

The native flora of Madeira is strictly what botanists call "palaearctic", i.e., characteristic of north-west Europe; between eighty and ninety plants are peculiar to the island and are found nowhere else in the world, while another hundred odd are peculiar to Madeira, the Canaries and the Azores. What is particularly interesting, to the botanist, is that some of these endemic species closely resemble European ones now extinct, but found in fossil rocks on the Continent, having survived in their ocean isolation. Unlike the wild flowers of the British Isles, which travelled overland when these were still joined to the mainland of Europe, the native plants of Madeira have all been brought to the great volcanic block, when it eventually emerged from the surrounding seas, by birds or ocean currents, since depths of over two thousand fathoms separate it from any mainland coast; the trade winds and what is known as the "Canaries current" set south-west from the Iberian peninsula to the island, and still bring seeds and straggling birds—over seventy different sorts of the latter have been reported, all of Mediterranean or palaearctic types.

Obviously, then, one expects the Madeira flora to be peculiar rather than rich, and this is the case; there are no wild iris, only four wild orchis, and a very narrow range of many common plants which on the Continent each show numbers of interesting varieties

—to give one example, there are only seven wild veronicas in Madeira, while Coste's *Flore de France* lists fifty-one! One reason, of course, for the relative absence of wild flowers in the island is the extreme density of cultivation—up to about two thousand feet almost every yard of ground is terraced and planted, on slopes so steep that elsewhere it would be thought impossible to use them, so that below the cultivation line the only places left for weeds are the sea-faces of the cliffs, the steep roadside banks, and the stony beds of the ribeiros. Those tiny rectangles of vines, wheat, barley, or sweet potatoes, each above its little bronzed terrace, looking like a patchwork quilt flung over the hill-sides, are one of the most characteristic features of Madeira. Above them come first the planted trees, mostly *Pinus pinaster* and eucalyptus, and then at last the open slopes with patches of the native woodland—the wild laurel, the Madeiran bilberry, which grows up to twenty feet high, and, mainly on the northern slopes, immense specimens of the tree-heath, *Erica arborea*, and the *Til*, a handsome evergreen known as the Madeira ebony, with an underbrush of myrtle, lesser heaths, and bracken. Very large trees, up to one hundred feet in height, are extremely rare in a wild state; some attribute this to the persistent tradition that the first colonists cleared the dense forests which then covered the island—the word Madeira means wood—by burning them, a task which is said to have taken seven years; a more probable reason is the persistent cutting of native wood for fuel, which goes on under the noses of the forest guards. Terrible ravages occurred during both World Wars, when coal was short.

The best way to see these upper reaches of the island is to follow the "*levada* walks", the paths carefully built beside them for the use of the men who undertake their maintenance. These are charming, often bordered with hydrangeas or blue and white agapanthus, so that from a distance they look like blue ribbons tied across the green hillsides; in the wilder parts, it is along these mossy paths that one finds the rare delicate ferns and the more exciting wild flowers, the great white daisy-like *argyranthemum*, the big wild Madeiran geranium, and the wild cinerarias, with their white leaves and brilliant mauve-pink starry blooms. (The most exciting of all, *Echium candicans*, with its trusses of blue bloom nearly a foot long, is only found on the dry slopes.) And many of these paths afford wonderful views of the amazingly steep and savage cliffs and ravines, with buttresses standing out, almost as slender and vertical as slices of green cake, into the still greener abysses below. Its volcanic origin gives to the mountain scenery of Madeira a quality of exaggeration that is sometimes almost nightmarish. And here it is necessary to give a word of warning to all but those with the strongest heads for heights, as to walking in Madeira. Some of the levada-paths, like that to the RISCO WATERFALL at the head of the RIBEIRA DA JANELA, are broad and pleasant; but the vast majority of all paths and tracks in the island, and even the motor roads, wind along the rims of almost vertical precipices, generally hundreds of feet in height, which turn many heads sick and giddy, and make even motoring a doubtful pleasure to some people—as for the paths along many of the levadas, they are barely a foot broad, and the flowing water on one side, and the sickening drop on the other make most normal heads swim. (More than one traveller has been reduced to taking off shoes and stockings and wading along the bed of the levada itself, up to her knees in water!) But as the inhabitants wander along these places with complete indifference, often burdened with heavy loads, they call all paths roads, and consider all excellent; and it is advisable to consult some reliable person beforehand about any particular walk.

Two good, though exciting, motor roads cross the island from south to north, that over the ENCUMIADA PASS from RIBEIRA BRAVA to SÃO VICENTE, and from Funchal itself through RIBEIRO FRIO down to FAIAL and SANTA ANA; from the latter road a branch, unpaved but perfectly good for cars, leads up to the so-called observatory below the PICO ARIEIRO, and an hour's easy walking, blessedly free from dizzy drops, brings one to the peak itself. It is also easy to drive from Funchal to CALHETA in about two hours, and by a branch road up the LOMBO DO SALÃO to a good turning place—an important matter in Madeira—from whence it is easy to reach either the PAÜL DA SERRA or, by the lower of the two tunnels before referred to, the FURADO NÓVO, the Risco fall. Anyone who has made these four or five trips, and in addition has driven, as far as the really horrible road will take him, up towards the GRANDE CURRAL, and pursued his way on foot till he can look into that terrifying chasm, with its peaceful village lying at the bottom will really have skimmed the cream of Madiera mountain scenery. But the astonishing thing about the island is that in so small a compass there should exist such varieties of landscape, vegetation, and even climate—those who go up to spend the week-end playing golf at SANT' ANTONIO DA SERRA take, and wear, tweeds and woollens, while in Funchal, only an hour and a quarter's drive away, people are perspiring in cotton frocks; and while up at the Serra the tropical plants which flourish at Funchal will not sur-vive, a regular English or Scottish garden, impossible down on the coast, can be produced. But to learn to know Madeira properly needs weeks of patient exploration.

Madeira's great primary sources of wealth are today, as they have been for centuries, wine and sugar—to which must now be added as a modern runner-up, bananas; subsidiary industries are wicker-work and embroidery, which last was said at one time to occupy seventy thousand women; even now it is a useful secondary means of support to practically every peasant household, and though the pay is small, work which can be done in odd minutes under a vine trellis on one's own door-step, or afield minding the goats, has many advantages over a better-paid factory life.

Prince Henry the Navigator, who sent colonists to the island almost immediately after its discovery in 1419, lost no time in laying the foundation of its economic life by having plants of the Malvoisie vine brought from Crete, and sugar-canes from Sicily—a sugar-mill is reported as early as 1452, barely thirty years after the annexation. Irrigation also was promptly attended to; the first docu-ment relating to water is dated 1461, and Funchal's own levada, that of Sta. Luzia, was built or at least begun in 1515. But by the early part of the 18th century the wine, and by the middle of the 19th the sugar industries had both passed mainly into English hands, where they remain today. The story of the English in Madeira is a curious and exceedingly interesting one, and remains to be written; but the fact is that apart from one unimportant French raid, the Spanish domination from 1580 to 1640, a brief English occupation during the Napoleonic wars and the visit of Napoleon on his way to St. Helena (when he took on board large quantities of old Madeira, which he paid for in gold louis) the island, like a happy woman, has no history, in the political sense—its history is really economic, and it is largely a chapter of English history. (The English almost decided to annex it after the occupation, but in the end, at the Congress of Vienna, agreed to leave it under the Portuguese crown; the Portuguese negotiator who was regarded as responsible for this happy result, though a Lisbonian, was given the title of Marquês de Funchal.) And, when all is said and done, Prince Henry the Navigator himself, Philippa of Lancaster's son, was half English!

In their present rather nationalistic mood the Portuguese tend to forget these things, or to slur them over, but they are worth recording. No Portuguese guide-book mentions, and few Portuguese today, for all their friendliness and courtesy, are likely to tell you that Madeira embroidery was started in 1858 by a Mrs. Phelps, who opened a school of it for girls, and taught with her own hands; nor that the wicker-work, which now brings in thousands of dollars a year, was begun at Camacha by W. Hinton and James Taylor, who sent to Italy for models, and had the first baskets made; nor that John Blandy about 1850 made and sold the first butter known commercially in Funchal, thus starting the famous trade in Madeira butter, not only to passing ships, but to the mainland. The visitor will not be told that the same James Taylor who helped to start the wicker-work also taught the peasants to make hay to feed their stock in winter, and introduced the art of rope-making; nor that John Blandy, foreseeing the failure of the Bourbon stocks of sugar-cane, saved that industry by importing fresh stocks, in 1873, from Mauritius; nor that almost all the exotic fruits, the guavas, avocado pears, and so on, now largely consumed or exported, were introduced by Englishmen like Veitch, Page, and Davies, together with the trees and flowering shrubs already referred to, which make the gardens of Madeira one of the wonders of the world. Perhaps the modern Portuguese really do not know all this—these are forgotten things. But they are in fact an essential part of the island's history, such as it is.

In the production of sugar there is a startling contrast between the factory at Funchal, which employs all the most up-to-date machinery obtainable for crushing, refining and crystallising, and the almost biblical methods of cultivation and transport. Where practically all land is terraced, and a plot over a hundred yards long a comparative rarity, agricultural machinery is useless—cultivation and cutting must be done by hand; moreover, the steepness of the mountain paths cause the bundles of cane to make the first part of their journey to the factory on men's shoulders down to the main roads, where they are collected on lorries and brought to the town. The factory of Wm. Hinton and Sons is a huge concern, running uphill for a whole block beside the Ribeira da Sta. Luzia. At the lower end the lorries bring in the purple or yellow bundles of cane, which lie heaped in a pile ninety feet across; from this they are raised and slung by overhead travelling cranes on to a conveyor belt, to be crushed, wetted, crushed again and wetted again, five times over, the juice all the while pouring out into great gutters, whence it is drawn up by suction into the huge evaporators, ten feet across by twenty feet high, where it is boiled or heated in a vacuum, at progressively decreasing temperatures, till crystallisation begins— there are also complicated processes of bleaching, straining and filtering, all by the most elaborate machinery, till the sugar reaches its final white crystallised state. The molasses, or treacly part, which will not crystallise, is distilled into alcohol, and used to fortify wine; the dry fibre is carried on a conveyor belt to stoke the furnaces. The whole place hums, rattles, drums and booms with the great machines, and the vistor remembers again, with astonishment, the barefooted men, staff in hand, whom he met treading the tiny sinuous mountain paths, with those huge bundles of cane on their necks.

Madeira wine, known to the English in Elizabethan times—along with sherry and Canary wine—under the generic term of "sack", was exported throughout the 16th century, but it took second place to sugar in importance till the latter part of the 17th, when two things happened. Charles II suddenly prohibited the import into the American colonies of any commodities save those shipped from English ports in "English bottoms", but made an exception in favour of the wines of Madeira and the Azores. This gave these wines practically a monopoly of the American market; and English merchants, like the famous William Bolton, realising what this could mean, hurried out to Madeira and began to encourage the peasants to scrap their sugar-canes and grow vines instead, and proceeded to build up a great export trade. In those pre-refrigeration days, when moreover tinned or bottled vegetables and fruit were unknown, the health at sea of passengers and crew alike depended on an ample supply of wine, the only anti-scorbutic available, and ships calling at Madeira on their way to and from America or the East Indies took wine on board for the round trip, as well, as in the case of merchant-men, for sale in America. This trade was further encouraged by the fact that with English merchants trading at Funchal it was not necessary to pay in cash—both traders and naval officers could pay by drafts either on their London agents, in the one case, or on the Navy Commissioners in the other.

This trade continued briskly throughout the 18th century, but curiously enough the later popularity of Madeira wine in England itself came via America, where travellers, and Army and Navy officers were regaled by Americans with the finer types of wine, privately imported by individuals and called either after their owners, or the ships which brought them.

The practice of fortifying the island wines with spirits began about the 1750's, and has continued ever since; but, unlike port, the alcohol is not now used to control fermentation at once, but is only added after this has been done by the application of heat—the wine, in huge *tonels*, is kept in chambers heated to a temperature of 100–160 degrees Fahrenheit for weeks or months, after which alcohol is added up to 10 per cent; it then goes into reserve to mature, ultimately to be blended as required. This dual process gives to Madeira an astonishing and unequalled resistance to age and climatic conditions—wines a hundred years old may, by the lucky, be drunk in Madeira, and are as bland, as delicate and virile at once, as vintage ports, which can rarely be drunk with satisfaction, after forty years. The three chief types of Madeira are known, from the vines which bear them, as Sercial, Boal, and Malvazia or Malvoisie, Madeiran descendant of the old Malmsey so fatal to the Duke of Clarence. Sercial is the dryest, Boal a wonderful half-way house between sweet and dry; Malvoisie is truly sweet, a positive nectar, yet light and fresh, without any of the liverish heaviness of brown sherry, for instance. Since those disastrous epidemics of oïdium and phylloxera in the last century, grapes have now to be grown on American stocks, as in the Douro.

The same contrast between ancient and modern methods is to be observed in the making of wine as in the production of sugar. Out in the country and up in the hills, at vintage time, the baskets of grapes are carried to the *lagares*, large square wooden troughs where six men, with well-washed naked feet, prance about on the bunches to the strains of a guitar till the juice is mostly pressed out and run off into a vat—a huge wooden block then presses the remaining skins and pipes. The "must" or new wine is promptly brought down to Funchal either in barrels on ox-sledges or, from the north coast, by boat; but if the paths are too small even for a sledge, in goat-skins slung on men's shoulders. One of these primitive processions of wine-laden men, with their tall staves and their grotesque four-legged burdens, is an unforgettable sight in the 20th century. But once in the Lodge at Funchal, all is modern,—electric pumps for racking from one vast *tonel* to another, a laboratory for testing, elaborate mechanical control of the temperature in the heating chambers, up-to-date methods of bottling and corking. Incidentally, for the benefit of those unfortunates who do not live by the robust precept that everyone must "eat a peck of dirt in his life", it may be worth mentioning that the two processes of fermentation and heating to 160 degrees (the level of pasturisation), completely eliminate any impurities which might conceivably arise from contact either with the skins of goats, or the healthy feet of peasants. A visit to the Lodge of the Madeira Wine Association, which now incorporates most of the famous firms, should on no account be omitted; the buildings are as old and picturesque as the methods are scientific and modern. Only—charming to those who still appreciate manual skill—the staves for the pipes (or casks) may still be seen being trued off by hand to the required thickness; no machine has yet been found to equal the delicate dexterity of man and a steel blade.

. . . . . .

In view of what has already been said about the relatively recent human occupation of Madeira, the intelligent traveller will not expect too much in the way of architectural variety—nor will he find it. What there is has charm—rather the charm of modest simplicity than of magnificence. Indeed, the contrast between the modesty of the buildings and the extravagant luxuriance of the vegetation is one of the outstanding features of Madeira. FUNCHAL, the capital and heart of the island, supremely exemplifies both. The visitor may well begin by going up to the little chapel of Santa Caterina in the new park behind the hideous gallows-like structure which encloses an admirable statue of The Navigator—a humble edifice, the 17th-century successor to the first church built in the island, of wood, by Zargo's wife in the year 1425, and first rebuilt of stone towards the end of the 15th century. The date 1425 is carved in stone over an obviously 17th-century doorway, under a charming square porch supported on six pillars of red basalt; against the white-washed wall is a holy-water stoup whose decoration of looped cables, coupled with the terrestrial sphere, suggests a Manueline influence. From the open space in front, over-hanging the harbour with its shipping and fishing -boats, there is a good view of Funchal as a whole—of the sea-front, with the picturesque yellow mass of the Governor's 16th-century palace, its curious towers joined to the main structure by covered passage-ways, and the square creamy blocks, first of Blandy Brothers' building, home of the firm which has brought so much prosperity to the island by its triple activities of bunkering, banking, and as shipping agents, and then of the Alfandega, or Customs House; beyond is the deeper yellow outline of the Fort of S. Tiago. Inland rise the towers of the Sé, or Cathedral, and of the Convent of S. Clara, while immediately behind the Chapel itself the grey walls of the Forte do Pico, built during the Spanish occupation in the 17th century, are outlined against the villa-strewn slopes surrounding the town—behind these, again, rise the grey-green mountains themselves.

The architecture of Madeira is mainly of two types, the Gothic of the earlier churches and the renaissance or baroque both of the later ones and of the civil buildings as well. Usually the most interesting thing, about the later churches in particular, are the carved and gilt retables framing the pictures or statues behind the altars, and in some of the earlier ones their wooden ceilings—the Madeiran builders had an ample supply of fine native woods to their hand, and made full use of them. The Cathedral in particular, built between 1485 and 1514, has a very fine carved ceiling of Madeiran juniper, which is really its most impressive feature, though the whole structure has a rather appealing simplicity. The Convent of S. Clara, founded in 1492 and frequently added to, presents a curious mixture of styles; its chief feature is Zargo's tomb, in a Gothic niche in the chapel. It had a charming galleried upstairs cloister round one of the courtyards, with delightful painted wooden chapels at the corners; but this, like so much else in Portugal, has fallen a victim to the purist ravages of the Commission on Ancient Monuments, who some years ago tore away the gallery, leaving the chapels exposed to the weather—they have already suffered greatly from this, and doubtless they will soon vanish too.

One group of buildings in Funchal can hold its own with any of its kind—the Camara Municipal, or Town Hall, at the eastern end of the Praça do Municipio, with the Igreja do Colegio, the Jesuit Church, close by, flanked on the south side by the charming two-storey cloister of the little disused church of São Luiz. (Where so much is being pulled down, it is a pity that the ugly wall which masks this last should not be removed or at least lowered.) Both Church and Camara are of a very austere and pure baroque, made the more striking by the contrast between their white-washed walls and the windows, doorways and angle-stones at the corners of almost black basalt. The Camara, built by that same Conde de Carvalhal who laid out Palheiro with so much taste, has an agreeable courtyard with an elegant staircase; the Count did not live to inhabit it, but his old house near the Church of São Pedro, now the Museum, also has a fine façade. Incidentally, the Museum is well worth a visit—the collection of stuffed fish, sharks and sea-beasts is unusually fine, and it is amusing to compare them with the strange creatures, freshly hauled up out of the depths, to be seen in the market of a morning—another visit that should be made; moreover, there is an admirable and almost complete display of the birds of Madeira, well arranged and clearly labelled.

Another particularly fine and interesting building, seldom much recommended in guide-books, is the Customs House itself. True, its fine façade is defaced with ugly ochreous paint, and further disfigured by a tin roof coming half-way up it, but it should not be missed. The actual date of the oldest part, on ground level, a vast groined and vaulted chamber supported on graceful pillars, is hard to ascertain; but though the island was only annexed in 1420, in 1477 a royal charter established a Customs House at Funchal, so that the existing structure is presumably of about that date—delightfully, it is still used for its original purpose, and bales and cases lie about in it. The same document prescribes the furnishing of weights and measures for the Customs Officers; another, a suitable provision of meat and wine. On the first floor is a room with one of the finest ceilings in the whole of Portugal, carved and painted, with ravishing shell volutes at each corner; the building also contains a tiny illuminated copy of extracts from the Four Gospels, dated 1616, bound in tooled leather adorned with rich metal work, for the purpose of swearing that one had nothing to declare!—a nice psychological touch. A chapel just inside the entrance was added in 1714; it is now used as an office.

The Colegio Church, near the Camara, typifies that wealth of gilded retables which are such a feature of Madeiran churches; the great one behind the High Altar dates from 1660, and the eight in the side-chapels are of varying degrees of merit, but all decorative and all exuberant—the general effect is of being in a huge painted room, rich with soft time-dimmed gilding. One of the chapels on the right has an amusing picture of the discoverer and his ship, and there are some attractive polychrome sculptures, notably a charming St. Michael in the second chapel on the left.

Funchal must have been much more interesting and picturesque fifty or even twenty years ago than it is today. Many of the earliest streets of old houses, with pointed doors and windows, either have been pulled down, or are in process of being removed to make room for broad avenues reminiscent of Buffalo or Detroit. One of the victims of this process was the house in which Christopher Columbus lived after his marriage to the daughter of Perestrelo, the Governor of the neighbouring island of Porto Santo—a fine double window from it has been rescued and is now in the garden of Quinta Palmeira, the residence of the late Mr. H. Hinton. Another blameless victim was Banger's Pillar, a great column of red basalt built on the foreshore in front of Blandy Brothers by one John Banger in 1798; it was used as a signal station, and was one of the most familiar landmarks of Funchal to generations of seafarers and travellers, as well as being a mariners' mark on all charts, and a feature of many of the early prints of Funchal—almost all engraved in London, and now extremely valuable. But in 1939, when the new sea-front road was being constructed the Portuguese authorities ruthlessly and needlessly removed one of the most striking features of the port. There is now an airport on Madeira and one on the neighbouring island of Porto Santo from where passengers are taken by boat to Funchal.

The various country churches display the same main features as those at Funchal, that is to say occasional Gothic arches, doors or windows, and delightful gilt retables. One of the earliest is that at SANTA CRUZ, on the way to S. Antonio da Serra, built in 1450, only twenty-one years after the discovery of the island; it has good Gothic arches and pillars, some lovely groining in the chancel, a touchingly primitive rose window over the West door, and amusing flying buttresses outside it—the beautiful juniper ceiling has unfortunately been painted over. Opposite, across the square, the very early Domus Municipalia also has charming doors and windows. There are pleasant Gothic fragments at MACHICO—where the legendary Englishman, Machin, and his bride are alleged to have landed and perished on their disastrous elopement from England in 1346; and at PONTA DO SOL, at ARCO DA CALHETA and CAMARA DE LOBOS (S. Clara), all on the south side of the island. As for the 17th- and 18th-century retables, they are to be found all over the place: particularly worth notice are those at RIBEIRA BRAVA, Ponta do Sol, and SANTA ANA. The last has particularly graceful retables to the two side altars, and the otherwise dull High Altar is flanked by two most curious niches containing small polychrome statues—they are formed of looped curtains surmounted by gilt crowns, a most delightful conceit. (Incidentally, this church was built in 1698 at a cost of 1,193 escudos; at today's rate, just under £15.)

Visitors to S. ANTONIO DA SERRA should make their way, down a lane near the Church, to the Fonte Velho, a charming spring gushing from three curved and plastered niches, overhung with fern-grown trees and hydrangeas—a sweet and gentle spot. Carved in the plastered walls are a long series of English names, locally believed to be those of the British Army of occupation between 1801 and 1814; in fact they are almost all of British residents—ninety-six of them—and cover dates from 1707 to 1827. Presumably the fountain lost its appeal as a picnic-place ten years before the accession of Queen Victoria.

There are quite a number of attractive polychrome sculptures in the island, a few of which are listed and illustrated in the "*Ilhas de Zargo*"; one of the best is the Madonna in the Parish Church at ESTREITO DA CALHETA. In this same village, in the tumble-down little chapel of the Magi, or Capela dos Reis, is a most lively and remarkable group in high-relief of the Adoration of the Three Kings and their train; it has been repainted with disastrous vulgarity, but nothing can destroy its vigour and freshness—the saucy soldier with the fat behind and his cap at a rakish angle is as much a portrait today as when his 17th-century creator modelled him.

Another curious feature of Madeiran churches are the paintings, either by actual Flemish artists, or by men working under a strong Flemish influence; at MADALENA DO MAR there is an alleged Memling, and another in S. Martinho at Funchal. In the church at

MACHICO there is an Adoration of the Magi which some believe to be Italian. Of course Portugal itself received a great influx of Flemish artists during the late 16th and early 17th centuries, and it may well be that wealthy Madeiran patrons imported some of them to decorate their local churches.

There is a very large literature about Madeira, which can be consulted by the enterprising in the library of the English Rooms at Funchal; permission is usually granted to serious inquirers. A short bibliography of the most essential books will be found at the end of this book, which lovers of the island must feel to be sadly inadequate, and a list of hotels in the Appendix.

THE AZORES

North and west of Madeira lies the archipelago of the Azores, possibly all that remains of the lost continent of Atlantis, a scattered group of nine islands in the open Atlantic, about a thousand miles to the west of Portugal. Being of volcanic origin, earthquakes there are frequent, and in 1812 a tenth island called Sabrina rose from the ocean, but sank again into the sea after a few weeks. The Azores were first marked on Catalan and Genoese maps in 1351 and 1375, but their effective discovery did not take place until 1431, when Gonçalo Velho Cabral landed and found them uninhabited. Ten years later Ponta Delgada, the capital of the island of São Miguel was founded, and largely settled by Flemings, sent by Henry the Navigator, who also caused the castle to be built.

The inhabitants have always been an exceptionally hardy and self-reliant race, and the physiognomy of the people shows to this day a strong affinity with the Portuguese type of the age of the discoverers, so vividly depicted in Nuno Gonçalves' great double triptych in the Art Gallery in Lisbon. The numerous Portuguese communities, both in Bermuda and certain parts of the United States have mostly emigrated from the Azores.

Owing to the damp Atlantic climate and the constant sea mists, the pasturage in many of the islands is exceptionally good, and they have always been renowned for their dairy products. Indeed, in the early days of colonisation it is known that cattle and sheep were sent from Portugal, which multiplied so rapidly that soon numbers were being exported back to the mother country. At the present time, in addition to dairy products, the principal exports are pineapples, oranges, wine and tea.

The easiest way of reaching the islands is by air, as many air-lines using the south Atlantic route call at Santa Maria, where a big aerodrome was built by the United Nations during the War,; they also constructed the military aerodrome at Lages on Terçeira Island. Boats sail frequently from Lisbon, via Madeira, but are apt to be booked up for months ahead. (Inquiries in respect of these should be addressed to the Empresa Insulana de Navegação, Rua Augusta 152, Lisbon.)

At the time of the Spanish domination of Portugal in 1580, the Azores backed D. Antonio, the Prior do Crato, for the succession, and were only forced into submission in 1583. A Spanish force landed earlier on Terçeira, but was confronted by herds of the half-wild island cattle, who were driven into them by the inhabitants: the latter then cut the unfortunate Spaniards to pieces as they retreated in confusion to their ships.

In 1591 there was an abortive English expedition under Cumberland against the Spanish occupation of the islands; but to English people, till World War II, "the Azores" normally recalled one thing only, the fight put up by Sir Richard Grenville in the little "*Revenge*" against a Spanish fleet of fifty-three ships, many of which were crippled before his crew, in defiance of his orders, surrendered. Tennyson's poem has made this sea-fight immortal.

After the Restoration, King Afonso VI of Portugal was confined in the castle of Angra on Terçeira for five years, till he was sent by his brother, later Pedro II, to his final prison in Sintra Palace in 1674, having first, in a fit of understandable madness, attempted to murder the Governor of Angra.

The Azores emerge again from their Atlantic mists into history, rather romantically, during the boring Miguelite wars, when Dom Pedro and the Marquis of Palmela made a prolonged rendezvous there with the Princess Maria, Dom Pedro's daughter, who subsequently became Queen Maria II of Portugal.

* * * * * *

The population of the Azores is about a quarter of a million, of which a hundred and twenty thousand live in SÃO MIGUEL, the largest island, 41 miles in length by 9 miles wide. It is exceedingly fertile, with both tropical and European flora, and is the chief centre of pineapple cultivation. Tea and tobacco are also grown. PONTA DELGADA, the capital (Hotel de S. Pedro and Hotel do Infante) has well-built shining white houses and most beautiful gardens. The Cathedral, with a Manueline door, contains a splendid baroque High Altar; indeed most of the churches in the island have good boiseries and azulejos. The Museum, which has an interesting natural history section, is in the old Graça Convent.

There is a good hotel, the Terra Nostra das Furnas, in the very lovely valley of LAS FURNAS, surrounded by high mountains with bubbling boiling hot geysers, iron and sulphur springs, and hot mud. Nearby a beautiful waterfall falls into the Lago das Furnas, which is stocked with numbers of fish. From SETE CIDADES, at the other end of the island, there is a most wonderful view, and two little lakes are set in the crater of an extinct volcano.

TERÇEIRA was where Vasco da Gama's brother died in 1499 on his way back from the first voyage to India. It is near São Miguel and is the second island in importance, with a population of seventy thousand, mostly engaged in agriculture. It possesses a unique breed of dogs, not unlike bulldogs in shape, called ''cães de fila''. ANGRA DO HEROISMO, the capital, is perhaps the most picturesque town in the Azores, with its wonderful hydrangeas and flowering shrubs. The Colegio church contains good gold-work and interesting pictures, while in the Cathedral Chapter House hangs a most singular set of portraits of the Bishops of Angra. The 17th-century fortress of S. João Baptista, containing the Governor's Palace, is most beautiful, this was the prison of the murderous King Afonso VI. At PRAIA DA VITORIA, the Misericordia church is remarkable for its particularly florid Manueline architecture.

The island of SANTA MARIA, where air passengers now land, is the most easterly of all, and is where Columbus landed in 1493 on his return from discovering America. The capital is VILA DO PORTO. The island is chiefly remarkable for the enormous number and varieties of fossils to be found, especially near the village of FIGUEIRAL. The soil is particularly suitable for the making of earthenware, and there are a great many kilns and small pottery works, which supply china to the whole archipelago.

GRACIOSA, one of the smaller islands, is also one of the least mountainous; there are two or three pretty little villages, the largest of which is SANTA CRUZ, and picturesque lakes are scattered about, as in all the islands.

The archipelago falls roughly into three groups, the second of which consists of São Jorge, Pico and Faial. The first of these is very long and narrow, with a high mountain range down its spine, giving wonderful views of the other islands. SÃO JORGE is chiefly given over to agriculture and stock and dairy farming, which produce excellent butter and cheese for export. The capital is the little town of VELAS.

PICO, the most mountainous of the islands, has a volcano that is not yet extinct but still sends forth sinister smoke from time to time. The whole island shows strong traces of its volcanic origin, with hardly any soil, and lava everywhere; there is so little cultivated land that all cereals have to be imported, the only crop being grapes from the tiny terraced vineyards. The summit of Pico, rising starkly seven thousand feet from the sea which washes it on three sides, is often covered in snow; from it the whole archipelago can be seen. The ascent is made with a guide from the village of MADALENA, and a night should be spent at PEDRA MOLE on the way.

FAIAL is mostly farming land, with a great number of peasant proprietors. HORTA, the chief town, faces Pico, only three miles away across a shallow channel. It is one of the best of the Atlantic ports, and is a submarine cable centre. The Public Library, in the 17th-century former Jesuit College, contains good azulejos and interesting pictures. The top of Caldeira, the highest mountain on Faial, consists of a very large and almost circular crater filled with amazing vegetation and lovely streams. A service of motor boats from Horta make the daily return journey to Pico.

FLORES, also agricultural, is the most westerly and remote of the islands, and is the centre of those anti-cyclones that the B.B.C. is so fond of attributing to the Azores, as it is a meeting point for the winds from every quarter. There is a strange gap in the precipitous coast-line which reveals a great amphitheatre of cliffs down which tumble innumerable water-falls. SANTA CRUZ, the capital, is remarkable for its great banks of hydrangeas everywhere.

The smallest island is CORVO, which is an extinct volcano, eight miles in circumference. The thousand inhabitants all live in elysian peace and amity, with unlocked doors and an ever-empty prison in ROSARIO, the single village, in which the clean white cottages are grouped round a little church. There is a special breed of tiny pale coffee-coloured cattle, not unlike miniature Jerseys, which yield exceedingly good milk. The summit of the island, Monte Gordo, is crowned with a secondary crater, in which lies a lake with a number of tiny islets, looking from above like the archipelago itself seen in miniature from an aeroplane.

The visitor familiar with the West of Ireland will be struck, in the Azores, by many resemblances—the white-washed houses, the intense greenness of the grass, and above all the small stone-walled fields. On many of the islands one might imagine oneself in Connemara or Ennis, save for the fact that the main crop is not oats or potatoes, but pineapples! Beautiful, remote, strange, it is well worth while to take ten days out of one's life to make the trip round these islands in one of the comfortable little Insulana boats from Funchal in Madeira—for the Azores, in spite of their great airport, do really belong to "other worlds than this".

MADEIRA

Scale: 1 cm. = 3·7 kilometres

APPENDIX OF USEFUL INFORMATION
For American Travellers

VISAS

U.S. visitors do not need visas, but their passports are stamped for a sixty-day stay on arrival in Portugal. This period can usually be renewed for a total visit of up to about six months. Those who wish to take up permanent residence in Portugal have to make special application for a resident's permit through a Portuguese Consulate abroad.

CURRENCY

The currency is in escudos, and the official rate for changing Travellers' Cheques is about 28 escudos to the dollar. Foreign notes can be changed at the Exchange Bureaux, or at a bank, of which there are several in the Rua do Ouro and other parts of Lisbon.

BANKS

All American and English banks have correspondents in Lisbon and Oporto. One English-speaking bank in Lisbon is the Bank of London and South America, Rua do Ouro, 40–48 [Tel. 324201].

ROUTES

Lisbon may be reached by air from the U.S. by the following airlines: Pan American Airways, Trans-World Airlines, Swissair, Iberian Airline and the Portuguese airline TAP (Transportes Aereos Portugueses). All have regular flights to Portela Airport just outside Lisbon, as do Canadian Pacific Airlines from Canada. By sea, the Greek Line, Hellenic Lines Ltd., American Export Lines, Inc., the Italia Sta. di Navigazione, Ca. Transatlantica Española and Zim, Israel Navigation Co., have regular sailings from the U.S., and from Central and South America there are numerous shipping lines including vessels of the Royal Mail and Blue Star lines. Freighters also leave New York every three weeks with a maximum of twelve passengers in second class accommodation. For information and details call East Coast Overseas Corp. in New York, WH 3–0200. Fast international services make it possible to come all the way to Lisbon by rail from any European capital, including London, by the overnight rail ferry. The Sud-Express, the Iberia Express and the Rapido make quick work of the journey between Paris or Madrid and Lisbon. Motorists (who should get a car triptyque from the American Automobile Association) can drive with an International Drivers Permit through France and Spain, or they may prefer to put their cars on a train. For details write to Portuguese State Tourism Department (S.N.I.), Pr. dos Restauradores, Lisbon 2 [Tel. 367031]. In Spain there are Government road-houses, and in Portugal there are either Government road-houses called *pousadas*, estalagems, or good hotels on all the routes from the Spanish frontier to Lisbon.

CUSTOMS
There are no special customs regulations except an allowance of only 200 cigarettes. Cigarette lighters may have to be declared as Portuguese residents pay a modest annual tax on them.

TRANSPORT
Taxis in Lisbon and all other big towns are equipped with meters and are modestly priced. The usual tip of 15 to 20 per cent should be added. Portuguese trains have a reputation for punctuality, but tend to be rather full even on the Lisbon–Estoril–Cascais line. Trolleys in Lisbon, Oporto and some of the bigger towns are frequent but are also very full. The buses in Lisbon help to relieve the transport problem and the new subway is proving its worth. Single tickets are about 5 cents.

LISBON HOTELS
Hotel accommodation is, relatively, one of the cheapest things in Portugal. A full list of hotels and pensions, with prices, is available at the Casa de Portugal, 570 Fifth Avenue, New York 10036 [Tel. 581–2450]. Ten per cent for service is added to hotel bills, plus a 3 per cent tourist tax. The best hotel in Lisbon is the Ritz, Rua Rodrigo da Fonseca [Tel. 684131]; this is a real luxury hotel with 300 beautifully appointed rooms and suites, all with bathrooms and terraces overlooking the city, and an excellent restaurant. Then come the Avenida Palace, the Condestavel, the Embaixador, the Fenix, the Florida, the Imperio, the Mundial, the Principe Real and the Tivoli, all First Class. Among the Second Class, but still excellent hotels, are the Atenas, the Borges in the Rua Garrett, the shopping centre, the Capitol and the Miraparque. These are all moderate in price, say from $10.00 a day with meals.

LISBON PENSIONS
Of the pensãos or boarding-houses in Lisbon, one of the pleasantest is York House, Rua das Janelas Verdes 32 [Tel. 662435], which is in a former convent and is cool and spacious. The Mansão Nazareth and the Mansão Santa Rita are both good, and the Residencia Avenida Parque is near the Avenida da Liberdade. The Casa de São Mamede, Rua Escola Politecnica 159, is in a large old palace with a direct trolley outside the door to the centre, and the Casa de São Francisco, Avenida da Republica 48-B, is in a modern building in the new part of the city near the bull-ring. All these charge from $6.00 a day, including meals and table wine; but the rooms do not have private bathrooms and baths are usually extra.

ESTORIL HOTELS
In Estoril the big luxury hotels are the Palacio with a large swimming pool and

APPENDIX

the Cibra, with prices from $15.00 a day. But there are excellent First Class hotels both in Estoril and Monte Estoril, particularly the Atlantico, right on the sea with a balcony to each room and a swimming pool; the Miramar, with a garden and big terrace; and the Monte Estoril and the Grande next door. These are all at Monte Estoril, about ten minutes walk from Estoril. The Paris is at Alto Estoril with lovely views of the sea. These hotels all start at about $9.00 a day for room and meals, though afternoon tea and table wine are extra. The Choupana Restaurant on the sea-front is excellent for dinner and dancing, as is the English Bar at Monte Estoril.

Between Estoril and Cascais, the huge Hotel Estoril-Sol, on the sea, is in the luxury class. The Baia, Cidadela and Nau Hotels in Cascais are all First Class and the Estalagem Albatroz and the Solar Dom Carlos are both very attractive.

ESTORIL PENSIONS

Among the numerous pensãos at Estoril there are the Casa de São Mamede, the Lar Sao Cristóvão near the pretty little station and the sea; and the Estalagems Belveder, Fundador, Lennox and Pimenteiras. At Monte Estoril the Zenith and the Royal start at $5.00 a day, meals and table wine included. The extras naturally cost less. Portuguese tables wines are excellent and the imitations of French liqueurs are good though sweet. Visitors staying in hotels or boarding-houses outside the Lisbon area should buy their drinking water in 5-litre demijohns or *garrafões*, which stay at the restaurant table or in the bedroom until used up. This is much cheaper than buying drinking water in bottles, although many hotels try to avoid supplying it this way. Most of the Estoril hotels have an arrangement whereby their visitors can have meals at certain hotels or restaurants in Lisbon and Sintra at no extra cost, by asking for a special voucher.

RESTAURANTS

Portuguese cooking is both ample and good. Among the best-known Lisbon restaurants are the *Aviz*, Rua Serpa Pinto 12-B, which is superb; *Tavares*, Rua da Misericordia 35; *Negresco*, Rua Jardim do Regedor 39; *Folclor*, Rua Nova da Trinidade 22-A; *Solmar*, Portas de Santo Antão 108; *A Caravela* (luncheons and tea room), Rua Paiva Andrada 8; *A Quinta* at the top of the Santa Justa lift and *La Gondola*, Avenida de Berna 64, serving Italian food, with meals in the open in hot weather. The two last named are closed on Sundays.

TEA ROOMS

There are several good tea rooms in and around the Rua Garrett or Chiado, and the Rua Augusta, the main shopping district of Lisbon. Tea (*cha preto*) or coffee and cakes can always be got in any of the numerous dairies or *leitarias* which are to be found in any town in Portugal. Cafés are everywhere and tea, as well as coffee, can be obtained in them.

NIGHT CLUBS

There are a few night clubs, or places where the visitor can go and dance after dinner in Lisbon, but their popularity varies from year to year. The Casino at

Estoril opens at 3 p.m. In addition to the gaming rooms where roulette, French bank and baccarat are played, there is a restaurant for dining or having supper, and dancing to a good small band. In Cascais, the *Canoa* and the *Van Gogo* are the smartest dancing places.

FADOS

Fados, the traditional songs of the Portuguese town worker, can be heard in a number of cafés and fado restaurants in the Bairro Alto in Lisbon. The best-known are *Machado's*, Rua do Norte 91; *Mesquita*, Rua do Diario de Noticias 107; and *Tipoia*, Rua do Norte 104.

CINEMAS

In Lisbon and Oporto there are large numbers of cinemas where all the popular American, English and European films are shown.

THEATRES

A few Lisbon theatres show straight plays and there are now several small experimental theatres. The revues in the two theatres in the Parque Mayer, an amusement park off the Avenida da Liberdade and in some other theatres are usually excellent. The São Carlos Opera House stages superb opera and ballet from time to time and attracts the best European companies. The National Theatre in the Rossio has recently burnt down and is being rebuilt at the moment. It usually presents classical or serious plays; the Coliseu in the Rua Eugenio dos Santos often has opera at popular prices, and always a good circus at Christmas.

CLUBS AND LIBRARIES

Particulars of the American Men's Luncheon Group and the American Women of Lisbon can be had at the U.S. Consulate, Avenida Duque de Loulé 39, Lisbon; in the same premises is an excellent American Library and Reading Room.

The Royal British Club for men in Lisbon is in the Rua da Estrêla. Visitors can usually be made temporary members. The Lisbon Ladies' Club, Rua Nova da Trinidade 1, 2nd floor, also accepts temporary members, as does the British Institute, Rua Luis Fernandes 3. All these have good English libraries.

SHOPPING IN LISBON

The best shops are in the Rua Garrett or Chiado, the side streets off it and in the *baixa* or low part of the town between the Rossio and the river. The big stores stock an increasing quantity of ready-made clothes but in Portugal most people buy material, of which there is an astonishing variety, and have it made up by one of the little dressmakers who exist all over the country. There are now several boutiques in Lisbon, and in Cascais; Gloria, Prisca and Tara are the best known. Portuguese shoes are good and inexpensive, but are made in Continental sizes. Stockings, however, are usually in American sizes. Imported cosmetics and scents are expensive, but reliable Portuguese equivalents can be bought. Soap is excellent. The hairdressers, chiropodists and manicurists are usually highly trained and very competent. Ready-made underwear is also expensive, but the big shops will have it made to measure. Furriers are excellent and fur coats can be cheaply and well re-modelled. Certain of the men's tailors are good and fit well, and still only charge the price of a pre-war, made-to-measure London suit. Women's tailors are also adequate and their charges moderate. Handbags and leather goods are expensive but of good quality, as are other dress accessories.

REPAIRS

All repairs can be done cheaply, quickly and well in Lisbon or any of the big towns. Watches, shoes, jewellery, invisible mending, ladders in stockings, hats re-modelled, indeed almost anything can be repaired or altered in Portugal.

LANGUAGE

Many educated Portuguese speak English or French. There is always a linguist in the big shops and hotels or pensions. Portuguese phrase books are available but the pronunciation is so unexpected that any visitor would take some time to become proficient. The daily newspapers can, however, be readily understood by anyone knowing French or a little Italian or Spanish.

CLIMATE

The climate of Portugal is delightful. In winter the hotels are heated and in the summer there are always at least three months without rain. The sun is never unbearably hot but it usually gets considerably cooler at sunset, so something warm should be brought even in the summer.

SPAS

There are an exceptionally large number of mineral water spas in Portugal, each of which has its season and specialises in the relief or cure of a number of diseases. Particulars of these spas are available at the Casa de Portugal, 570 Fifth Avenue, New York 10036 [Tel. 581–2450].

GOLF

Eighteen-hole golf courses are to be found at Estoril, Carregueira near Lisbon, Bussaco and Penina, near Portimão in the Algarve, which is a Championship Course. Others are shortly being opened in the Algarve. Hotel Urgeirica at Canas de Senhorim, Miramar near Oporto, Pedras Salgadas and Vidago have nine-hole courses.

TENNIS

There are good lawn tennis courts all over the country at every hotel, spa or seaside resort.

SKI-ING

Snow ski-ing takes place in the Serra de Estrêla, referred to in Chapter X. Water ski-ing takes place at every resort. For details apply to S.N.I., the Portuguese State Tourism Department, Pr. dos Restauradores, Lisbon [Tel. 367031].

FISHING

Fishing is still good in certain parts of the northern rivers and the Serra da Estrêla lakes, as well as in the sea-water lagoons in various parts of the country. Tunny-fishing is practised off the Algarve or southern coast of Portugal.

SHOOTING

Little shooting is preserved and there are most complicated regulations covering the import of sporting guns even by tourists.

USEFUL ADDRESSES

The American Embassy and Consulate: Avenida Duque de Loulé 39, Lisbon [Tel. 55141].

In Oporto the American Consulate is at Rua Julio Dinis 826 [Tel. Porto 0263094].

The English Church of St. George (C. of E.) is in the Rua da Estrêla, Lisbon, behind the Parsonage, which is at No. 4 [Tel. 663010]. The Scottish Presbyterian Church is at Rua Arriaga 11 [Tel. 662640]. The English College (R.C.) is in Travessa dos Inglesinhos [Tel. 323405]; and the Irish Dominican Church of Corpo Santo (R.C.) is in the Largo do Corpo Santo, Lisbon [Tel 323208].

At Estoril, St. Paul's Church (C. of E.) is in the grounds of the Hotel Paris.

In Oporto, St. James' Church (C. of E.) is in the Largo da Maternidade.

The British Hospital in Lisbon, Rua Saraiva da Carvalho 49 [Tel. 663837], has English nurses and an English-speaking doctor is in attendance at the surgery every morning and late afternoon.

The American Consulates have lists of doctors who have worked in the U.S.

The British Hospital in Oporto is at Rua da Bandeirinha 12 [Tel. Porto 0221202]; this also has English nurses and an English dispenser.

SHIPPING AND AIRLINE OFFICES

The main agencies in Lisbon are:

Pinto Basto (Italian Line), Praça Duque de Terçeira 20 [Tel. 361581].

Messrs. Rawes (Royal Mail), Rua Bernardino Costa 47 [Tel. 370231].

Garland Laidley (Blue Star Line), Caes de Sodre 24 [Tel. 320441].

Carlos Gomes (Greek and Hellenic Lines), Largo Vitorio Damasio 4 [Tel. 668086].

Sociedad Maritima Argonauta (Grimaldi-Siosa Line), Avenida D. Carlos 1, 72D [Tel. 665054].

The American Express Co. (Star) is at Avenida Sidónio Pais 4A [Tel. 538971], where train tickets can be bought and places reserved. There are branches at Praça dos Restauradores 14 and in Estoril at Avenida da Nice 4 and in the Hotel Estoril-Sol, Cascais.

The airline offices in Lisbon are:

Pan-American World Airways, Praça dos Restauradores 46 [Tel. 362181].

Trans-World Airlines, Avenida da Liberdade 258 [Tel. 58121].

Guest Air-Lines (TAP), Pr. Marquês de Pombal 3 [Tel. 538851].

Swissair, Avenida da Liberdade 220 [Tel. 533171].

Canadian Pacific Airlines, Avenida da Liberdade 261 [Tel. 556192].

APPENDIX

MADEIRA HOTELS

The famous Reid's Palace Hotel at Funchal is now open with prices from $20 a day. The Hotel Nova Avenida is also in the luxury class, as is the Santa Isabel, the Savoy, the Golden Gate and the Monte Carlo.

The Miramar, the Santa Maria and the Atlantico at Funchal are all good. Their prices start at about $10.00 a day inclusive.

ENGLISH PERIODICAL

The Anglo-Portuguese News, published fortnightly at 14 cents, can be bought at any large news-stand. It is of great use to visitors as it contains announcements of events of interest to English-speaking people, shopping articles and articles in English on Portuguese historical, topographical and current subjects.

BIBLIOGRAPHY

ANGLO-PORTUGUESE NEWS, THE, Bound Volumes from 1937 onwards.
BAEDEKER, K. *Spain and Portugal*. (Allen and Unwin) 1913.
BECKFORD, WILLIAM. *Travel Diaries*. Ed. by G. Chapman. Two vols. (Constable) 1928.
BELL, AUBREY F. G. *Portugal of the Portuguese*. (Pitman) 1915.
BORROW, GEORGE. *The Bible in Spain*. (Dent. Everyman's Library) 1931.
BROWN, A. SAMLER. *Brown's Madeira, Canary Islands and Azores*. (Simpkin Marshall) 1922.
CAMPBELL, ROY. *Portugal*. (Reinhardt) 1957.
CHEKE, MARCUS. *Dictator of Portugal. The Marquis of Pombal*. (Sidgwick and Jackson) 1938.
    Carlota Joaquina, Queen of Portugal. (Sidgwick and Jackson) 1947.
COUTINHO-PEREIRA. *Flora de Portugal*.
CROCKETT, W. D. and CROCKETT, S. G. *A Satchel Guide to Spain and Portugal*. (Allen and Unwin) 1930.
ESTRADAS DE PORTUGAL. Several volumes. (Lello & Irmao, Porto) n.d.
FULLERTON, ALICE. *To Portugal for Pleasure*. (Grafton) 1945.
GALLOP, RODNEY, *Portugal, a Book of Folk Ways*. (C.U.P.) 1936.
GIBBONS, JOHN, *Afoot in Portugal*. (George Newnes) 1931.
GOLDRING, DOUGLAS. *To Portugal*. (Rich and Cowan) 1934.
GOODALL, AGNES M. *Portugal: Peeps at Many Lands Series*. (Black) 1909.
GORDON, JAN and CORA. *Portuguese Somersault*. (Harrap) 1934.
GUIA HOTELARIA E TURISTICA DE PORTUGAL E ILHAS. Lisboa.
GUIA DE PORTUGAL. Four vols. (*Biblioteca Nacional de Lisboa*) 1924, 1927, 1944, 1964. Two more volumes are in preparation.
HUME, MARTIN, *Through Portugal*. (London) 1907.
INCHBOLD, STANLEY. *Lisbon and Cintra*. (Chatto and Windus) 1907.
KELLY, MARIE NOËLE. *This Delicious Land — Portugal*. (Hutchinson) 1956.
LEES-MILNE, JAMES. *Baroque in Spain and Portugal*. (Batsford) 1960.
LIVERMORE, HAROLD V. *A New History of Portugal*. (Cambridge University Press) 1966.
MACAULAY, ROSE. *They Went to Portugal*. (Cape) 1946.
MARDEN, PHILIP S. *A Wayfarer in Portugal*. (Methuen) 1927.
MORISON, SAMUEL ELIOT. *Admiral of the Ocean Sea*. (Atlantic Monthly Press, Boston) 1942.
MUIRHEAD, FINDLAY. Ed. by. *Southern Spain and Portugal*. (MacMillan, The Blue Guides) 1929.
MURRAY's *Handbook for Portugal, Madeira, Azores and Canaries*. (Murray) 1887.
NAPIER, SIR WILLIAM. *English Battles and Sieges in the Peninsular*. Reprinted (Murray) 1910.

THE SELECTIVE TRAVELLER IN PORTUGAL

PORTUGAL, MADEIRA, AZORES. (English edition, Hachette) 1956.
PORTUGAL, MADÉRE, ILES AÇORES. (Hachette, Paris. *Les Guides Bleus*) 1964.
PRESTAGE, EDGAR. *The Portuguese Voyages of Discovery.* (The Anglo-Portuguese Society) 1939.
ROSENTHAL, E. *Peeps at Portugal.* (The National Council of Turismo, Lisbon.)
SALTER, CEDRIC. *A Fortnight in Portugal.* (Percival Marshall) 1957.
SANCEAU, ELAINE. *Henry the Navigator.* (Hutchinson) 1946.
SANTOS, REINALDO DOS. *A Escultura em Portugal.* Vol. I. (Academia Nacional de Belas Artes, Lisboa) 1948. Further volumes are in preparation.
SANTOS SIMÕES, J. M. DOS. *Alguns Azulejos de Evora.* (Evora) 1945.
    A Casa do Paço da Figueira da Foz e os seus Azulejos. (Figueira da Foz) 1947.
    Os Azulejos do Paço de Vila Vicosa. (Fundaçao da Casa de Bragança) 1945.
SITWELL, SACHEVERELL. *Sacred and Profane Love.* (Faber and Faber) 1940.
    Spanish Baroque Art with buildings in Portugal, Mexico and other Colonies. (Duckworth) 1931.
    Portugal and Madeira (Batsford) 1954.
SMITHES, M. F. *Things Seen in Portugal.* (Seeley, Things Seen Series) 1931.
TAIT, C. WILLIAM. *The Birds of Portugal.* (Witherby) 1924.
WALFORD, A. R. *The British Factory in Lisbon.* (Instituto Britanico em Portugal, Lisboa) 1940.
WATSON, WALTER CRUM. *Portuguese Architecture.* (Constable) 1908.
WRIGHT, DAVID and SWIFT, PATRICK. *Algarve* (Barrie and Rockliff) 1965.
WYATT, HONOR. *The Young Traveller in Portugal.* (Phoenix House) 1955.
YOUNGER, WILLIAM and ELIZABETH. *Blue Moon in Portugal.* (Eyre and Spottiswoode) 1946.

MADEIRA BIBLIOGRAPHY

Hand-book for Madeira. JAMES YATE JOHNSON. (Dulau) 1885.
Plants Seen in Madeira. MICHAEL GRABHAM. (H. K. Lewes & Co.) 1934. London.
Elucidario Madeirense. Two vols. PADRE F. AUGUSTO DA SILVA and CARLOS AZEVEDO DE MENEZES. (Funchal) 1940 and 1922.
Ilhas de Zargo. Two Vols. ED. E. N. PEREIRA. (Funchal) 1939 and 1940.
Power's Guide to the Island of Madeira. (George Philip & Son, London) 1951.
Baedeker. Madeira, Azoren, Die Kanarische Inseln. 1934.
Guide Bleu. Portugal, Madére, Açores. (Hachette) 1964.
A Manual Flora of Madeira. R. T. Lowe. (Van Hoorst, London) 1868.
Madeira — Wine, Cakes and Sauce. ANDRÉ SIMON and ELIZABETH CRAIG. (Constable, London) 1933.
The English Church in Madeira. LT.-COL. H. A. NEWELL. (Oxford University Press) 1931.
Madeira and the Canaries. ELIZABETH NICHOLAS. (Hamish Hamilton) 1953.

INDEX

u

INDEX

INDEX

INDEX

INDEX

INDEX

INDEX

INDEX

287

INDEX

INDEX

INDEX

INDEX

INDEX